TJ Schneider - July 1977

THE COMPLETE
DOBERMAN PINSCHER

CHAMPION RANCHO DOBE'S STORM

Ch. Rancho Dobe's Storm set records unparalleled by any dog in modern show history. His career was meteoric throughout and was climaxed by his second successive best in show award at Westminster. He was then retired at the age of 38 months.

Storm's "batting average" was tops. He was shown only 25 times and was never defeated in the breed. He won 22 working groups en route to 17 all-breed best in show wins. His champion offspring are myriad with many best in show winners among them.

F. F. H. Fleitmann, a great authority on the breed, said in an article comparing Germany's Dobermanns with those of America, "the Germans have not yet produced a dog to beat Storm. But then there is quite a difference between Storm and the next-best American dog."

THE COMPLETE
DOBERMAN PINSCHER

Milo G. Denlinger
Gerda Umlauff
C. W. Sloan
John T. Brueggeman
Kenton E. Smith
Mrs. Bob Adamson
Anne F. Paramoure

Revised Edition
Illustrated

1972

HOWELL BOOK HOUSE INC.

845 Third Avenue, New York, N.Y. 10022

ISBN 0-86705-110-7

Acknowledgments

THE compiling of this volume, The Complete Doberman Pinscher, required three years of preparation and research to make it all that the word "complete" implies. Our task might never have been completed without the help of the following contributors, to whom we wish to express our appreciation.

We are especially grateful to Miss Gerda Umlauff, daughter of Peter Umlauff, who was for many years President of the Doberman Pinscher Club of Germany and judged the first Doberman specialty in America. Gerda worked for her father as his secretary, after his death preserved his records and therefore, is better qualified to write on the Doberman in Germany than any other living authority. It is with deepest appreciation of Miss Umlauff's untiring efforts that we dedicate this book to her father, Peter Umlauff.

We are also deeply indebted to Mr. C. W. Sloan for his unusual chapter and illustrations on the gait of the Doberman. This chapter is very essential, especially on a breed such as the Doberman.

We wish to express our appreciation to Mr. John T. Brueggeman for his chapter on the character and temperament of the Doberman, a study of which should be very beneficial to those not thoroughly acquainted with the character of the breed.

We appreciate the assistance of Mr. Kenton E. Smith for his help in obtaining illustrations, his chapter on American Kennels and his discourse on the standard.

Mrs. Bob Adamson, in her contribution of the chapter "Illena and the Seven Sires", has set forth an invaluable record of the outstanding blood lines of the breed in America.

We are deeply grateful to Mrs. Anne F. Paramoure, whose chapter on the bloodlines of the Doberman in America required one year of tedious and extensive research to compile.

It is with great pleasure that I submit this book on the Doberman Pinscher, which is the fifty-fourth in a series of publications on dogs and dog subjects, and it is my hope that it will be accorded the same warm reception by the fancy as my previous efforts.

MILO G. DENLINGER.

CH. SULTANA VON MARIENBURG

Sultana's history-making record includes winning of 35 all-breed Bests in Show and 89 Firsts in the Working Group. Winner of two consecutive National Specialties in 1967 and 1968. Owned by Mary Rodgers Shea, Sun Valley, Calif. Handled by Rex L. Vandeventer.

Contents

STROLCH AND HIS 7 YEAR OLD PLAYMATE
The dog was awarded German Life Guard Medal **for**
saving the child's life when the boy
broke through the ice

Character of the Doberman

by

Gerda M. Umlauff

NE of the earliest descriptions of Doberman temperament comes from a police officer of the name of Grobatscheck, who was invariably accompanied by one of the breed when making his daily rounds. This dog, a male named Troll, was reported by his master to be an excellent watch dog, keen, alert, dependable, and very obedient. When hunting, Troll would leave the trail of a hare at the command "Back!" and return at once to his master. The latter claimed that he was better in the field than many gun dogs and was a very rapid retriever. He would find his quarry, fetch it, and lay it at his master's feet uninjured while another dog was still figuring what to do. Troll was also clever at catching rats, hamsters and fitchews.

Troll was also very good at finding lost objects. His handler would often hide something during his round, without the dog's being aware of it. After several hours, Troll

11

could be sent back for it, and would return with the missing article. He would also pick up and carry at command any article found lying in the street. If he was left on guard over any article in a public place, Troll would allow no one to remove it, nor would he permit anyone to touch his master. He would also stop any person indicated on the street, even at a distance, and hold him until his master's arrival. However, Troll would not bite unless commanded to seize someone.

When on night patrol, Troll would go about 30 paces in advance, but would return to heel promptly on command, only a soft hiss being required to call him back. When ordered to go on he would again take the lead, and would bark a warning when any one approached. When ordered to watch a prisoner he would do so, growling at the slightest movement and not allowing a single step without orders. On one occasion Troll located six tramps sleeping in piles of straw and herded them before him without allowing one to escape.

Troll would also retrieve objects from the water, and if he started to fetch the wrong article would leave it and go on to the right one when told "That is wrong!"

On returning home, Troll would fetch his master's slippers and take away his boots without being told. He was definitely a one man dog, paying no attention to strangers. No one else could call him, and he refused food from anyone else.

This and similar stories give a good picture of the Doberman character. Nevertheless, no sooner was the breed recognized than calumnies were spread about it. Whether due to grudges or envy, there were many disparaging remarks made. It was claimed that the Doberman was a great barker, that his brain was small, and that the breed was losing ground and would soon die out. These were some of the less serious claims, while the more malignant were charges of viciousness and treachery, and even that a Doberman would bite his own master.

Such remarks, which have been made regarding more than one breed, nearly always follow a regular form. If they are questioned, and an attempt made to trace them to their source, it almost invariably turns out that the person reporting such a story has no personal knowledge of the breed, has never owned one himself, and his information is all hearsay. The neighbor of the grandfather of his aunt's sister's cook heard it from somebody else.

Statements of this sort, which breed specialists and fanciers will heatedly deny, are partly due to the fact that many people lack experience with dogs and do not know how to behave toward them. No one should handle a strange dog without the owner's knowledge and permission, for many dogs do not like to be touched by strangers. Dogs feel a sense of responsibility toward their owners, their homes and their belongings, and will resent any apparent tampering with them. To be alert and keen, a good watch dog is entirely distinct from being cross, vicious or treacherous.

Moreover, in any breed there are individual differences as well as good and bad specimens. Behavior is to a large extent the result of education and training. "Like master, like man" is a proverb which can be equally well applied to dogs. As every experienced fancier knows a dog's behavior is a reflection of the care and training he has received, and a careless master makes a poorly behaved dog. There are Dobermans who seldom bark, and then only with good reason. On the other hand, it is easier for an expert to restrain and direct a dog which is full of life and energy than to instill force and responsiveness into a dull, sluggish one. Of course, the trainer must know what he is about and be able to do his work properly. And the methods suitable for directing a team of oxen might not work out satisfactorily with a high-spirited thoroughbred.

The statement that dogs with narrow heads are lacking in brain power seems to have little basis in fact. The proportions, or even the size of the brain appear to have little effect upon its quality.

Time has shown that the Doberman is far from dying out. Back in the middle 1920's, the German club registered 11,000 Dobermans in a period of 18 months, and up to 1940 there were already more than 400 U. S. champions of the breed, while the succeeding decade, in spite of the war,

13

added many more. In 1968, 11,585 Dobermans were registered in the U.S., and the breed ranked 17th of all breeds.

Naturally the fanciers of any breed and the clubs which promote its interests rejoice in its popularity. However, experience has shown that for a breed to become suddenly fashionable is not desirable. In the long run, it is the slow, steady gain which fosters a breed's best interests. Then the newcomers who are attracted to the breed can be educated thoroughly and become acquainted with its fine points, while extending their breeding operations gradually. On the other hand, when a breed becomes suddenly fashionable there is a sharp increase in demand for stock which cannot be filled immediately. This naturally sends up the price, and a flock of newcomers are likely to try to cash in. Since these new breeders have no real knowledge of the breed and are looking primarily for high returns in cash they are likely to do two-fold damage. Instead of keeping up the quality of the stock by culling vigorously and breeding only from the best bitches they breed anything available, including many bitches which should never be used at all. This is partly due to lack of knowledge, and also in many cases to lack of sufficient funds to buy first rate stock in a rising market. On the other hand, even where such novices can afford to buy the best they are often unable to recognize it. This results in the uninformed pursuit of championship titles, such as a case reported from the 1920's when a German Sieger who had proved a disappointment as a sire was sold to an agent for $30 (120 Marks in those days) and resold in America for $1,200. Even where the uninformed novice is lucky enough to acquire really first class stock the breeding results are often disappointing, since he lacks the knowledge and experience to select breeding partners which are both suitable individuals and of compatible bloodlines.

No responsible breeder with the welfare of his breed at heart, desires to see the market flooded with inferior stock which sooner or later brings down the price below the cost of production. Then the followers of fashion turn to something else, leaving the serious breeder to face the inevitable slump and spend years, perhaps, in getting the breed on its

14

feet again. Such a development occurred in Germany after the first World War, when there was a rush of Doberman breeders, most of whom soon disappeared again. Since then the wheat has been winnowed from the chaff and the Doberman breed more or less stabilized. Disturbed by a second World War, the breed is once again struggling back toward a normal condition, which it is hoped can be maintained for some years to come.

As to the final count in the charges made against the Doberman's character, that he will bite his own master, this is another case in which the incidents reported on hearsay evidence usually prove impossible to substantiate when a serious attempt is made to trace them to their source. Or if not, they prove to be instances in which an untrained, confused, or frightened dog is brutally or unintelligently handled. In one case the owner of a Doberman male went running to a club official for assistance reporting that his dog was locked in a room which he was afraid to enter. On inquiry, it proved that the dog had been allowed from the time he was a puppy to sleep on a certain couch. Now that he was grown, the master suddenly decided that this was no longer permissible. Naturally, the dog failed to understand, and when he persisted in seeking his usual place, the master applied a whip so unsparingly that the dog resented it, and chased him out of the room. As any trainer knows, consistency is one of the most vital factors in training, and to eliminate a habit which has endured for months or years requires the most careful and deliberate retraining—not abrupt harsh measures with a whip. The type of owner who adopts such a course is unquestionably asking for trouble and is not likely to be the dog's "master" in any but a purely legal sense.

Any breed as alert, active and intelligent as the Doberman demands the right treatment if he is to prove a success. A lively, four-footed fellow of his size needs plenty of work and exercise to keep him in good health. If he does not, there is something wrong with him. If such a dog is kept in small quarters, with only short runs out of doors on the leash, he will inevitably become discontented or ill, and very likely both. Inheriting his physique from a long line of ancestors who were truly working dogs, he cannot overnight accommodate himself to life as a sedentary parasite. For his own sake and his master's too, he needs plenty of room and active exercise if he is not in actual service as a working dog, which few American Dobermans are today.

For this reason, also, the Doberman is not well-suited to a kennel life. He wants something to learn, something to do, and the companionship of a master who recognizes this and can handle him intelligently. How close his attachment to his owner can be is shown in a number of incidents. A German police officer in Berlin reported that a young Doberman was sent by his owner to a training kennel, where he remained for eight months. Previously, the dog had been kept on a large farm, where he was never allowed in the house, and he was quite young at the time he was sent to be trained. When the dog was brought home the trainer requested the owner to keep at a distance while the dog went through his exercises, in order not to divert his attention. The demonstration was nearly finished, with the master stationed nearly 100 yards away, when the dog recognized his scent and rushed to him at once. His joy at the reunion was clearly evident as he tried to wag his short tail and quivered all over, and it was not without difficulty that he was finally persuaded to finish his demonstration of training. The owner was much astonished, as he believed the dog would have entirely forgotten him after such a long interval, considering his youth when he was sent away.

A different type of memory was shown by a Doberman bitch who belonged to a farmer in California. As reported in a letter to his family in Germany, this man owned four Dobermans whom he used as watch dogs. Because there was no market for puppies in his vicinity, so that he saw no chance of disposing of the young dogs, he destroyed the bitch's next litter. When she proved to be again in whelp, she suddenly disappeared as the whelping date approached and repeated searches failed to reveal any signs of her. After several weeks her owner concluded that she must have met with some accident or had been destroyed by some beast of prey. However, at the end of three months the bitch reappeared at the farm, accompanied by six strong, healthy puppies! Evidently she recalled the loss of her previous litter and feared a repetition of it. Consequently, she had hidden herself away with complete success and had managed to raise her puppies safely and to somehow provide them with food until she felt it safe to return.

Still another type of remarkable memory was shown by the famous German bitch, Senta v.d. Moorinsel, a granddaughter of Carlo Viktoria. Senta was known as the "talking dog". A bitch of the highest intelligence and an excellent brood matron as well, she attracted the interest of many animal psychologists. Contemporary newspapers reported that one university professor spent a week on the North German island where she lived in order to observe this remarkable bitch, and her ability to "talk" inspired long and learned scientific dissertations. Senta's pedigree was not complete, but she has carried on through her grandson, Fedor v. Buetersburg. Her career may be compared to that of "Intelligent Hans", the "speaking horse" of Germany.

In attempting to present a true picture of the character and temperament of the Doberman we must not, in justice, forget the opposite side, which has been generally ignored and passed over. In other words, those Dobermans which are not keen enough, for some enthusiasts at least. Soon after the turn of the century they are mentioned as occurring from time to time. Writers on the breed have spoken of shyness and lack of temperament in certain individuals, named and unnamed, and quite recently there was a discussion of this phase in the German Club's breed paper. Some years ago a prominent German fancier is reported to have disposed of his male for this very reason, that he was not sharp enough. Others, however, have no objection to dogs of this type and prefer them not too keen. One old gentleman cannily remarked: "If I put a sign by my garden gate saying: 'Warning! Doberman!' that is all that is necessary. The dog doesn't need to be sharp. Just the sight of him is enough to impress strangers." To which the writer

17

might add that the less strangers know about dogs the more likely they are to be impressed.

However, the policy of the German Club is to issue certificates as to suitability for breeding purposes which will in the future make it impossible to breed from nervous or untrained animals. Since training includes certain tests for temperament, this requirement would automatically eliminate many unsuitable animals. Moreover, it is impressed upon the breeder that it is his duty to eliminate promptly any puppies in a litter which are shy or nervous, as has been generally done by responsible breeders in the past. A dog with undesirable mental or physical characteristics has absolutely no place in any intelligent breeding program. Nevertheless, it is well for the conscientious breeder to remember that Dobermans, like many other dogs, may have very decided likes and dislikes. Character and temperament can be complex matters, and a highly bred, intelligent dog may be quite fearless and yet avoid strangers. The fact that a one-man dog does not make friends readily and does not care to be handled by strangers means only that he is not hail fellow well met, and is no indication of shyness. Home environment, too, plays an important part. Where a litter has had little experience with strange sights and people, the first venture into a large world may bring very different reactions. The more intelligent puppy may be watchful and wary of the unknown, while his apparently more aggressive brother is simply more headlong and heedless. A single set test, therefore, cannot always be decisive, although a dog which is fundamentally shy and nervous will react promptly to sights and sounds.

Every Doberman breeder should be convinced of the importance of breeding dogs with real working abilities. In spite of the growth of Obedience Training during recent years, the importance of training seems to be more generally understood in Germany than in the United States, and a larger proportion of the dogs there are actually trained and worked. What the novice often fails to understand is that in order to retain the qualities characteristic of a working breed, they must be exercised. Race horses are bred from racers and drastically weeded by the test of actual performance. Bench show success attests a dog's conformation but not his working qualities. While breeding from trained stock will not in itself directly increase the trainability of the subsequent puppies, it does mean that the parents have passed a test. If all dogs which are unable to take training are eliminated from the breeding program over a number of generations, the resulting progency are certainly more likely to retain their working breed character than the product of generations of ancestors whose ability to take training is completely unknown, and a number of whom might have had to be eliminated as unsuitable if they had been tested.

The Doberman might, because of his versatility, be compared to an actor with a large and varied repertoire. The breed has many abilities. He is a keen, incorruptible watch dog, an affectionate house dog, a jolly friend to children, a good comrade with other animals. The fancier who loves the breed and has time to spend with his dog will always find new and interesting sides to his character. For such a one there can be no other breed and in his case it is "once a Doberman—always a Doberman!"

HERR DOBERMANN, ON LEFT, AND HIS FRIENDS
Taken in Germany, 1870. A very rare photograph

Origin of the Breed

THE origin of most breeds of dogs is veiled in obscurity and we can only conjecture as to their beginning. Before the days of dog shows, pedigree records were not kept. Breeding was haphazard and based on working qualities rather than refinement of type.

Transportation was difficult and breeders of a local community were forced to use the local studs. It was natural for the farmer who kept dogs for herding cattle to breed his bitches to a neighbor's dog that excelled in herding qualities. Likewise the hunter selected as a suitable mate for his bitch, a stud that was famous for pointing game.

While these early breeders knew nothing of the Mendelian theory, they believed that "like begets like," and through many generations of inbreeding a type was established in the local community which in time reproduced itself.

Not so in the case of the Doberman Pinscher! We know definitely where and when it originated. Although there are vague stories of dogs similar to the Doberman previous to the time that Herr Karl Friedrich Louis Dobermann owned a black and tan Pinscher who accompanied him on his rounds as night watchman in the town of Apolda, we do not give credence to these stories.

Herr Dobermann was born on February 2, 1823, and while a young man, worked as an official of the court of aldermen. He was later given the position of dogcatcher and administrator of the chamber of accounts at Nieder-rossla—Apolda, as well as flayer and official of the tax office. He was also employed as the night police officer and selected a likely specimen from the dog pound to accompany him on his rounds, not only as a guard but to scent out an intruder.

This dog he called Schnupp, and he undoubtedly did not consider him fit for breeding purposes because records show that Schnupp was castrated at nine months of age.

Herr Dobermann was interested in breeding dogs and it was not sufficient for a dog to be worthy of the duties of a guard, but he also wanted to breed a type that would reproduce itself with the same qualities.

Among his friends were a night watchman, Herr Räbel, and a watchman on the tower Böttger, who were also interested in dog breeding, and they collaborated with a shepherd in a neighboring village.

Early in the year 1870, Herr Dobermann owned a black male with red markings and a lot of gray undercoat. This type was more common in later years. His son, Louis Dobermann, master of woven goods at Apolda, has described this male, Schnupp, as "a dog of such great intelligence as is seldom found. He was clever and fearless and knew how to bite. My father could not have chosen a better one."

When Herr Dobermann first acquired Schnupp, he lived in an apartment where he was unable to breed dogs; but in 1874 he moved to a larger apartment, and in 1880 purchased a house situated so that he could breed a few dogs

APOLDA

The native town of Herr Dobermann as it looked 100 years ago. This photograph was smuggled out of the Russian Zone after considerable risk and bribery

23

and train them. He acquired a female of the same color as Schnupp but with less gray undercoat. He named her "Bismarck," but a superior officer warned him that it was unlawful to give a female dog the name of a great states-man, so he changed her name to "Bisart." It is said that Bisart was very keen and her master had to be careful with her. When she was in season and accompanied Herr Dobermann on his rounds, no other protection was needed than to allow Schnupp to accompany him. Should the local "gallants" approach her, it was only necessary for Herr Dobermann to say to Schnupp, "Let's get rid of the other dogs." Schnupp would immediately chase them off.

Louis Dobermann tells us that his father bred some very good puppies from Bisart. They were almost all black with red markings, but in each of the first three or four litters there were one or two puppies that were black with red and white markings. Because of their sturdy bodies, they were very popular with the public and Herr Dober-mann did not destroy them.

One of Bisart's daughters, named Pinko, had a natural bobtail, and he kept her for breeding purposes. He used a bobtailed stud with Pinko as he believed that from these he would get puppies with short tails, thus eliminating the necessity of docking; but the result was only one bobtailed dog in a litter. Among Pinko's get there were a few blues.

A review of the prices Herr Dobermann obtained for his puppies is very interesting in comparison with what is be-ing asked today. A male puppy five to six weeks old sold for two Deutschmarks, fifty pfennig. A female of the same age would bring one Deutschmark, fifty pfennig. It is said that the dogs were of the best quality, with their tails and ears cropped. At that time, four marks and twenty pfennig were valued at one dollar.

The town of Apolda in which Herr Dobermann resided is located in the state of Thuringia, and beginning with the year 1860, on the first Sunday after Whitsuntide, there was held each year a dog market or dog show by an organized group, for the promotion of breeding purebred

24

KARL PETER UMLAUFF
(February 21, 1869—June 9, 1937)

An outstanding pioneer of the breed, Peter Umlauff was president of the Dobermannpinscher Club of North Germany (later the Dobermannpinscher Club D.V.) for thirty years. A judge of both bench shows and police trials, he was the first German judge to be invited to officiate at Westminster Kennel Club (1923). Mr. Umlauff was father of Gerda Umlauff, a co-author of this book.

dogs. The government of Apolda surrendered the entrance fees to this show, which were fifty pfennig for each dog, to the club to be used as prize money, for buying certificates, and to pay the necessary bills. The market was situated in the old part of Apolda and the dogs were arranged in six groups and classified as luxury dogs, hounds, house dogs, butcher dogs, etc. It is said that nearly one hundred dogs were exhibited, and they were accommodated on two benches forming a right angle. The show began at eight o'clock in the morning and remained open until one in the afternoon. There was music by a band. We quote from an interesting report on the dogs benched in the market place in one of these shows: "In the first part, which was designated 'dogs of luxury,' there were, among others, four big Pinschers, two of very good quality. In the next there was a very good smooth-haired, brindled white and brown German dog, with brown ears, powerful and well built, and two brown giants, undoubtedly of German parentage, while among the others were four gray colored dogs which seemed to have mixed blood. This gray color is the same that had been seen in hounds since 1860. There was a gray Pointer of pure German stock with a tail, however, which was too strong and with red haws in his eyes. There was a two-year-old bitch of nice appearance, with a litter of two beautiful puppies, all belonging to the same kennel. They were the best dogs among the grays. The breeder had known their ancestry for several generations and had owned some of the stock himself. He said it was a pure breed. Another kennel had an exhibit of twelve house dogs, all of poor quality with the exception of a Pinscher."

Herr Dobermann always attended this dog market and was on the lookout for any dog that seemed to have the qualities necessary for training and he was especially interested in types bordering on the Dobermann Pinscher as we know him.

Older specialists affirm that the Doberman breed existed before Herr Dobermann helped to popularize it. Never-

26

JAMBO V. HAMBURG
One of Peter Umlauff's Dobermans with his trainer,
policeman Kruger

theless, after his death on the ninth of June, 1894, the breed was named for him.

Formerly, these dogs were occasionally called "Thuringia Pinscher" or "Police-soldier dogs." The name "Schnupp" was a popular name for dogs at the beginning of the century.

Records show that at a dog show in Apolda, an heirloom photograph showing Herr Dobermann and his friends was given as a prize; and it is doubtful if these early dog breeders would have given such recognition to Herr Dobermann had he not been actually the originator of the breed that we now know as the Doberman Pinscher.

The word "Pinscher" meaning Terrier, after the word "Dobermann" has not been used in Germany since 1949, as it is now recognized that the name is not appropriate for this breed.

The first dog show to be held in Germany was at Hamburg in 1863, but it was not until 1876 that the first "German Dog Stud Book" was founded; and in the same year there came into being the first dog magazine to be published in Germany. This was a weekly journal, *The Dog, Organ for breeders and fanciers of purebred dogs*, consisting of four pages, commercial size, with pictures.

From an issue printed in 1882 we quote: "In the German dog shows there is some confusion about the English Black and Tan Terrier or Manchester Terrier, and our shorthaired Pinscher. The Pinscher's head is not shaped like that of the Greyhound breeds. The Pinscher seems to be gaining more and more in favor with the public." In a show report of that same year at Hanover, we quote: "There have been no great numbers of the German Pinscher, but some very good specimens."

Undoubtedly breeders used various crosses in these earlier years, and in one magazine there appeared an article in which the author tried to explain the numerous crosses that had been tried out in order to duplicate Herr Dobermann's breeding. These crosses of miscellaneous dogs were made in great number and the results had been useful, clever, elegant, courageous, and alert dogs. It

28

seems that all of the ancestors of the German Dobermann gave of their best quality of body and spirit, because the Dobermann excels as a runner and as a jumper and is useful for each purpose; both his size and his practical short hair are of great advantage.

There have been many speculations advanced regarding the origin of the Dobermann. We will not try to examine them all. It is better to rely on known facts.

An old breeder, Mr. Albert Ammon, wrote: "My grandfather, in the years 1830-1860, owned an inn with a slaughter house at Grobenbodungen, in Worbis, Saxony, near Thuringia. I always spent my holidays at my grandfather's, and when there, Audi, a great butcher dog, was always with me. Audi was a bitch nearly 65 cm. high, black with much undercoat and red markings, a little white spot at the chest, long ears, and a curled tail. The butchers seldom owned horses and carts. They used to drive the cattle for hours and hours. I remember very well that on one occasion, when my grandfather was driving his cattle from the Harz Mountains, Audi had her puppies en route. Grandfather gave her to a friend and drove his cattle with another dog which he borrowed, arriving home very late at night. He was indeed astonished when the next morning he found Audi in the stable with seven puppies. She had walked the distance seven times in four hours, and each time she brought a puppy with her.

In later years, when I bred Terriers and Collies, I read of a Mr. Göller who offered for sale the new breed, Dobermannpinscher. In the year 1899 I bought my first dog of this breed from Mr. Göller. At once I noted the resemblance between this new breed and Audi, my grandfather's dog of decades before, with only one difference: Mr. Göller's dogs had no cropped ears and tails.

Concerning this similarity, Mr. Göller said: "I am quite convinced that it was principally the German Shepherd dog, the smooth haired Pointer, the blue Great Dane, and the German smooth haired Pinscher which played a remarkable part in the creation of this breed. Those dogs that I bought in the villages had no undercoat, or very little, but red markings, short, absolutely black hair like hounds, little marked lips, and long toes. Those dogs which came from Apolda were more like German Shepherd Dogs and Pinschers."

It is very interesting to hear the conclusion of Mr. Richard Strebel, one of the most prominent German dog specialists, who believed that the Doberman does not belong to the Pinscher group; that is to say, the Terriers. He supposed that this breed came from the Shepherds, that it is probably a cross between the Shepherds and the Pinschers. It was his supposition that there had been crosses of the Shepherds of Thuringia and the Black and Tan Terrier of England, and that the Doberman had inherited not only the coat of what we know as the Manchester Terrier but also his disposition, which is keen, alert, quick, and fearless.

German Champion 1949
HELLA GERMANIA 889/48
Breeder-Owner: A. Schneider, Remscheid

30

Early Breeders and Champions in Germany

by

Gerda M. Umlauff

FTER the death of Herr Dobermann, several promoters who admired the character and temperament of the dog Doberman sponsored, endeavored to improve its appearance and establish a breed of dog that could be recognized by the national kennel club of Germany.

The breed of today can be traced back to the 1890's, when the first animals entered in the Dobermannpinscherverein stud book were whelped. Recorded history thus dates back about fifty to sixty years. Before that time opinions vary and the truth must be a matter of conjecture and circumstantial evidence. Certainly, the ancestors of the present Doberman were quite different from the show stock of today. A contemporary show report describes the breed in 1899 as coarse and heavy-headed, inclined to be long and wavy-coated, with thick undercoats, often

31

grey in color, and straw-yellow markings. White spots on the chest were common, and the general appearance resembled a Rottweiler. Various authorities have claimed that the ancestry of the breed included the old German Shepherd Dog (not to be confounded with the modern breed of that name), the Rottweiler, and even some Great Dane, Setter, and Weimaraner blood. Dachshunde and smooth-haired German Pinschers (now practically extinct) are also mentioned. The original Thuringian stock, whatever it was, is said to have been crossed with Rottweiler or other cattle dogs used to drive northward the cattle bought in Switzerland and southern Germany.

A decisive part in developing the Doberman was unquestionably played by Herr Otto Göller, who was, like Herr Dobermann, a resident of Apolda in Thuringia. It is said that he was encouraged and spurred on to active breeding by a well-known merchant, Herr Oskar Vorwerk of Hamburg, who had already become known as the creator of a new breed of poultry.

The dogs in the neighborhood of Apolda had a reputation as exceptional guard and watchdogs. In fact, the early representatives of the breed of whom there is record seem to have been notably sharp, if not actually vicious in temperament. The occupation of dog breeder was not highly esteemed in 19th century Germany, and Göller and his young wife are reported to have been hesitant, at first, about agreeing to Herr Vorwerk's suggestion. However, Göller's enthusiasm was eventually aroused, and he seems to have taken the lead in pushing the new breed. Apparently he began to buy up dogs which had been raised in the neighborhood of Apolda, selecting what seemed the most suitable out of a rather mixed group.

Before long this attracted attention and brought about a rise in prices. Another problem which soon arose was the matter of proper quarters for so many animals. The dogs, quartered together in a large rented building in the village, made so much noise that the authorities intervened. It proved more satisfactory to distribute the dogs about the neighborhood individually or in small groups, instead of attempting to operate a single large kennel. This has remained the usual German practice.

It seems likely that the early breeders of Dobermans lacked a clear aim and specific principles on which to work. Each probably had his own ideal, and there was at first no club, no stud book, and no breed standard. Modern theories of breeding and knowledge of Mendelian laws were unknown, and progress was necessarily a matter of trial and error.

Except by constant reference to the stud books in which many of the foundation dogs were later registered it is not even easy to tell who was actually the breeder of notable individuals. There were then no fixed rules regarding names. Dogs frequently bore the kennel name of owner rather than breeder and often changed names with ownership. Some of them consequently appear under three or four different and confusing aliases.

As appears to be commonly the case when a new breed is developed or an old breed is introduced into the show ring, there are many early registrations, most of which left no permanent influence. Gradually a few prepotent sires and dams, who possessed the inherent ability to pass on desired qualities to their get, came to oust the less potent strains. After a number of generations it is found that practically every important show dog or sire traces back to a very small number of sires. In some breeds all male lines go back to a single dog. Even when, as in the Doberman, this does not seem to be the case and two or three or even four appear to divide the honors, it is quite possible that could they be traced sufficiently far they would all be found to be related.

Sometimes a line is prominent for a time and then disappears completely, or is carried on only through daughters. This was the case with Prinz Matzi v. Groenland, whose parents, Bosco and Caesi, produced the earliest litter in the stud book. Prinz Matzi, whelped in 1895, was an early Sieger, reputedly the first Doberman in Hamburg. Bred by Gustav Krumbholz of Wickerstedt, whose Ilm-Athen kennel later became one of the most important influences upon the breed. Prinz Matzi v. Groenland was sold by Göller to Herr Vorwerk. Groenland was the kennel name of Goswin Tischler. Thueringen was the kennel name used by Herr Göller of Apolda, and Ilm-Athen the name used by Gustav Krumbholz of Wicker-stedt, tho Krumbholz has also been used as a kennel name. The career of Prinz Matzi (formerly Fritz) under his new name and ownership was not a fortunate one. For one thing, he was not house-broken, and worse still, he celebrated his arrival at Hamburg by attacking a Great Dane for which his master had just paid 1,100 marks. Prinz Matzi proved an effective fighter, for he tore the Dane to pieces and was promptly shipped back to Göller. "Before I shoot Matzi we will use him for further breeding," wrote Vorwerk, his enthusiasm for the breed apparently unquenched. He was thereupon sold to the president of the breed club in Frankfurt. In this area he was one of the earliest sires, his best son being the winning Siegwart v. Hochheim, but his line has not carried on. His get are said to have been inclined to have long coats, a fault for which Prinz Matzi was himself criticized, as well as for a heavy, coarse body and light eyes. Herr Vorwerk, however, was afterwards made an honorary member of the Dobermannpinscherklub of Apolda, and of the Dobermannpinscherverein, because of his contributions to the development of the breed.

A second dog who was important in the 1890's was Junker Slenz v. Thüringen, whelped in 1897 and bred by Herr Muenzenberg of Giebichenstein, but carrying Göller's kennel name. Slenz was by Rambo out of Elly, both unregistered. Slenz' son, Leporello v.d. Nidda (later v. Main), out of a Troll v. Groenland daughter, Flora v. Groenland (later v.d. Nidda), was a handsome dog who had little influence in Germany but who holds an important place in Switzerland. Slenz also sired three good bitches: Thinda v. Thüringen, Veronika v. Thüringen (winner of 15 firsts), and Walpurgis v. Thüringen. Slenz, like Prinz Matzi, was at stud in Frankfurt. His sons, in addition to Leporello, included Schill v. Deutz and perhaps

34

MODERN V. SIMMENAU #42114
German Champion, 1929

Erbgraf Zingo v. Thüringen. Zingo was a son of Freya v. Thüringen, one of Göller's important early winners, with 22 firsts to her credit. Freya was a daughter of the unregistered Schnupp and Helmtrude. Freya was accidentally mated to both Slenz and Graf Belling v. Thüringen, as was duly recorded in the stud book. Subsequently, Göller is said to have been convinced that Graf Belling was actually the sire. However, Philip Gruenig, an outstanding German authority on the breed, claims that Zingo's descendants are of a clearly distinct physical type from those of Graf Belling. In particular, he cites Thina v. Aprath and her get. Thina, a daughter of Thinda v. Thüringen, would have been a double Slenz granddaughter if Zingo were actually by Slenz, and this close inbreeding would naturally tend to fix and perpetuate any characteristics derived from him. The fact that Zingo's descendants today are all through female lines, like the rest of Slenz' descendants, is perhaps an additional bit of circumstantial evidence.

The two principal male lines which have left descendants still important at the present time are those through Lux v. Groenland and Landgraf.

Goswin Tischler of Apolda, whose kennel name of von Groenland was derived from the name of the street in Apolda in which he was born in 1859 and not from the island of Greenland, was, together with Otto Göller of von Thüringen kennels, the most important breeder in the early days of the Doberman. In 1898 his black and tan bitch, Tilly I v. Groenland (NZ 17), whelped a year earlier, produced a litter of five which were to make breed history. Tilly's parents were unregistered and are generally given as Lord and Schnupp, or, more elegantly Lord v. Dennstedt and Schnuppine v. Dennstedt. She was a ·full sister of Dobber v. Berghof 4, who played a minor role in the development of the breed through his daughters Merigarda and Betty v.d. Haardt, both out of Tilly's daughter Krone v. Groenland (also called Korvins Krone). The name of Schnupp or Schnuppi was a common one at this time for both dogs and bitches, therefore it is impossible to say whether the Schnupp and Schnuppi who produced Nero, sire of Lux v. Groenland, and Moora, double granddam of Prinz Matzi v. Groenland, were the same pair, though it is quite possible. Nor can we say with any certainty whether Nero's dam was also the dam of Tilly I. Should this be the case, Tischler's famous litter by Lux out of Tilly would result from the breeding of a Schnuppi daughter to a Schnuppi grandson, and since such strong inbreeding appears in the early generations of most breeds when carried back sufficiently far, and is not otherwise found to the usual extent in the Doberman, it seems highly probable that this was the case. If so, Schnuppi or Schnuppine v. Dennstedt would appear to be one of the most powerful influences in the formation of the breed. It may have been the same or another Schnuppi who was the dam of Theolinde v. Thüringen, who, when bred to Nero, produced Siegerin Gerhilde v. Thüringen. The male Schnupp who was the sire of Nero and the grandsire of Lux v. Groenland may also have been the same as the Schnupp who sired Moora, granddam and perhaps double granddam of Prinz Matzi, and dam of Rudelsburg Schnuppe, dam of Siegerin Veronika v. Thüringen.

The other litter recorded out of Tilly I v. Groenland produced Troll v. Groenland, sire of Flora v. Groenland (later v.d. Nidda), who was the dam of Leporello v.d. Nidda, important in Switzerland. Troll was sired by Lord v. Groenland, about whom nothing seems to be known, but considering the frequency with which names were changed at that period and the fact that both were unregistered, it seems at least possible that Lord v. Groenland was identical with Lord v. Dennstedt and that Tilly I produced Troll when mated back to her own sire. A dog called Schnupp also sired Freya v. Thüringen, the dam of Graf Wedigo v. Thüringen, who was sired by the Lux-Tilly son Graf Belling v. Thüringen. And a bitch called Schnupp v. Thüringen was the dam of Adele and Alarich v. Thüringen, whelped in 1897.

In addition to Lux v. Groenland, the other important tail male ancestor of modern Dobermans is the unregistered

Landgraf, who sired Baron Winfried v. Thüringen whelped in 1899, out of the bitch Hertha. While Landgraf's breeding is unknown, an early pedigree records him as by Neff out of Schnuppe, and once again the interesting question arises whether this Schnuppe was the same bitch which produced Tilly I v. Groenland and Nero. Since two strong male lines such as those of Lux and Landgraf nearly always have a common origin when it can be traced—as is shown in the history of many breeds of dogs, and of cattle and horses as well—this is certainly a tempting theory.

Whatever their original relationship, the two lines from Lux and Landgraf have carried on for more than fifty years and are today represented in full force in America through the descendants of Lux v.d. Blankenburg (including Ch. Dictator v. Glenhugel) and Stolz v. Roeneckenstein (including Ch. Alcor v. Milsdod). However, although both Lux and Landgraf are still strongly represented, the male line from Lux has dwindled in recent years, though his influence on the breed remains of tremendous importance.

The chart on the opposite page shows the descendants of Lux v. Groenland.

Greif v. Groenland made his greatest contribution to the breed as the sire of Prinz v. Ilm Athen, whose dam, Lady v. Ilm Athen, was part Manchester terrier. Prinz, whelped in 1901, was one of the great sires of the breed, and his owner, G. Krumbholz of Wickerstedt, had a decisive influence upon developments. Almost all of Prinz' progeny were black with clear, dark markings, and in the field of color his dominance was profound. He left many great descendants, including three notable sons, Peter v. Ilm Athen, Graf Edel v. Ilm Athen, and Sturmfried v. Ilm Athen. All three are repeatedly found behind modern pedigrees, though none of them is any longer prominent in male line. Peter sired Graf Benno v. Thueringen, already mentioned as the grandsire of Theo v. Funkenburg. The influence of the above dogs can be seen in the pedigree of Graf Belling v. Berlin, the sire of Troll v.d. Blankenburg.

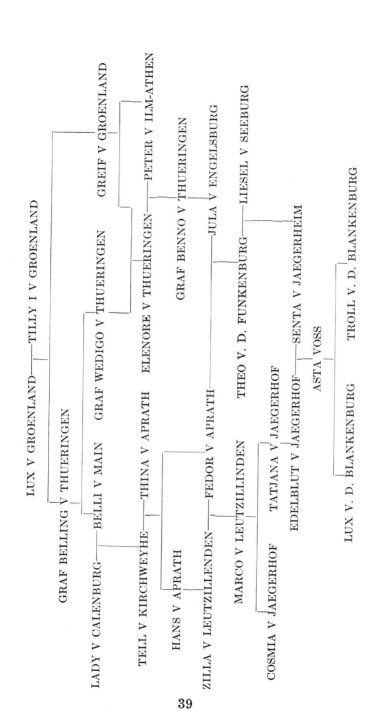

39

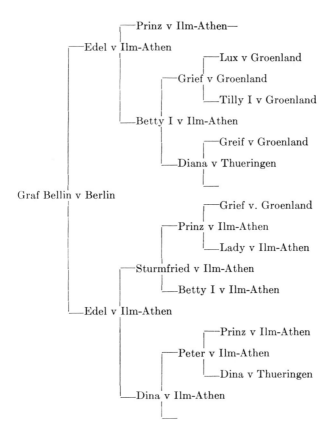

┌─Prinz v Ilm-Athen—
┌─Edel v Ilm-Athen
│   ┌─Lux v Groenland
│   ┌─Grief v Groenland
│ │   └─Tilly I v Groenland
│ └─Betty I v Ilm-Athen
│   ┌─Greif v Groenland
│   └─Diana v Thueringen
│   └
Graf Bellin v Berlin
│   ┌─Grief v. Groenland
│   ┌─Prinz v Ilm-Athen
│ │   └─Lady v Ilm-Athen
│ ┌─Sturmfried v Ilm-Athen
│ │   └─Betty I v Ilm-Athen
└─Edel v Ilm-Athen
      ┌─Prinz v Ilm-Athen
   ┌─Peter v Ilm-Athen
 │   └─Dina v Thueringen
└─Dina v Ilm-Athen
   └

Sturmfried v. Ilm Athen, whelped in 1906, was three years younger than Peter, and was out of the blue bitch, Betti I v. Ilm Athen, a daughter of Greif v. Groenland and Dina v. Thuerigen. Dina, herself a Greif daughter, was the dam of Peter as well as the granddam of Sturmfried, who was consequently a double Greif grandson, with Greif a third time in the previous generation. Sturmfried was a black dog of great nobility, a more refined edition of his double grandsire Greif, and a consistent transmitter of the rich markings inherited from his paternal granddam, the part Manchester Lady v. Ilm Athen.

Moritz v. Burgwall left another son, Bodo v. Elfenfeld (out of Eddie v. Elfenfeld), who was mated to Hispa v.

40

NETHERLAND CHAMPION GRAAF DAGOBERT OF NEERLANDS STAM
Best Doberman 1948, 1949, 1950
Sire: Ch. Waldo v.d. Rhedenvelt   Grandsire: Ch. Troll v. Engelsburg

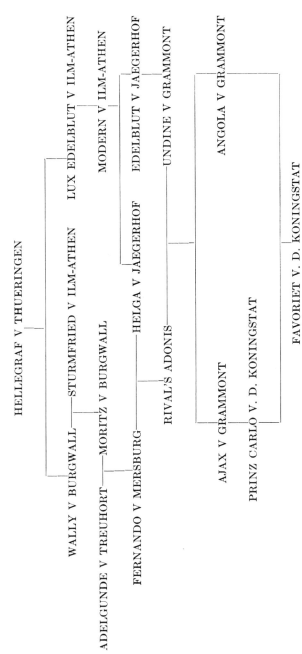

HELLEGRAF V THUERINGEN

WALLY V BURGWALL——STURMFRIED V ILM-ATHEN

LUX EDELBLUT V ILM-ATHEN

MODERN V ILM-ATHEN

ADELGUNDE V TREUHORT——MORITZ V BURGWALL

FERNANDO V MERSBURG——HELGA V JAEGERHOF

EDELBLUT V JAEGERHOF

UNDINE V GRAMMONT

RIVAL'S ADONIS

AJAX V GRAMMONT

ANGOLA V GRAMMONT

PRINZ CARLO V. D. KONINGSTAT

FAVORIET V. D. KONINGSTAT

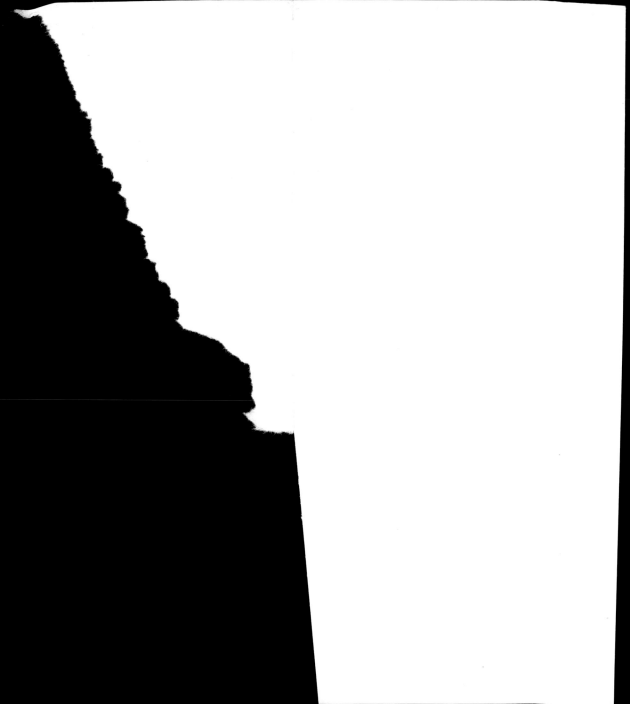

Maco Kennels
Certificate of Pedigree

MACO's
REGISTERED NAME

( ) 6-17-73
AKC NO.   DATE OF BIRTH

#1
BLACK+RUST MALE
COLOR   SEX

G.M. Cox
BREEDER

Ch. Adel's Bourbon
sire

AKC NO.
Walkers
BREEDER
Black+Rust.
COLOR #1

Ch. Brown's Dian
SIRE

AKC No.
Black+Rust
COLOR

AKC No.
Black+Rust
COLOR
Hillcrests Ho
DAM

#1
Black+Rust.
COLOR

J. McGowan
BREEDER

AKC NO.
Quailway's
dam

Signed this 26 day of August 19 73

Marge Cox
PO Box 163 Duchation, Ola
775-2776

Silberberg to produce the litter sisters, Borste and Brunhild v. Falkenhain. Borste was of substantial importance
as the dam of Alex v. Simmenau, to be discussed later.
Moritz was also the sire of Gudrun v. Hornegg, an important bitch too often passed over. Mated to Alex v.
Simmenau, she produced Lotte I v. Simmenau, a double
granddaughter of Moritz v. Burgwall, while by Arno v.d.
Gluecksburg Gudrun was the dam of Burschel v. Simmenau, who holds unchallenged position as the sire of
Lux v.d. Blankenburg.

Sturmfried's influence was likewise of prime importance
through his daughter, Lotte v. Ilm Athen, dam of Prinz
Modern v. Ilm Athen, who belongs to the now dominant
male line of Hellegraf v. Thueringen.

Whelped in 1904, Hellegraf was one of the greatest
sires the breed has ever seen and the tail male ancestor
of every Doberman champion finished in the United States
for a number of years past. Oddly enough, he was a
brown, and it is curious to observe how his color has to
a large extent disappeared, while his influence in other
respects remains so strong. A powerful dog of great
beauty and nobility, Hellegraf was hard to fault, though
it is reported that his shoulders might have been tighter
and his muzzle a trifle less pointed. His ancestry can be
traced back in male line over four generations to Landgraf
and Hertha, beyond which it is doubtful. Given in one
place as by Neff out of Schnuppe, Landgraf is also reported to have been by Alarich v. Thueringen out of his
litter sister, Adele v. Thueringen, who were by Prinz I
v. Thueringen out of Schnuppe v. Thueringen. Alarich,
whelped in 1897, the same year as Junker Slenz, is one
of the earliest sires who proved of real importance. His
sister Adele, small, crooked, and unimpressive by modern
standards, was nevertheless the dam (by Graf Wedigo v.
Thueringen) of Prinz Weddo v. Thueringen, whose daughter, Beda Frischauf, alias Nora v. Ried, was the dam of
the very important Sieger, Lord v. Ried. Whether or not
he was by Alarich out of Adele, Landgraf sired Baron
Winfried v. Thüringen early in 1899, and Winfried sired

Landgraf Sighart v. Thueringen, whelped in November, 1900, whose dam, Ines, was certainly by Alarich out of Adele. Sighart was mated to Glocke v. Thueringen, also known as Ullrich's Glocke, a notable winner and a sister to Graf Wedigo. Sighart and Glocke were the parents of Hellegraf. Another Sighart son deserving mention was Hans v. Thueringen, later known as Junker Hans v.d. Ronneburg, whose dam, Merigarda, was by Dobber v. Bergerhof, full brother to Tilly I v. Groenland, out of Krone v. Groenland (called Korvin's Krone), litter sister to Greif v. Groenland. Hans sired Immo v. Isenburg, later called Max v. Kaiserring, whose dam, Hulda v. Isenburg, was a daughter of Junker Slenz. Immo was the sire of Luna II v.d. Pfalz, whose daughter by Lord v. Ried was Helga v.d. Pfalz. Helga, another bitch insufficiently known, was the dam of Leuthold v. Hornegg by her own sire, Lord v. Ried, and of Gudrun v. Hornegg by Moritz v. Burgwall.

Hulda v. Isenburg, who was likewise known as Hulda v. Zavelstein, was also mated to Normann v. Frauenlob, a double grandson of Graf Belling v. Thueringen, and produced Nora Frischauf, the granddam of Lord v. Ried on his dam's side.

The descendants of Hellegraf v. Thueringen are shown on the following chart:

FILIPPO, ITALIAN CHAMPION 1949

44

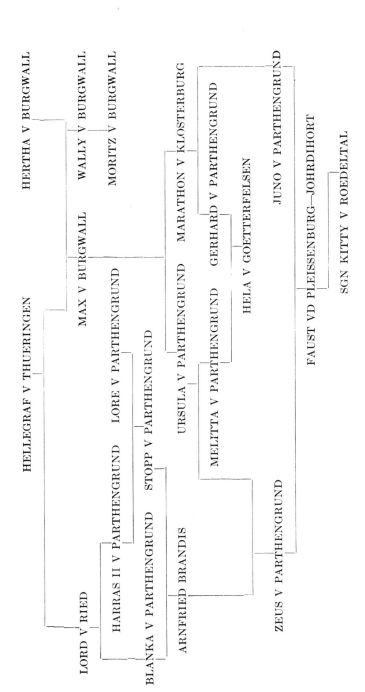

HERTHA V BURGWALL

WALLY V BURGWALL

MORITZ V BURGWALL

MARATHON V KLOSTERBURG

GERHARD V PARTHENGRUND

MAX V BURGWALL

HELA V GOETTERFELSEN

JUNO V PARTHENGRUND

SGN KITTY V ROEDELTAL

HELLEGRAF V THUERINGEN

URSULA V PARTHENGRUND

LORE V PARTHENGRUND

MELITTA V PARTHENGRUND

STOPP V PARTHENGRUND

FAUST VD PLEISSENBURG—JOHRDIHORT

HARRAS II V PARTHENGRUND

ARNFRIED BRANDIS

LORD V RIED

BLANKA V PARTHENGRUND

ZEUS V PARTHENGRUND

Note Max v Burgwall is sometimes called Max vd Klosterburg.

45

F_1 F_2 F_3 F_4 F_5

Hispa v. Silberberg
    Borste v. Falkenhain
        Alex v. Simmineau
            Lotte I v. Simmineau
Hiede v. Silberberg
    Sybille v. Silberberg
Bayard v. Silberberg
    Sybille v. Silberberg
        Adela v. Ostern
            Claus v.d. Spree
      Arno v. Gluecksburg
        Burschel v. Simmineau
            Lux v.d. Blankenburg
                Alto v. Sigalsburg
            Leddy v.d. Blankenburg
                Alex v. Finohoehe
            Claus v.d. Spree
Helga v. Jaegerhof
Rival's Adonis
Edelblut v. Jaegerhof
    Asta v.d. Voss
        Rappo v.d. Blankenburg
            Asta v.d. Finohoehe
      Lux v.d. Blankenburg
      Troll v.d. Blankenburg
        Dora v. Siesengrund
        Asta v. Stolzenburg
            Figaro v. Sigalsburg
    Undine v. Grammont
    Urian v. Grammont
        Benno v. Roemerhof
  Roland v. Gersbach
        Artus v. Rheinerft
  Asta v. Starkenburg
        Artus v. Langerode
        Achim v. Langerode

CH. TROLL V.D. EVERSBURG # 48/716
Best Doberman in Germany in 1952
Sire: Ch. Alex v. Kleinwaldheim   Dam: Ch. Christel v.d. Brunoburg
Owner: W. Hillebrand, Dortmund, Germany

F¹	F²	F³	F⁴	F⁵

Alex v. Finohoehe
    Stolz v. Roeneckenstein
    Lotte v. Roeneckenstein
   Arno v. Wiechselburg
    Comtess v. Steyerberg

Lord v. Warteburg
Waldo v. Strengbach
Artus v. Hoernsheim
Betty v. Jaegerhof
   Asta v. Starkenburg
Selma v. Jaegerhof (also called Thea)
Elfrieda v. Elsass
   Lotte II v. Stresow
    Horst v. Stresow
  Freya v. Stresow

More prominent than the Max v.d. Klosterburg line from Hellegraf, however, was that of Hellegraf's son, Lux Edelblut v. Ilm Athen, the sire of the famous Prinz Modern v. Ilm Athen and grandsire of Edelblut v. Jaegerhof. Lux Edelblut himself was one of those sires whose value is not recognized until too late to make adequate use of him. Whelped in 1908 out of Schnuppe v.d. Saale, who is said to have been a granddaughter on her sire's side of Glocke v. Thueringen, the dam of Hellegraf, Lux Edelblut was a black and tan dog who is said to have ended his days on a chain as watch dog at a brewery. Not until his son, Prinz Modern, was at the height of his glory was Lux Edelblut's value recognized, and by then it was too late to make use of him.

Prinz Modern v. Ilm Athen was out of Lotte v. Ilm Athen, a daughter of Sturmfried and Schnuppe v. Ilm Athen, whose breeding is unknown, so that both Modern's grand-dams are of uncertain origin. Nevertheless, he proved a most prepotent sire, who transmitted his qualities with exceptional vigor. Whelped in 1909, Prinz Modern was a medium-sized, elegant dog, who is criticized as lacking

48

in sharpness. Owned by Councillor Harry Peek of Düsseldoff on the lower Rhine, an active center of Doberman breeding at that period, he was given ample opportunity at stud, and bitches were sent to him from all over Germany as well as from Belgium and Holland.

Although Edelblut, whelped in 1913, was in his prime during World War I, which was unfortunate for his breeding career, he nevertheless suffered less than many of his contemporaries, since he was located in the Rhineland, in close proximity to Holland, and this was the area in which most of such breeding as was done at that time was carried on. This may have been the source of rumors current at the time that Edelblut was tremendously overused at stud, though as a matter of fact the records show that up to 1924, when he was eleven, he had served only 104 bitches, an average of ten per year. Nevertheless, Edelblut appears today in the pedigree of every important Doberman.

There seems to be no important male line from Edelblut today, but his daughter, Asta v. Starkenburg (dam of Achim and Artus v.d. Langerode, granddam of Alex v.d. Finohoehe and other important individuals), and his still more important daughter, Asta Voss (dam of Lux and Troll v.d. Blankenburg), were unquestionably two of the most influential factors in breed development. Asta v. Starkenburg was a double granddaughter of Prinz Modern v. Ilm Athen.

Sieger Lord v. Ried, the other outstanding son of Hellegraf, has already been mentioned as a son of Nora v. Ried (also called Beda Frischauf), who was by Weddo v. Thueringen. Lord was whelped in 1907 and made a sensation when first shown at Frankfurt. He was bred by A. Freyer of Lampertheim, Ried, in Hessen, and never changed hands. From his sire, Hellegraf, he derived great nobility and imposing size, his markings were clear and of good color, and his head in good proportion. He was larger than the average dog of his time, and not perfect in either front or rear. His breeding included five lines to Graf Belling v. Thüringen. The fact that Lord remained

49

throughout his entire life in a single locality probably limited his breeding opportunities, and many of the bitches bred to him were not suitable.

Among Lord's important daughters were the blue Liesel v. Dambachtal (out of Leska v.d. Wartburg by Lord v.d. Wartburg), who was the dam of Lea v. Weissenfels. Lea produced the noteworthy Dora v. Weisengrund (to be discussed later), Ch. Dyno v. Wiesengrund, and many others. Another Lord daughter, Blanka v. Parthengrund, was the dam of Arnfried v. Brandis; and another, Nora v. Elsass (bred to Prinz Modern v. Ilm Athen), was the dam of Elfriede v. Elsass, dam of Freya and Lotte II v. Stresow. Lotte's son, Horst v. Stresow, whelped in 1922, was the outstanding sire of his day in Russia. Helga v.d. Pfalz, still another Lord daughter, has been mentioned as the dam of his most important son, Leuthold v. Hornegg, from whom is descended the most important male line in the breed today with the exception of that through the Blankenburg dogs. Leuthold sired Achim v. Langerode, sire of Alex v.d. Finohoehe, who in turn sired Stolz v. Roeneckenstein, whence comes the line to Ch. Alcor v. Millsdod.

DESCENDANTS OF LORD VOM RIED

F₁   F₂   F₃

Harras II v. Parthengrund
Sepp v. Kraichgau
    Rino v. Romerschanz
        Troll v. Albtal
    Cryano v. Kranichstein
        Orste v. Kranichstein
Bodo v. Hoernsheim
    Alex v. Simmineau
Roland v.d. Haide

Roland's two sons, Salto v. Rottal and Bluto v. Isarstrand, in spite of their faults, both influenced the breed in America, Salto as the sire of Ch. Benno v. Burgholz, one of the earliest Siegers imported, and Bluto as the sire of Ella v. Siegestor, the dam of Helios v. Siegestor. Helios, through whom the Stolz v. Roeneckenstein line comes down, was bred by H. Renner of Munich. Stolz' breeder was O. Roenecke of Leipzig, where M. Eckner's Wiesengrund kennel was also located. The Blankenburg and Spree kennels were both located in Berlin, Sigalsburg at Chemnitz (now in the Russian Zone) and Simmenau, owned by C. Winkler, at Mertschuetz.

ESTER GERMANIA # 47/184 SchH 1
Best of Breed at 11 months, Dusseldorf, 1949
Sire: Friedo v. Furstenlager
Dam: Draga Germania

Dog Show in Hannover, Germany, September, 1949 (870 dogs)

52

The Doberman in Germany Since 1945

by
Gerda M. Umlauff

THE EVENTS of 1945 had a profound effect upon Doberman breeders and fanciers, for that year marked the beginning of the worst period the breed has ever experienced in its native country. But despite the shortage of food and the other hardships encountered, Dobermans produced during the next few years were of surprisingly good quality. The results achieved speak well for the average German fancier's integrity and regard for breed interests. There were faults in the dogs produced, it is true. Chief among them were lack of uniformity in size, and heads somewhat lacking in quality. Also, food shortages were reflected in the rickets and poor chests of some of the dogs—indicating sickness or feeding deficiencies.

When the currency was stabilized in June 1948, matters began to improve. Two months later it was possible to again print the independent Doberman magazine, to unite Doberman fanciers again into one large club, to use a single studbook, and to limit strictly the number of Sieger titles awarded each year.

Among the outstanding Dobermans shown in 1948 were Pan v. Heibertshausen, 58031; Tell v. Hinterborn, 56696; Roland v.d. Ambornquelle, 58200; and the bitch Bärbel v. Heibertshausen, 57693. A fault particularly prevalent at that time was missing teeth, although the fault was not found among the red Dobermans.

After the various small clubs were combined into one large club in 1949, it was decided to hold the Sieger show in Frankfurt. With an entry of 132, divided by sex and color, four Sieger titles were awarded. In black and tans the Sieger was Asko v.d. Walzenburg, 47/220, and the Siegerin was Hella Germania, 48/889. In reds the Sieger title went to Casso v. Kleinwaldheim, 46/288, and the Siegerin title was awarded to Afra v. Bad Heidelberg, 74415.

In other parts of the country three other shows were held the same year, and the main faults noted and discussed seem to have been missing teeth and light eyes. In some cases the forehand was weak. Very often, croups were too sloping.

In the Russian Zone, the black and tan male winner was Barro v. Rehwalde, 58563, SchH I, and the bitch winner was Asta v.d. Brundiekshöhe, 59904, SchH II at the Sieger show in Leipzig. In reds the winning male was Sally v.d. Schanzenhöhe, 59218, SchH II, and the winning bitch was Draga v.d. Vogelweide, 57218, SchH II.

The 1950 Sieger show took place at Dortmund. The black and tan Sieger title went to Troll v.d. Eversburg, 48716, SchH I, and the Siegerin title went to Britta v.d. Salzestadt, 1200. In reds the Sieger was Egon v. Fasanenheim, 758 (another dog from the same kennel, Carlo v. Fasanenheim, made his American championship). In reds the bitch title went to Cilly v. Klockenhof, 63053.

By the latter part of 1950, the lack of teeth, which had been such a prevalent fault immediately after the war, had largely disappeared, although light eyes were still somewhat common. A new fault which began to appear at this time was the large white mark, like a star, which was to be found on the chests of some Dobermans. Also, at this time, the bitches seemed somewhat prone to faulty coats—showing a thick, wooly undercoat, not only on the sides of the neck but also on the shoulders —to a degree which had not been known since the very early days of the breed before 1906.

To improve the breed and to aid in the elimination of existing faults, it was suggested that some form of breed inspection be inaugurated, and that certificates be issued showing suitability for breeding purposes.

Outstanding stud dogs in Germany during the latter part of 1950 were the following: the black and tan Rex v.d. Ambornquelle, 58201, a dog of excellent temperament and one that did not have the fault of missing teeth (in his pedigree were the kennel names v. Glasshof, v. Notburgstal, v. Hessenstolz, d.h. Neckartrasse, and v. Oberton); the black and tan Tell v. Hinterborn, 56696, whose pedigree included the v. Fürstenlager and v. Sandberg lines and who was considered especially suitable for Fürstenlager, Pfeddersheim, Sandberg, and Rauhfelsen bitches; Boris v. Rehwalde, 58562, SchH III and the Russian Zone Sieger for 1948, as well as his brother Barro v. Rehwalde, 58563, SchH I (v. Wiesengrund and v. Simbach lines appear in their pedigrees); and Hasso v.d. Neckarstrasse, SchH II, Messenger Dog, and a Russian Zone champion in 1947 and 1948, who carried v.d. Bismarcksäule and v. Rauhfelsen lines.

Four other black and tan males were rated as outstanding at this time: Bodo v. Wellborn, 59028, with v. Hinterborn and v. Kleinenborn bloodlines; Alex v. Kleinwaldheim, 57139, with v. Simbach and Südharz lines; Benno v.d. Schwedenhecke, 57363, SchH I, with v.d. Nievelsburg and v. Friedewald lines; and Bodo v. Raffturm, 1/4747-224, SchH II, with v. Hühnerhof and v.d. Nymphenburg lines.

There were only three red sires of importance at this time: Albert v.d. Wackermühle, 58037; Blitz v. Schwanengold, 59269, SchH I, from v. Friedewald and v.d. Neckarspitze lines; and Fels v.d. Barlinge, 54218, whose pedigree included dogs from v. Steiger, v.d. Bismarcksäule, v. Zwingfried, v. Schwetzingen, v. Ludwigsburg, v.d. Hebelgruft, v.d. Engelsburg, and v.d. Domstadt lines. The last-named kennel calls to mind another familiar name—that of Ch. Blank v.d. Domstadt, who appears in many American pedigrees.

At the general meeting of the Doberman Club in Cologne in 1951, the judges' association passed the following resolution concerning the Standard for the Doberman in the show ring:

1. *Teeth:* only Dobermans with completely faultless dentition may be awarded the Sieger title. "Excellent" may be awarded if two teeth are missing (not more than one in each jaw), or when small spaces are present between the teeth. "Very good" may be awarded if not more than three incisors are missing in both upper and lower jaws; or when spaces between the teeth are so large as to constitute an impairment to the general appearance. "Good" may be awarded if each jaw is lacking two incisors. Lack of more than four incisors or lack of molars is considered to be a disqualifying factor. The foregoing rules are applicable only to dogs of a generally faultless appearance.

2. *Color:* only the following colors will be recognized— black with red, brown with red, and blue with red.

3. *Disposition:* more emphasis should be placed on the disposition of the Doberman. Dogs manifesting nervousness, shyness or cowardice should be put down.

4. *Size:* if a dog is $\frac{1}{4}$ to $\frac{1}{2}$ inch oversize, it should not be held against him if he is of good general appearance.

In the Russian Zone of Germany, fawn-colored Dobermans were bred during the early 1950's.

Champion Dobermans in Germany in 1951 were the black and tan male Igon v. Naunhof, 64406; the black and tan bitch Nixie v. Württemberg, 64990; the red male Ajax v.d. Wertachbrücke, 56374; the red bitch Tonka v.d. Priorei, 63543; and the blue bitch Adda v.d. Geer, 63687.

The 1952 Sieger show was held at Dortmund with 93 Dobermans in competition. Results were as follows: black and tan male, Bordo v.d. Angelburg, 65523; black and tan bitch, Jette v.d. Geilenberge; red male, Etzel v. Romberg, 65564, SchH II; and the red bitch Corry v.d. Priorei, 66744. At the 1952 Sieger trial, the Sieger title was awarded to the male Artus v. Weideneck, 64623.

The 1953 Sieger show was held at Mannheim and the fol-

56

lowing Dobermans were awarded titles: black and tan male, Boris v. Felsingpass, 69192; black and tan bitch, Elsa v. Rurtal, 68072; red bitch, Hede v. Felsingpass, 64415. The black and tan Sieger male and the red Sieger bitch had the same sire and dam but were from different litters. At the 1953 Sieger trial, the male Artus v. Weideneck, 64623, was awarded the Sieger title for a second time.

The quality of the Dobermans benched at the 1953 Sieger show was first class. During the years immediately preceding this show, many top black and tan bitches had been seen, but at the 1953 show, the males were of the best quality. There were five males that were altogether so excellent that each was worthy of the Sieger title. The title was finally awarded to Boris, a German-born dog that had been sold to Switzerland.

Of the sixteen black and tan bitches, twelve were awarded the "Excellent" rating. In contrast to the red bitches, the red males were of poor quality.

In 1954 the following Dobermans were awarded Sieger titles: in black and tans, the male Lux v. Naunhof, 69671, and the bitch Jette v.d. Geilenberge, 68606, who had been awarded the title in 1952; in reds, the male Bodo v. Wolterskrug, 63833, and the bitch, Astried v.d. Walgernhiede, 66453; in blue and tans, the bitch Anett v.d. Priorei, 70076. At the Sieger trial, the male Artus v. Weideneck, 64623, was awarded his fourth Sieger title.

A 1955 issue of the club magazine stated that two cases of cryptorchidism had been noted in Dobermans, and it was decided that in such cases, permission for breeding would not be given. Also, that such males could not be awarded a prize at a show.

At the 1955 trial, the Sieger title was awarded the bitch Anni v. Neckarrhein, 64963. Siegers of the champion show were the following: in black and tans, the male Arras v.d. Georgsburg, 68738, and the bitch Senta v. Württemberg, 69109. In reds, the male Barri v. Weideneck, 70847, and the bitch Freya v. Romberg, 69894. Of the foregoing Siegers, all but one—Senta—were trained as protection dogs.

At the world's championship show held in Dortmund in

May 1956, 4,000 dogs were benched, including 86 Dobermans. In his report, the president of the club said the quality of the dogs exhibited was very good, and there were few with missing teeth. On the other hand, it was noted that the markings of many Dobermans were too pale in color. World's Champion titles were awarded the black and tan male Lump v. Hagenstolz, 70473, and the red bitch Freya v. Romberg, 69894.

The International Doberman Club (I.D.C.) was founded May 10, 1956, at Dortmund, with representatives present from Germany, Austria, and France. The Honorary President of the club is His Royal Highness Prince Philipp von Hessen.

Also in 1956, important instructions for breeding were given, and it was stated that in some cases breeding could be forbidden—for instance, if the stud dog was not yet eighteen months of age and the bitch not fifteen months; if the dogs had serious faults; and if either dog was ill or in poor condition. Bitches were to be permitted to have only one litter per year and were not to raise more than six puppies from a litter. Otherwise, pedigrees for the puppies were not to be issued.

At the 1956 Sieger trial, the famous male Artus v. Weideneck was again awarded the title. Sieger titles were also awarded in 1957 to the following: Prinz v. Hugenottendorf, 71146; Carmen v. Felsingpass, 71553; and the red male Harry v. Südbezirk, 74742. The working champion title was awarded in October 1957 in Berlin to the bitch Els v. Möllensee, 67991.

Beginning in 1957, registered pedigrees were issued for Doberman puppies only if the sire and dam were examined in advance and their desirability for breeding determined. The examination and subsequent rating are called ZuchtTauglichkeitsPrüfung, abbreviated ZTP. The ZTP has two parts: 1.) a determination of the quality of the dogs. The stud must have been awarded at least a "Very Good," and the bitch a "Good." 2.) a determination of the character of the dogs. They must either have been examined as protection dogs or their character and behavior must have been determined by a judge to ascertain whether the dogs are shy or nervous. If they are, permission for breeding is to be withheld.

1958 champions were Dieter v.d. Dykschen, 74325, Julchen

v. Wellborn, 75250, and the red bitch Gitta v. Romberg, 71772.

In 1958, the following new instructions for judges were issued:

1. Dogs must be judged according to the Standard.

2. Dogs with a missing tooth could be awarded only "Very Good," not "Excellent."

3. Males were to be no higher than 65 cm, bitches no higher than 62 cm. (1 inch equals 2½ cm.)

4. True type was to be stressed—a strong body, and a long and dry head.

5. Light eyes and light or dirty markings were declared faults.

6. Males with only one testicle were not to be awarded a prize. Names of such males were to be published in the club magazine and the dogs were not to be used for breeding.

7. The behavior of the dog in the ring was to be rated.

8. Acceptable colors were black and tan, red and tan, and blue and tan, only.

9. The title of champion was to be awarded only if the dog was at least eighteen months old; the CACIB (International championship title) was to be awarded only if the dog was at least fifteen months old. The title of champion was to be given only to dogs that compete in the open class or in the working dog class.

10. Judges were not to be allowed to handle strange dogs in the ring.

Later in 1958, the following additional instructions regarding the ZTP were given: from the 1st of January 1960, only Doberman males with completely faultless dentition could be used for breeding. A bitch could be used if only one tooth in the jaw was missing, but all other teeth were to be complete, otherwise the bitch could not be used. Testicles were also to be examined.

Examination of the Doberman character was to be determined in the following way: a man was to go close to the dog to determine whether he showed evidence of nervousness when a chair was dropped nearby or when someone shouted at a distance of 20 meters. A man with a stick was to threaten the dog. Shy dogs and those biting from fear were not to be

59

used for breeding. All German breeders agreed to these new regulations.

1959 Siegers were the black and tan male Dirk v. Goldberg, 76137; the red male Fan v. St. Clemens, 76046; the red bitch Blanka v. Alt-Hilken, 76006; and the black and tan bitch Citta v. Fürstenfeld, 76173. The champion title for work was awarded the male Frido v. Egelsberg, 71933.

Also in 1959, instructions for judges were changed in some points: the height of males was to be 66 to 68 cm., but no higher than 70 cm. Height of bitches was to be 63 to 66 cm., with a maximum height of 67 cm.

Also, if two teeth were missing, the dog was not to be rated higher than "Good" at the shows. If three or more teeth were missing, the dog could not be given a prize and was not to be judged. In such cases the name of the dog was to be published in the club magazine and the dog could not be used for breeding. The same was true if the dog was overshot or if a male had only one testicle.

In 1960 a resolution was adopted and published that first class dogs could acquire the Title "German Champion" if they were awarded, the CAC three times, provided they had been given an "Excellent" rating and had won first prizes; also provided they were at least fifteen months old, and an interval of twelve months had elapsed between the first and the third CAC. In addition, the dog must have passed an examination as a protection dog first class.

The 1960 working champion was the bitch Herba v. Rehwalde, 73674. Bench show titles were awarded the black and tan male Cito v. Fürstenfeld, 76169, and the colored Afra v. Wappen zu Bremen, 76786.

Sieger titles awarded in 1961 went to the black and tan Titus Germania SchH I, 76078; the bitch Ember v. Weinberge, SchH I, 76803; the red Falk v. Niddatal, SchH I, 76301; and the bitch Sonny v.d. Reeperbahn, 76668. The Sieger award for working dogs went to Fred v.d. Blütestadt Orsoy, 74597.

By 1962 the quality of the Dobermans in Germany had improved greatly. Almost no dogs with teeth faults were to be found at the shows. Most Dobermans had a complete set of incisors, whereas formerly, two—often from the underjaw—

were missing in many cases. (The four incisors were often so well set, however, that the fanciers did not realize there should have been six.) Character had improved, too, and on the whole, the benched dogs exhibited good manners.

Nine international shows took place in 1962. Of the 225 Dobermans benched, 143 merited the award "Excellent," 77 were classed as "Very Good," and only 5 were "Good." Two were prohibited from breeding.

Sieger titles were awarded to the black and tan male Graaf Cito v. Blue-Blood, NHSB 253796 (a dog whelped and owned in the Netherlands) ; the bitch, Ina v. Fürstenfeld, 77492; the red Hardes v. Nömmegarten, 76626; and the red bitch Bella v.d. Kieler Förde, 77143. The show was held in Berlin and 43 Dobermans were benched. The 1962 Sieger of the working dogs was again Fred v.d. Blütenstadt Orsoy, 74937.

Among outstanding Dobermans in Germany are Titus Germania, 76078, son of the world champion Lump v. Hagenstolz, 70473; Falko v. Hagenstolz, 76522, also sired by Lump; Dirk v. Goldberg, 76137; Dirk v. Ehrenreichen, 77060; Jago vom Fürstenfeld, 77551.

Among the famous kennels are Germania, von Neckarstolz, von Forell, von Niddatal, von der Vogelaue, von Weinberge, vom Haus Jünemann, von Schöntal, vom Andreasstift, and vom Eichenhain.

INTERNATIONAL DOG SHOW, MONTE CARLO, MAY, 1952
Princess Antoinette of Monaco (in center) congratulating the trainer of
Youki du Quartier Turenne # 1905, whelped October 15, 1950
Sire: Filou v. Bad Heidelberg   Dam: Anny de Saint-Richard
Owner: H.R.H. Prince Rainier III du Monaco   Breeder: M. Lampert
Winner of international beauty prize

62

The Doberman Outside Germany

by

Gerda M. Umlauff

HE Doberman is one of the
breeds of dogs which are known far outside the country
of their origin and are no longer confined to the country
in which they were first developed. Today the breed
is found in almost every country in the world, and this
general recognition occurred surprisingly soon after the
Doberman first became established as a recognized breed
in Germany.

Once the Doberman had won laurels at home for his
beauty, general utility, and outstanding performance in
police work, it was not long before representatives of
the breed were exported abroad. Shipments to Russia
are known to have been made by 1907, and to the United
States about the same time or not long afterward. Dutch
breeders played so important a part in the development
of the modern breed in Germany that their contributions

63

cannot well be considered separately. Dobermans went to Holland about 1904 and the earliest specimens were for the most part purchased from or through Otto Goeller of Apolda. The Koningstad kennel of Ch.L. an Akkeren, the Grammont kennel of H. Kloeppel, and the Roemerhof kennel of Mynheer Le Noble, all at The Hague, and Rivals kennel of Mynheer van der Schoot at Franeker, all had an important influence on the breed in Germany or the United States. Sieger Troll v. Albtal, whelped in 1912, was one of the sires imported into Holland who proved his value as a producer and carried down to the present time through such important dogs as Benno v. Roemerhof, Prinz Carlo v.d. Koningstad, and Prinz Favoriet v.d. Koningstad. Rival's Adonis, the best in Holland in his day, was whelped two years later, by Fernando v. Merseburg out of Helga v. Jaegerhof, the latter a full sister to Edelblut v. Jaegerhof and the former a Sturmfried grandson. Urian v. Grammont was an Edelblut son and from his sister Undine v. Grammont by Rival's Adonis came the excellent Ajax and Angola v. Grammont. Angola was the dam of Prinz Favoriet, Prinzessin Elfrieda, and Prinzessin Ilisa v.d. Koningstad in Holland before her purchase by White Gate Kennels of Philadelphia.

A number of Dobermans from Holland accompanied their masters to the Dutch East Indies, where the breed adapted itself well to life in the tropics. Black and tan dogs and reds were about equally popular, but the blues never obtained a good foothold.

The van Neerlands Stam kennel was established about 1910 and has produced many outstanding Dobermans. Probably the most important bitch produced by the kennel was Ch. Gravin Diana. The most important dog was Ch. Graaf Dagobert van Neerland Stam, 27 times awarded the CACIB, who was later sold to Italy, where he did very well, also. Important lines represented in the kennel are Troll v.d. Engelsburg, Gazelle v.d. Bismarcksäulte, and the Koningstad line.

Perhaps the first country outside Germany to become interested in the Doberman was Switzerland, where a

64

Dobermannpinscher Club was organized as early as 1902. Volume 8 of the Swiss all-breed stud book (SHSB) contained the entries of five Dobermans, one of which was Swiss bred. Switzerland was fortunate in beginning with some stock of excellent quality and breeding, and has developed its own strain, with a minimum of judicious importations over the years. One of the foundation bitches was Gertrud I v. Frauenlob, a daughter of the Prinz v. Ilm Athen son Graf Siggo v. Hohenstein out of Hilde v. Hessen, a litter sister to Belli v. Hessen. Gertrud was mated to Leporella v.d. Nidda (later v. Main), whose dam, Flora v. Groenland, was a double granddaughter of Gertrud's own maternal granddam, Tilly I v. Groenland, one of the foundation bitches of the breed. Leporello's sire was Junker Slenz v. Thüringen, whelped in 1897, an important dog in his day in Germany, still found at the back of most pedigrees. Leporello's line, of minor importance in Germany, proved of great value in Switzerland through his daughter Gertrud II v. Frauenlob. Hans v. Aprath, litter brother to Fedor v. Aprath, also played an important part in the Swiss strain through the v. Tale, Lentulus, Berneck, and v.d. Baerenburg kennels.

In the late 1920's another infusion of German blood took place, through the mating of Edel v.d. Barbarossahoehle to the Swiss Britta v. Beundenfeld, which produced Donar v. Beundenfeld, while a little later Egil zum Ziel was imported into Switzerland, where he sired Jenny v. Hagburg and Resl v.d. Baerenburg, among others. From 1921 to 1932 Swiss Doberman registrations ran in the neighborhood of 150 per year, indicating a steady popularity and fairly even production without extremes.

During World War II, in spite of Swiss neutrality, dog breeding suffered, as elsewhere in Europe, from food shortages, as well as from the general disturbance of the times. Young stock was lacking in bone, but, with no outside resources to draw upon breeding had to be done from what stock was available. In a report published in 1949 by the breed warden of the Swiss Dobermannpinscher Club it was stated: "I remember with deep appreciation the sincere attempts of our small group of earnest breeders to utilize to the best possible advantage the limited amount of stock at their disposal. That they have not been entirely successful in fulfilling all requirements for the proper maintenance of the breed is to be ascribed to the very difficult conditions prevailing during the war years. Admittedly, the conditions were no better in other countries than in ours. Indeed, they were rather worse. However, other countries for the most part had a far broader basis for breeding operations, and as soon as conditions began to improve they were able to accomplish a much quicker recovery. Hence they were more quickly in a position to raise the standard of the breed by suitable matings, and selection was more feasible than in a country as small as Switzerland".

With this situation in mind, Swiss breeders sought to improve their stock by again importing German dogs, by giving great care and study to selective breeding, and by consulation with German breeders. Among the importations was Hera Germania. Of the individuals carefully chosen to carry on the breed may be mentioned Thermes de la Mertzau and Gudo v. Leyerhof, among others. Swiss Doberman breeders seem to have worked together eagerly to repair the damage caused by World War II and are intent upon a common goal. Above all other objectives they are intent on breeding sound, substantial dogs, with good jaws and the proper number of teeth. As they point out on all occasions, their dogs are being bred as a strain of utility dogs, which will not be able to fulfill their tasks adequately without the correct number of healthy, sound teeth.

When passing in review the outstanding Dobermans of Switzerland at the present time we may note in particular Ary v.d. Dobermanntreu, Dox v. Langhag, and Baldo v. Ardigo. Most preeminently, however, the ideal of a bench-show winner is incorporated in the American-bred bitch, Champion Westphalia's Artemis.

It was natural that in Austria, a German-speaking country and a near neighbor, the Doberman should have been

VELPO DU JARDIN DES ROSES
First prize, Paris, 1948
Owner: Madame Langlais, Des Recollets Kennels, Sarthe, France

enthusiastically received in the early days of the breed. However, the stock developed there was of a decidedly heavy type, which strongly suggests the Rottweiler in appearance. It is perhaps for this reason that histories of the breed and lists of important kennels and individuals make little mention of Austria as compared with either Switzerland or Holland. Also, the Austrian Doberman-Pinscher Club (öDPK) was not formed until 1919. Upon their thirtieth anniversary in 1949 this club held a specialty show in conjunction with the International Dog Show in Vienna. Two of the more outstanding Austrian kennels which may be mentioned are v. Philippsheim, owned by Herr Ludwig and Herr Prochaska, and v.d. Scholle, owned by Herr Dr. Joseph Bodingbauer.

According to the rules of the Austrian Club, only dogs which have been classified as "excellent" or "very good" at a regular show or special examination can be used at stud, while for bitches the rating must be at least "good." For many years Dr. Bodingbauer has advocated unification of all working dogs. He has also urged the establishment of character tests for young dogs (*Jugendveranlagungsprobungen*), in addition to and not to be confused with the regular working trials for young dogs (*Jugendveranlagungsprüfungen*). The latter are comparable to Obedience Tests in this country in that they grade a dog on the results of training which he has already received. The character tests proposed by Dr. Bodingbauer, on the other hand, attempt to forecast whether or not a youngster will respond satisfactorily to training. Here the dogs are classified as "very promising", "promising", "less promising," and "unpromising." The objective, of course, is to save the owner or trainer from wasting further time or money on a dog of inferior quality. Particular attention is paid in such tests to those characteristics which qualify a dog for training in protection, including courage, alertness, aggressiveness, and the instinct to protect.

Information as to the popularity of the Doberman throughout the rest of Europe is rather fragmentary. Although the breed had gained a foothold in Hungary and

68

German Champion 1959; Swiss Champion
CITTA VOM FURSTENFELD 96173
Breeder-Owner: Herman Palmer, Furstenfeldbruck

German Champion 1960
Champion of Netherland 1959
CITTO VOM FURSTENFELD 96169
Breeder-Owner: Herman Palmer, Furstenfeldbruck

69

Bulgaria before the war, present conditions in those countries are such that no news is available. However, in an earlier day the Doberman in Bulgaria had penetrated even to the Court itself. Back in the 1920's the King of Bulgaria owned a Doberman which often accompanied him as a hunting companion. Honorary membership in the German Doberman Pinscher Club was offered to His Majesty, King Boris, who was pleased to accept in a letter expressing the conviction that the value of his Doberman as a versatile working dog was exceptional, and that the animal was exceedingly intelligent and sincerely attached to him.

In Czecho-Slovakia the Doberman had many friends and fanciers. A number of excellent German-bred dogs were sold to that country during the years between the two World Wars, and various kennels produced home-breds of high quality. The most notable importation was probably Alex v.d. Finohoehe, sire of Stolz and Lotte v. Roeneckenstein, whose great value as a sire was largely overlooked until after he had left Germany. To appreciate his immense value, it is sufficient to say that the leading American sires of today are descended from Alex through either Stolz or Lotte, or both. His Czech get included Nixe Meirling, Baldur v. Delmenhorst, and Asta v.d. Goldflagge.

Judging by show reports of the years before the Second World War, the browns rather than the black and tans seem to have been the dominant color in Czecho-Slovakia. No doubt this was due in considerable part to the importance of Alex v.d. Finohoehe, who was himself a brown. Alex, then Sieger of Moravia and Czecho-Slovakia, is said to have been the model for the two bronze Doberman statues, a little more than life size, which stand on either side of the main entrance to the New Savings Bank in Bruenn, CSR, as symbols of vigilance.

There is also said to have been great interest in the Doberman in prewar Russia. During the early 1920's the dominant influence there was Horst v. Stresow, son of Troll v.d. Blankenburg and Lotte v. Stresow, a Burschel

v. Simmenau daughter. He was followed by the Lux v.d. Blankenburg son, Artus v. Eichenhain. The Blankenburg blood was further intensified in the bitches Bona v. Seehagen by Lux and Asta v. Goldgrund by Troll, Asta's litter sister. Alli v. Goldgrund went to the United States, where she produced at least five champions. Asta v.d. Spree, another early pillar of the Russian Dobermans, was, like Lotte v. Stresow, a Burschel v. Simmenau daughter.

The early interest in the breed in Russia and Finland seems to have been from the point of view of police service.

The interest in Dobermans in Sweden seems to be a fairly recent growth. In 1949 Mr. A. Dalzell, a prominent British judge, made a report on breed activities there, with some interesting particulars about the Swedish standard. He commented upon the large number of cropped Dobermans (not found in England) and their superior expression and alertness when compared with dogs with natural ears. The quality of the Swedish-bred dogs in competition was very good, but not equal to those which were passed on by the same judge in South Africa in 1948. The principal faults which were noted in the Swedish dogs were poor feet and faulty gait, and too heavy heads. A few specimens even reminded him of Rottweilers. However, there were a number of good heads also. For the most part the dogs were of correct size, and the body proportions left nothing to be desired. Mr. Dalzell's report concludes with the statement that this intelligent breed is steadily gaining popularity in Sweden.

Dobermans have been bred in Norway with good results since the early 1920's. It is almost impossible to import a dog into Norway because of the severe quarantine laws. Despite this fact, however, two imported Dobermans have had an important influence on the breed in Norway in recent years. They are Carri, 14687/59 (bitch), and Anios Duke, SKKR 9238/59 (dog) imported from Sweden.

Brazil has some good representatives of the breed, also. Especially important are Dobermans from the line of Ch. Alex v. Kleinwaldheim. Among those that have had an outstanding influence on the breed in Brazil is the bitch Tongri v.d. Scholle, whose sire was champion of the CSSR. And Tongri's red son Saturno de Marigny was one of Brazil's most outstanding Dobermans.

Another outstanding bitch of recent years was Ch. Flama v. Tabajara do Norte, dam of Tempest de Marigny and Victoria de Marigny, sired by Conny v. Fürstenfeld. A dog from this litter, named Vanguard, became the property of the governor of the new state of Guanabara.

The Doberman has always had friends among the French fanciers, who have endeavored to raise the quality of their stock by suitable importations. The Saar district, which formerly contained flourishing branches of the German club, was especially fertile ground for the breed. Saar kennels had excellent stock, but since the war the breed has not yet regained its former high standard there. However, a number of experienced breeders and fanciers have organized in a combined effort to revive and strengthen interest in Doberman breeding. Naturally, breeding activities in the Saar have stimulated interest in the breed in France and have had a good effect on it there. An exceedingly attractive and stylish bitch may be mentioned in the black and tan Vedda de l'Ile-aux-Saules, who carries Troll v.d. Engelsburg blood on her sire's side, and Notburgatal and Ludwigsburg on her dam's. As a brood bitch, if suitably mated, she promises to produce excellent stock which will be of value for the general improvement of the breed.

In Italy the Doberman is well represented, and there are few shows at which the breed fails to appear in competition, although the type does not always agree absolutely with German ideals of beauty. The most important Italian kennels are: Milano, Diavoli, and della Sfinge, of which the last mentioned contains the largest number of dogs.

In South Africa the interest in Dobermans dates back many years. Its beginning can be traced even before World War I, to a bitch from the v. Fernsicht kennel of

72

Herr Oscar Carlsson in Hamburg. Balmung v. Zinsgut, whelped in 1924 by Rival v. Kranichstein out of Brangaene v. Weingarten, went to South Africa at too early an age to leave progeny in Germany. His litter mates, Baldur v. Zinsgut and Bajadere v. Zinsgut, came to the United States, where Bajadere mated to Ch. Big Boy of White Gate produced the dam of Ch. Princess Latosca of Westphalia and the latter's sister, Princess Latona, grand dam of Ch. Westphalia's Uranus. Balmung promptly won his championship in his new home, and left descendants of excellent quality there.

The British judge, Mr. Dalzell, who passed on the breed at Port Elizabeth, South Africa, in 1948, drew an entry of fourteen Dobermans. The Challenge Certificate and Best of Breed awards went to the dog Ch. Astor v. Arras, a leading sire which is described as of marvelous proportions, with faultless head, perfect eyes and ears, and of excellent temperament. Reserve male was Peerless of Kinross, a very close second and extremely high class. His head, body, and movement were all excellent and the deciding factor seems to have been the behavior of the dogs in the rig. Several good browns were also shown, but they were not quite equal to the black and tans in quality. The bitch Certificate went to the beautiful Hurricane Straffer.

At the Johannesburg show the winners were Canadian Chief of Westphalia in dogs and Tanser's Matilda in bitches. However, the most outstanding Dobermans in South Africa are said to be police-owned and these are never exhibited at bench shows. They are used exclusively for police work. Most South African Dobermans are of a strong, robust type, but vary considerably in size and carriage of ears, a point which does not seem to have been fully stabilized. It is interesting that the police do not care to mingle their dogs of working quality with the show bloodline, and that Lux v.d. Blankenburg decendants were recently imported from the Mannerheim kennels of Dr. Shute in Canada.

73

FRITZ, OWNED BY ALEXANDER KORDA
An example of show type Dobermans in England

The Doberman Pinscher in England

by
Gerda M. Umlauff

NGLAND is practically new at breeding Dobermans. Even though the first imports arrived in England in 1909, the breed did not become popular until after World War II. Much of the Doberman's popularity can be attributed to its services as a war dog and later to an American movie in which a highly intelligent and well trained Doberman portrayed a Police dog named Rodney. However, the unfortunate conditions of the two world wars and the rigid quarantine regulations have kept the import rate at a low level. Not only does the six-months period of quarantine at 30s. per week constitute a considerable expense, but the importer also runs the risk of losing the dog from disease. Nevertheless, determined breeders continued importing dogs and the interest in the Doberman increased so much that in 1948 the "Dobermann Pinscher Club" in England was founded. (The British continued the usage of the double "n" in honor of the German originator, Louis Dobermann).

According to Mrs. Curnow, Secretary of the Dobermann Pinscher Club, two hundred Dobermans are now registered with the British Kennel Club, fifty per cent of which were registered in 1951. The black and tan variety is by far predominant; only 10 per cent of all registered dogs are brown with red.

Next to the question of cropping ears, the size of the Doberman is the most hotly disputed issue. Dobermans in England range from 24 to 28½ inches in height. This caused an American expert, Mr. P. Roberts, to remark: "Size seems to be the question mark at the moment. I believe 25 to 27 inches for a bitch and 26 to 28 inches for a dog is about the ideal—though I would prefer a well-made small one rather than a badly made dog that was up to full measure. Size should automatically come when the desired type, make and shape are more firmly established". (*British Dog World, 1951*).

The shape of the ear on the Doberman in England remains the subject of many arguments. A number of British breeders admit that the uncropped, pendant ear robs the Doberman of his alert expression and appearance. Attempts have been made to breed Dobermans with a v-shaped ear, similar to that of the Fox-Terrier. This would undoubtedly be more attractive than the uncropped prick ear as found on the Bull Terrier. It is widely believed that a cropped ear is much to the dog's advantage in the ring.

A factor of importance, though often neglected, is the environment in which the puppy grows up. It is necessary to give a puppy much personal attention and affection if it is to develop into an intelligent specimen of good disposition. Many a young dog of good physical appearance fails to develop into an alert and responsive animal because of this lack of attention. It goes without saying that disposition in a dog is equally important to physical qualities. The Doberman has often and wrongly been defined as a vicious and unpredictable animal. This reputation followed him to England where many people spread it in

ADEL OF TAVEY

Male, whelped June 6, 1948. First litter Dobermans bred in England
Sire: Derb v. Brunoberg   Dam: Beka v. Brunoberg
Breeder: Mr. A. Curnow Owner: Mr. Wm. Bolitho, Lancashire, England

ignorance of the true facts, and it may be the reason for overemphasizing on a quiet and friendly disposition in the selection of sire and brood matron. However, this practice is just as detrimental to the breed as selecting suitable mates by their physical qualities only. Even though physical and mental characteristics deserve much consideration in the mating of dogs, a careful study of the blood lines is the first step toward improving the breed.

Dobermans have been imported in England from South Africa, the United States, Holland, France and Germany. Almost all of these imports, however, can be traced back to German ancestry. The Tavey Kennels' (owner Mr. A. Curnow) first imports from Germany in 1947 were Derb v. Brunoberg and Beka v. Brunoberg. Several months later the Dutch female Roeanka v. Rhederveld, dam of the well known Champion Graaf Dagobert v. Neerlands Stam, followed, and after about one year Mr. Curnow obtained a Graaf Dagobert daughter, Anja v. Scheepjeskerk, now a Utility Dog. In 1950, the Tavey Kennels imported a Graf Dagobert son from Holland, Waldox v. 'h Aamsveen. Recently, the excellent Tasso v. Eversburg was imported from Germany and his influence on the British Dobermans will no doubt be a very favorable one.

One of the brood matrons at the Tavey Kennels, Brunno of Tavey, was whelped in quarantine by the Dutch import Pia v. Dobberhof (Sire Benno v.d. Schwedenhecke). According to Mr. Curnow, Benno was not too good a show dog but an excellent sire. He passed on to his get a quality particularly desirable for the breed in England: small ears. One of his daughters, Elegant of Tavey, recently won "Best in Show" over 500 competitors at London.

A well known breeder of Dobermans in England is Mr. L. Hamilton Renwick, owner of the Birling Kennels. In his kennels we find Rachel, a promising young female, and Birling Roimond, a solidly built male of excellent appearance and many good qualities. Roimond was mated to Frieda v. Casa Mia, a South African import, and the resulting litter of ten contained the female Britta of Upend, which was later sold in Ireland. A litter brother to Roimond, Roque,

78

sired the very promising Birling Kwal, a beautifully developed, strong dog, high spirited and full of energy.

In 1947 Mr. Hamilton Renwick imported the black and red colored female Britta v.d. Heerhof and the male Bruno v. Ehrgarten. Later he obtained from the United States the female Quita of Terry Run, a very lovely bitch of blue and red color with an excellent head. Another of Mr. Renwick's purchases was a brown with red colored female which had been whelped in England by Billa v.d. Mulde and resulted from a mating to the German male Bill v. Blauen Blut. Also in 1947, the female Beka v. Brunsberg, black and red of color, was imported. She is well proportioned and comes close to meeting the standard in all respects. Carta v. Emsperle was imported by Mr. Louis Levy of London in 1948 but died soon afterwards. Mr. Levy then imported the black and red colored male Vetr du Diamant Rose, whose dam had won considerable honors in Paris. Vetr's pedigree includes such significant names as Asso v.d. Wertachbruecke and Reichssieger Ferry v. Rauhfelsen.

In 1949, Bob v. Langenhagen, a black and red colored male, and Arno v. Forstschutz were imported in England. Mrs. Korda, owner of the Vyking Kennels, imported the brown and red colored female Asta v. Hangeweiher, ex Aga v. Kaiserstadt, by Casso v. Kleinwaldheim. The black and red colored male Dolf v. Pleistal (by Tasso v.d. Eversburg, out of Hall v.d. Huenerburg) was imported in Scotland. An employee of the quarantine kennels in Hertfordshire imported the brown and red colored female Helga v. Kleinwaldheim.

Mrs. Bass of London-Feltham is one of the most enthusiastic fanciers of the breed. While in Malaya, she kept eighteen Dobermans unrestrained on her premises. Her personal protection dog was Golf v. Simmenau who had all desirable qualities of an excellent watch dog. He was able to prove his devotion to Mrs. Bass by saving her life as many as four times. He obeyed her commands only and even though he was friendly to the extent of letting strangers touch him, he would have attacked any intruder most fiercely. He was most gentle with children and friendly toward all personal visitors of the house. He knew all of the servants and remained quiet as long as they did not bring strangers into the house at night.

The Crufts Show is always a good place to assess the progress of various breeds in England. Evidence of the Doberman's popularity lies in the fact that at a show held in the early 1960's, there was a total of 122 entries, with 71 Dobermans entered in twelve classes. The exhibits were a good lot, with bitches somewhat better quality than dogs. Particularly promising and vigorous were entries in the puppy class. This was in contrast to the situation a few years earlier, when English Dobermans were inclined to show a lack of strength in build.

Heads were not faultless, for in many cases there was lack of fill under the eyes. Some of the dogs appeared too elegant, and consequently were faulted. Also, in some cases angulation at the shoulder was not good, and markings and eyes were too light in several cases. However, all the Dobermans shown were in very good condition and had wonderful coats, making an excellent impression.

Despite the breed's comparative newness to England, the demand for the breed is good. With judicious use of carefully selected bloodlines—preferably including Doberman lines imported from Germany—the breed can look forward to a rosy future in England.

The Doberman As a Police Dog in England

by

Gerda M. Umlauff

PON his initial appearance in England, the Doberman's elegant physique and aristocratic carriage immediately captured the fancy of British breeders. Soon, however, it became apparent that in addition to his most appealing physical characteristics the Doberman combined remarkable intelligence and agility with many other qualities of a working dog. It was then that the interest of the British Police began to center on this new breed. The Surrey Constabulary Kennels were the first ones to train Dobermans in police work. The results were excellent and the Doberman soon was reputed to be superior to the Alsatian, previously used for this type of work in England.

Realizing the advantages of the Doberman, the kennels of the British Police began a select breeding program. The background of both the prospective sire and brood matron was carefully checked and only those were mated that originated from a strain of proven trained working dogs. The breeding stock was to a large extent imported from Germany where generations of the Doberman had been developed into excellent police dogs. The dogs of the Surrey Constabulary, of course, are of pedigreed ancestry and registered with the English Kennel Club.

In their attempts to breed outstanding working dogs the British did not neglect the appearance and temperament of the Doberman. The British police was determined to supply its forces with dogs that were reliable in their work as well as elegant in appearance and full of esprit. Even though the dogs would be well qualified to compete in the conformation ring, they are never exhibited there but participate in all of the field trials. Their achievements in the latter have not been equalled by any other breed.

Ulf v. Margarethenhof (S. Z. 57281, formerly of Werneuchen, Germany,. owner Mr. Thuerling), owned by the Surrey Constabulary kennels at Guildford, was an outstanding police dog and the first and only Doberman to win a Field Trail Championship in England. Ulf became a police dog due to the post-war food shortage in England. His former master, an American officer, left England after World War II and as none of his British friends were able to provide for so large a dog, Ulf was given to the British Police in the care of Sergeant Darbyshire. Since that time Ulf has obtained the titles of T. D. (Tracking Dog), U. D. (Utility Dog), and C. D. (Companion Dog), scoring "excellent" in all of these trials. Ulf also became the winner of both the 1949 and 1950 Open Police Dog Trials with the remarkable achievement of scoring "excellent" in each one of the various phases involved.

Donathe v. Begerthal and Astor v.d. Morgensonne (47/ 111), both German imports, also belong to the Surrey kennels. Donathe, one of the highest scoring females in the field trials (C. D. and U. D. with "excellent"), was bred to Ulf in 1949. The result of this mating was a litter of six in January, 1950, in which both the black and the brown variety with red markings were represented. One of these young dogs, Mountbrowne Joe, was presented to

82

Gin von Forell 77172
Bred by Ernst Wilking,
Munster, and owned by
Mrs. M. Bastable,
England.

Champion of Belgium
Alfa vom Wappen zu Bremen 76786
Breeder-Owner: Mrs. M. Huber, Bremen

German Champion 1962
INA VOM FURSTENFELD 77492
Breeder-Owner: Herman Palmer, Furstenfeldbruck

the English Kennel Club as a future stud dog while four others were purchased by various police units and one remained in the home kennel. The kennel usually retained one or two young dogs out of each litter for breeding purposes. It is interesting to know that five dogs of the above mentioned litter obtained both their C. D. and U. D. with scores of "excellent" in each, and the sixth scored "excellent" in his U. D. In August, 1950, Donathe whelped a litter sired by Astor v.d. Morgensonne. This litter consisted of five puppies, all of them black with red markings. Donathe is soon to be mated with Dober v. Oldenfelde (11/18), a German import, belonging to the Lancashire police force.

The British Police records are a tribute to the abilities of the Doberman as a working dog. In one case, which occurred in 1949, a Doberman tracked down a burglar who had fled a distance of 3½ miles. Even though one hour had elapsed when the dog and its handler arrived at the scene of crime, the dog immediately picked up the trail of the burglar. The man had fled cross country and the dog followed the trail thru a field in which wheat was being harvested. The officer handling the dog learned from one of the laborers there that the suspect had actually passed thru this location.

In 1950, a woman was attacked with an ax on a lone country road. Police thoroughly combed the surrounding area without result. A Doberman, arriving 20 hours later at the scene of crime, without hesitation picked up a trail that after 300 yards led to the discovery of a bloodstained piece of clothing that the suspect had worn. The dog then led police to two different shelters that contained the suspect's fingerprints. No trail was found from there. The suspect was apprehended the following day as he attempted to sell articles stolen from the shelters. In this case the dog performed the remarkable task of finding the trail after 20 hours even though it had been crossed by police in their search.

In 1951, a man was reported missing from a lone shack that he occupied. Blood and bloodstained pieces of clothing were found in the shack and the dog picked up a trail that

85

led over rough ground and thru a refuse pit to a deep pond. The man was found drowned in the pond.

The methods of training Dobermans for police work in England are similar to those in other countries except, perhaps, for being on a more rigid scale. The basic training consists of obedience work to which later obstacle courses and speed tests are added. Much emphasis is being placed on strict obedience of all commands so that the handler can control the dog when distractions occur. In fact, the dog is trained to the extent that it will not relieve itself without its handler's permission. The advanced training involves retrieving, tracking and quartering with particular emphasis on man-work and scenting.

Argus of Aycliffe, called "Charlie," is one of England's most famous police dogs. Bred by the Durham Constabulary Police Dog Section, Charlie began his work in the police service at the age of sixteen months. Before he was six years old, he had assisted in bringing about the arrest of 70 persons accused of breaking the law.

At a Midland District police dog trial, ten German Shepherds and eight Dobermans were entered in competition. First prizes were awarded one German Shepherd and five Dobermans, but the best record was made by Charlie with his master, Constable Regan, who earned thirty-six points from a possible total of forty.

The Durham Constabulary has, in addition to dogs bred locally, a number of Dobermans imported from Germany.

While there seems to be no objection to the docking of tails on Dobermans in police work, the cropping of ears is prohibited. According to the rules of the English Kennel Club, dogs with cropped ears are not eligible for registration in England which consequently bars them from competing in the conformation ring. This rule applies to the progeny of dogs with cropped ears. Dogs which had their ears cropped before being imported to England may compete in the field trials.

The breeding of fine Dobermans in England is now well advanced and many of the promising young dogs are exported for police work in other countries.

At work—
CHARDAS VON WAPPEN ZU BREMEN 77628
Breeder-Owner: Mrs. M. Huber, Bremen

JAGO VOM FURSTENFELD 77551
Owner of several "Excellent" awards at the shows, Jago has been trained
as a police dog. Bred by Herman Palmer, Furstenfeldbruck, and owned
by Jakob Bambach, Dreieichenhain.

The Doberman As a Police Dog in Germany

by

Gerda M. Umlauff

S FAR BACK as man and dog have lived together, which is thousands of years, the dog has made himself useful in various capacities, as hunter, guard, burden bearer and fighter. And from time to time dogs of exceptional prowess or intelligence have won a place in literature or legend.

A forerunner of the modern police dog employed in trailing criminals was the dog Carpillon, owned in the middle of the 13th century by a bell-ringer of Notre Dame. Carpillon accompanied his master everywhere, but one day when the latter paid a visit to the barber Galipáud he told Carpillon to wait outside the door. Carpillon waited in vain for his master's reappearance, for the barber was a criminal who had already cut the throats of a number of his customers and sold their flesh. He killed the bell-ringer and dropped his body through a trap door, but Carpillon, waiting outside, no doubt scented something amiss. His loud barking attracted attention. He confronted Galipaud and brought to light the victim's blood stained cap, which the murderer was trying to hide. Attracted by the dog's behavior, the bell-ringer's friends took action and Galipaud was imprisoned and duly executed. It is said that he was burned at the stake, doubtless for the sacrilegious crime of trafficking in human flesh. And a monument to Carpillon was erected on the site of the murderer's house.

Carpillon's breeding is quite unknown and it is extremely improbable that he had any direct influence on modern police dogs, but it is likely enough that such incidents were the seed from which the idea of training dogs to assist in the capture of criminals eventually grew.

The Doberman's career in police work goes back nearly fifty years. As early as 1906 a policeman with a trained representative of the breed competed in a police dog trial in Germany. The following year a trained German Doberman by the name of Bell v. Neroberg was entered at a trial at Breda in the Netherlands. This was an international competition, with dogs from Holland, Belgium, France and Germany competing. Among the rigorous conditions was the requirement that whenever a dog refused to perform any exercise he immediately had to drop out. Bell made an excellent record and delighted the spectators, one of whom purchased him at the close of the contest.

In 1912 a Doberman bitch named Hertha v. Ravensberg was instrumental in solving a burglary at Kiel. A workman's house had been robbed of 150 marks, and thirty-three hours later a constable with his police dog was called in. Hertha took the scent at the window through which the thief was believed to have entered the house and followed the trail to the apartment of another workman. From there she led the way to a cornfield, which the occupant had mowed the day before, and then along the road to a pasture where forty cows were feeding. Here she located the man and barked at him. He denied taking the money, but Hertha investigated some nearby underbrush where she found and brought to her handler a little bag containing the amount stolen. Thereupon the man confessed the crime and was subsequently condemned to serve seven months imprisonment for the theft.

It seems strange now to read in some of the old magazines that in those days not all policemen were pleased at the success of the dogs in police work, although it was becoming constantly better known. From reports of the time, we learn that many of them avoided calling upon the services of the dogs whenever possible. This was not due to any doubt of their ability, but because the men were afraid that their superiors would think the dogs' work more valuable than their own! This point of view has long since been forgotten, however.

An interesting state of affairs at the present time is reported from Hamburg, where a Doberman enthusiast recently visited the kennels in which dogs are trained for police service. Among the three dozen dogs in training there was no Doberman, although the handler was a Doberman fancier of long experience, who owned a bitch of the breed and had been breeding for years. In answer to inquiries he declared that it was a matter of money. The state, being poor, was forced to buy dogs as cheaply as possible. Although Dobermans are no higher in price than is reasonable, costs considered, German Shepherds are cheaper. Also, since there are many more Shepherds than Dobermans there are more cross-bred Shepherds. While the police prefer good looking dogs without too mixed an ancestry, there are unpedigreed dogs available which make a good appearance and are very, very cheap. These dogs the police will accept, and so it seldom happens nowadays that they have a chance to use Dobermans. The leader regretted this, in the light of his twenty years of experience. As trainer at the police school for dogs and handlers he had had opportunities to work with all breeds. Though he had found advantages to all of them he preferred the Doberman. The breed's good qualities include his racy body build, sharp and aggressive temperament, firmness and working ability. The Doberman has an excellent nose and shows more endurance than other breeds, a factor of importance in large districts in which the policeman with whom he works must use a bicycle.

About the year 1928 the German Railways used Dobermans as watch dogs and guards. It was their experience that good dogs could replace several men. They were used largely at night.

During the last war, when all food was severely rationed, a man who owned a sheep reported to the police that it had been stolen from his yard. A policeman with his Doberman was sent to the man's house to investigate, with unexpected results. It took only a few minutes for the Doberman to lead the way upstairs to the attic, where the sheep had been slaughtered by its owner's orders. Of course, by not requesting the proper permits for this action, the man had hoped to avoid the loss of ration points for some months which the possession of so much meat would entail.

In service with the Swiss police today is a Doberman male named Dox v. Langhag who has made a remarkable record. He is a member of the service dog group of the Basel-Stadt police department, and although now twelve years old is still a good trailer and a reliable protection dog of first class quality. He is very gentle and friendly at home and among his acquaintances, but will attack fearlessly when need arises. Dox is a big, strong dog and became an excellent trailer while still young, being employed in many difficult tasks. Many a traveller without a passport, many a gang which felt secure in a hide-out, has trembled when Dox approached and found an attempt at flight both useless and painful. In October 1947 Dox proved successful when ordered to hunt for a missing man. A large district had to be searched, full of rocks, caves and difficult going. A number of police with their dogs were taking part in the search and several of the dogs had to be rescued by their handlers because of the dangerous nature of the terrain. Consequently a lot of time passed and when darkness fell it was decided to call off the hunt. Dox, however, kept going. He led his handler to an inaccessible cavern, and here they found the body of the missing man, partly devoured by foxes. Dox is also known to be a terror to smugglers, who are said to avoid those sections of the border where he is known to be working.

At the close of the War one of the first Dobermans imported into England after 1945 from Germany was a black and tan male, Ulf v. Margarethenhof. Being fully trained, he was promptly employed in the service of the English police. After a very short time he attracted much favorable comment by tracking down a criminal. The trail was three and a half hours old, and Ulf followed it successfully for over three miles.

In closing this chapter it is well to re-emphasize the often repeated statements of German experts about training Dobermans. Success is to be expected only when the dog is in competent hands. Not every handler is suitable, and one can be fairly sure that in 90% of the cases where a handler does not care to work with a Doberman or condemns the breed outright he has been unsuccessful with one in the past. A policeman who hopes to succeed with a trained Doberman must himself have a quiet, steady temperament. If he is nervous, the dog will be nervous, too, while if he is too easy-going himself, a Doberman with plenty of temperament may make the handler nervous. The handler must know what to do, and what he wants his dog to do. He must be firm as well as patient. The right man will achieve success and gain new friends for the breed.

AJAX V. ELSTERSTRAND, *Called "Caesar"*
Army messenger dog who ran 17 km. in 30 minutes
See Chapter "Dobermans in Military Service"

94

The Doberman in Military Service

by

Gerda M. Umlauff

ISTORY relates that men have used dogs as aids in fighting as long as they have known war themselves. True and unforgettable stories of service dogs of various breeds are related. Two Dobermans of the first World War deserve mention for their performances. The male, Schreck von Péronne, was an army messenger dog, who carried through his alloted task and delivered a message of great importance in spite of having had one leg smashed by a shot so that he finished the journey on three feet. Another male, Hans, who came from the Westfront War Dog School, carried messages several times in one day over a distance of some six miles. In the Chemin-des-Dames and Winterberg areas Hans carried telephone cables a distance of more than half a mile within a period of two minutes under hostile artillery and rifle fire. He is reported to have been exhibited to the Kaiser when the latter visited the front.

Such accomplishments could certainly not be achieved except by the careful selection of the best and most suitable dogs. It was the task of the officers engaged in this service to study the available animals and develop plans so that sufficient numbers of the right sort would be ready when needed. There were two principal methods of doing this. One was by establishing army breeding and training depots. The second was to obtain suitable dogs from private owners in case of war. Both methods were used in Germany.

The operation of the Heereshundeanstalt, or Army Dog Office, is described by Dr. Brückner, a former scientific assistant there, to whom is due a complete and detailed description which deserves the careful attention of Doberman breeders and fanciers. His account was published shortly before World War II and was intended not only as an accurate report of his experiences but as a guide to Doberman fanciers who were desirous of knowing what type of dogs were desired by the authorities and had proved able to fulfill the duties required of them.

To begin with, the author states that it is necessary to refute the false statements by enemies of the breed that Dobermans are treacherous. This he can do from first-hand experience. In any case, such a statement is nonsense, because a dog is an animal and not a human being. He does not have the same type of intelligence as a man, but acts from instinct and experience. Neither does he understand good and evil in the human sense.

Dogs are required by the government for several purposes. They are used as messengers on the firing line, as Red Cross dogs to discover the wounded and guide rescuers, and as guard dogs for sentry work and scouting. For these uses the dogs must be physically suitable and free from faults of temperament. They must be strong and vigorous, and preferably bred from a working strain. Dobermans, like other breeds, when bred solely for the bench without regard to character may become too re-

96

A Marine Dog Fastens His Teeth on the
Weapon Arm

Devildogs Were Constantly Employed During the Operation of
Securing and Extending the Bougainville Beachhead

fined and elegant. Nervousness and other temperamental faults are likely to creep in, and the dogs become unsuited to hard, practical work. While a show dog may quite well have brains as well as beauty, the surest way to keep up the intelligence of the breed is to train all breeding stock and eliminate from the breeding program such animals as cannot make the grade.

At the time when these experiments were made, some of the Doberman breeders had produced dogs which were over-refined, too short in body and with long, thin legs and greyhound heads. They also lacked coat, having thin hair and insufficient undercoat, which did not afford adequate protection in bad weather or rough country. Some of these dogs were over-sensitive, irritable, and unreliable in disposition. Bitches of this type would sometimes destroy their litters, or were likely to transmit their faults.

The Doberman desired for Army training is a sound, normal animal, powerfully built, not too high on the leg, with a wedge-shaped head, strong bones, and sturdy without being coarse. His manners are serious and most men will treat him with respect. He should be in good, hard condition, with plenty of endurance and able to stand a lot of work. Dr. Brückner declares that dogs of this type are unsurpassed in their performance by the best workers of other breeds, who attain equally good results at trials only with great difficulty.

These dogs must be very resistant to weather, especially cold. They are alert, never disconcerted, and full of personality. They also require first-class noses for good trail work.

During the years from 1933 to 1938 the German Army Dog Office bred 71 Dobermans, 48 of which were of very good quality. Of the remaining 23, 9 dogs met with accidents or suffered from illness, 2 were born dead, and the other 12 were not suitable for training, being gun shy or otherwise too nervous.

Under the German system, the puppies were regularly tested when three, five, and six months old. The tests

PRACTICING LANDING OPERATION

MARINE DOGS GO THROUGH A VIGOROUS COURSE OF ACTION

99

included obstacles to be surmounted within a three-minute period, such as a staircase, a trench, a ditch of water, a narrow bridge over a trench, a wall about 14 inches high, and so forth. It was also noted whether the youngster followed his kennelman for a certain length of time off leash, without being called. The results were set down in accordance with a point system. Of course, these preliminary tests were made before the puppies had been formally trained.

At the second examination the results of the first were confirmed and the young dogs were timed on their efforts to get out of an enclosed kennel with a trellis fence having several openings, partly open and partly shut. Not the speed but the manner in which the dog attacks the problem is observed. The final examination is a test of character, made at six months of age. This includes the dog's behavior on the street in heavy traffic. Still more important is his reaction under fire, when rockets are exploded with smoke and sparks. The value of these tests is shown by the fact that out of the dogs from the German Army Dog Office so examined, 90 per cent proved satisfactory in service.

Dr. Brückner was the chief of the German Army Dog staff during World War II and commanded the 45,000 dogs in service during that time. He has known a great many dogs, and declares that the best Doberman of them all was Ajax v. Elsterstrand, known as Cäsar. Cäsar was a messenger dog of the highest quality and transmitted his abilities to his get, notably his son Rino. Both these Dobermans were awarded gold medals at the Grüne Woche show in Berlin in 1939. Cäsar would carry a message over a distance of 10½ miles in the average of three-quarters of an hour. Once in the summer of 1938 he completed the distance at night in only 30 minutes! This is an outstanding performance and indicates extraordinary stamina and endurance. It is likewise claimed that Cäsar succeeded in following a special trail over half a mile long, laid on dry ground in a pine wood after a period of 90 days, and another track on a wet lawn after 46 days, although other dogs failed at the end of five. No doubt he did follow a trail, but it may be questioned whether after so long an interval it could be the same one.

Cäsar performed in fine style and illustrates the difference which Dr. Brückner reports between the Doberman and other breeds. The Doberman, he declares, usually follows a trail with his nose rather high, but is as sure a trailer as the breeds which work close to the ground. As a result, a Doberman can follow the scent, especially when artificially laid, very fast. When in training the breed is inclined to be a trifle more headstrong than some other breeds, particularly the easily handled German Shepherd. However, he enjoys working and learns quickly. In spite of a fondness for running he is more serious about his work than the whirling Airedale, who is the playful rascal among working dogs. The Doberman is a speedy runner, undoubtedly faster and with more endurance than the Boxer or Rottweiler, and better adapted in conformation to different types of terrain, such as moor, rock, or sandy beach. In this respect other breeds show certain weaknesses, as for instance the Giant Schnauzer, which is too heavy, with a lack of agility and body power. Consequently the Doberman is a born messenger dog, and in addition a first-class tracker, guard, and Red Cross dog. The breed will always give satisfactory results when properly bred for working qualities.

A report by a Captain Dressler on 16,000 dogs examined for their fitness for military service records the following results: The breeds examined included German Shepherds, Giant Schnauzers, Airedales, Rottweilers, Dobermans, Boxers, Great Danes, Gundogs (presumably Setters, Pointers, and the German Short-hairs), Hovawards, St. Bernards, Hungarians, and cross-breds. Out of the total number only 18.8% were pronounced suitable for training. Out of 196 Dobermans there were 96 chosen—32%. Among the other breeds, Airedales had 33%, Boxers 32%, Giant Schnauzers 29%, Rottweilers 28%, German Shepherds 22%, all other purebreds 18%, and crossbreds 10.5%. These proportions might have varied in other parts of the

101

country, since some of the breeds are more popular in one locality and others in another.

Captain Dressler's report states that at first the German soldiers on the Western Front were not anxious to have messenger dogs and thought them superfluous, as they had had no experience with them in the infantry. Very shortly, however, they changed their minds, for they soon saw how effective the dogs were in saving the lives of soldiers or in bringing help in time to allow treatment to be begun early. From then on they wanted so many dogs that the training depot could hardly keep them supplied. On one section of the front 12 messenger dogs out of 200 in service were reported wounded, seven of them so badly that they could not return to duty.

It has been observed that when a dog is wounded in such a way that he realizes the source of the injury and connects it with his work, he may be spoiled for further service. One such dog, while carrying a message during a battle, was wounded and knocked over by the concussion. He managed to get to his feet and finished his task, but was of no further use as a messenger. However, another dog who was running through a minefield when it exploded without injuring him completed his mission and continued to be entirely reliable as a messenger.

Dobermans may also be used as transport dogs in army service. However, since the amount they can handle at a time is quite limited, their usefulness in this field is limited also. To be satisfactory, they must have endurance, speed, and a certain fondness for the work. The Doberman does not always show sufficient endurance at a trot and is inclined to change into a gallop, especially on soft ground. Rugged, powerful dogs with short-coupled bodies, rather than the gazelle type, are the most suitable. The Doberman is likely to be at a disadvantage in the matter of coat, which is often thin and lacking in undercoat. In contrast to the Great Dane, the Doberman usually has sufficient natural oil, but the single outer coat fails to retain the body warmth sufficiently. Consequently the

102

breed is likely to be sensitive to bad weather, the transport dogs suffering particularly.

During the period from 1939 to 1945 dogs served with the German army, navy, air force, customs, police, labor service, etc. Dobermans ranked second in number, being surpassed only by German Shepherds. The soldiers who handled dogs were all volunteers, who asked for this type of service. There were always more applications than could be accepted, so that there was never any lack of handlers in the army. That the men are strongly attached to their dogs is clearly evident. Not only was no case of ill-treatment of a dog brought before the courts during the entire war, but many cases have been known in which soldiers carried their wounded or exhausted animals out of the danger zone.

To sum up the wartime performance of the breed with German troops, the Doberman is rated as an especially good messenger and guard dog. They were diligent and unexcelled companions by day or night for those on lonely guard duty. If necessary, they could round up and watch fugitives, and attack when required. They were also very successful in locating wounded men, whether friends or enemies. On the other hand, the short, slick coat which adds to the breed's attraction as a house dog, so that he is always clean and elegant at home, is a handicap to his employment in service wherever the climate is extreme. On the Eastern front the severe cold is said to have eliminated the problem of distemper from the battlefields, but the short-haired Doberman could not stand the climate. In very hot regions, such as Africa and southern Italy, difficulties were also encountered. The powerful ultra-violet rays during the heat of the day made it necessary to keep the dog under cover as much as possible between ten and three o'clock. The black color which absorbs heat may have played its part in this, while the absence of undercoat eliminates the insulating effect which is provided when a thick undercoat is present.

Dobermans have also been used as guides for the blind before, during, and since the War. The success of one such dog is described by his master, who reports that he lost his sight four days before the close of hostilities. Six months later he obtained a Doberman male called Fango as a guide. He received three months' training, as is the case with Guide Dogs in this country. Fango evidently lives in Berlin, for he takes his master back and forth on the underground. This trip involves a walk of ten minutes through heavy traffic, then the subway, with a change at the next station and many stairs, and a further walk of ten minutes. After a few times he knew the way perfectly. "I could have no better comrade," writes Fango's master. "He gave me back my self-assurance, and I feel now that my fate will be bearable only with a Doberman as a companion."

A WORKING DOBERMAN
Used in rescue work in the Swiss Alps

The Doberman
As a Working Dog

by

Gerda M. Umlauff

OBERMANS are natural work-
ing dogs. Their intelligence, alertness, and powerful
bodies make them especially fitted to perform various
types of useful work. And among the members of the
breed there have been many who have accomplished striking tasks without any regular training.

There was, for instance, a Doberman male who was
alert to put out fire and would pounce growling upon
any lighted cigarette ends he saw dropped in the street.

Another Doberman, named Strolch, who belonged to
Herr Lehnshak, the inn-keeper in a village near Königs-
berg/Neumark, was featured in the German newspapers
in 1931 and aroused widespread interest. It seems that
Herr Lahnshak's son, a boy of seven, had been enjoying
himself coasting on the frozen pond at Hohenwutzen.
Without his knowing it, some fishermen had cut a hole

in the ice. Somehow the boy fell into the hole and sank before the eyes of his playmates. He would undoubtedly have drowned but for Strolch, who jumped into the hole and managed to hold the boy above water until help could reach them from the shore. The boy was unconscious when he was pulled out. The fact that the two year old Strolch was untrained made his rescue the more remarkable. The following year he was exhibited at the big Berlin Jubilee Show of the Kartell für Hundewesen (the German equivalent of the AKC) and was decorated by the Tierschutzverein (Animal Rescue League) with a collar and medal for life-saving. His appearance with the boy he had saved aroused a tremendous amount of interest.

Another rescue by a Doberman took place in Berlin during a display of fireworks. Two rowboats on the Spree River collided and a man and a woman fell overboard. The former managed to cling to one of the boats, but the woman woudd probably have drowned if a Doberman who was walking with his master on the bank had not gone to her rescue. He promptly jumped into the river, swam to the woman, and held her up until help arrived.

Many Dobermans are very fond of swimming. Some even appear to enjoy it in winter when there is ice on the water. Even those who do not seem to take to swimming naturally will usually learn without difficulty if they are handled in the right way. There is a story told of a Doberman who was employed some years ago by a band of smugglers. He had been carefully trained to avoid under any circumstances any person wearing a customs officer's uniform. In order to do this it was sometimes necessary for the dog to swim the river which ran through the district, a task which he sometimes performed several times in one night.

Stories like these have been told about the breed as far back as Dobermans were known, and breeders and fanciers could well have been expected to be eager to train their dogs for police and protection work. However, according to Doberman history there have seemingly always been two factions. One of these put appearance before all else and declared that conformation would suffer in the case of working dogs; that the muzzle would become too broad if the dog was trained to fetch and carry; that the chest would be over-developed by jumping over obstacles. Their views appear in the statement: "My dog is too good for training. He will only be exhibited at bench shows!" Some, on the contrary, expressed the view: "My dog is not good enough for bench shows. He is only suitable for training." This, as has happened in other breeds, tended to divide the Doberman into two types, an aristocracy of show dogs and a proletariat of working dogs. The working dog, of course, needed strong bones and a good physique. The show dog exhibited great elegance, but this sometimes degenerated into over-refinement or nervous instability.

Instances have been reported in the newspapers in which so-called watch dogs have been carried off by thieves along with the valuables they were supposed to guard. No such occurrences have been reported in the case of the Doberman and "Cave canem" (Beware the dog!) seems to be written invisibly on every house which a Doberman guards.

In many cases the opponents of training were to be found among breeders, who did not seem to realize the important part played by exercise of mind and body in the development of power and beauty. A dog as full of temperament as the Doberman needs work as much as his daily food, and shows it by the eagerness with which he applies himself to learning whatever he is taught and the evident enjoyment with which he performs. He has an excellent nose, plenty of courage and energy, and is also a splendid jumper and can readily follow a bicycle, One male, Kasso v.d. Axthöhe 48271, made a record of 6.7 metres (21 feet, 11 inches) at five years of age, and scaled 7.4 metres (24 feet, 3 inches) the following year. He also jumped a trench 5 metres wide, and ran a hundred metres in only 17 seconds.

On the basis of these qualifications, training grounds

were built in Germany, but it quickly became apparent that Dobermans could not be properly trained in such restricted areas. Unless they were also worked in public, under a variety of conditions, they would not perform properly when taken away from the grounds to which they were accustomed, like a child who behaves only at school under the teacher's eye. Night training was also carried on, and the results proved very satisfactory. In one instance a Doberman bitch, Helebarde v. Nibelungenhort, called Hella, was employed in the search for a young farmhand who had been missing for two days. Hella's master brought her to the farm in the evening and gave her the scent from a pair of socks belonging to the missing man. She followed the trail, accompanied by men with lanterns, to a nearby stable, climbed up a ladder to the loft, and began to bark. There the missing man was found hidden under some sacks in the hay. Two nights before, the young fellow had been drinking heavily with other workmen until five in the morning, and had then hidden himself away to avoid punishment and sleep undisturbed.

While not ordinarily considered a hunting dog, the Doberman's excellent nose equips him to perform satisfactorily in this field. It is reported that before the War a Russian fancier who owned several Dobermans was accustomed to killing three of four bears annually, only about 100 kilometers from Leningrad. The usual method was to leave meat as bait for the bear and keep watch for him from a high perch out of his reach. On this occasion the light was poor and the hunter wounded his bear without killing him. The bear took flight, and the hunter went to the neighboring farm to fetch a Setter and Pointer which he had there. His two Dobermans accompanied him also to the scene of the shooting. An attempt to get the gundogs to trail the wounded quarry proved unsuccessful. They evidently recognized the bear's scent and refused to follow it regardless of urging. Then the hunter tried his Dobermans on the trail, and they set off full tilt. He followed as fast as he could through the undergrowth and after about ten minutes heard them barking. When he arrived on the scene the bear was dead, with the dogs furiously biting at his coat. The owner was convinced that they would not hesitate to attack a live bear, and intended to make the experiment with them, but whether or not he did so is unknown.

The late Herr Otto Settegast, a Doberman specialist, used to tell the following story of a Doberman friendship for another dog. There was a young baker who had taken over his parents' business upon their retirement. The young man had two dogs, an old Leonberger and a young Doberman. Every morning he sent the Leonberger to carry a basket of fresh bread to his parents, who lived in another part of town. One morning the old dog refused to go, and the following morning he did the same. On the third day the young Doberman, who had never accompanied him before, went with him. Shortly afterwards the baker received word that his Doberman had knocked down a man and would not let him get up. When he hurried to the spot he found that this man had been throwing stones at the Leonberger when he made his morning trips, until the latter refused to go by himself. The Doberman had defended his friend, having apparently learned in some way that his escort was needed.

The first championship working dog trial of the German Doberman Club since the War was held at Hamm in Westphalia on October 15, 1950. It was recognized that proper Doberman breeding meant breeding for working qualities. It is now vigorously stated that breeders must concentrate their efforts on producing stock which is thoroughly suitable for working purposes. There must be more working trials than formerly, with better prizes offered, and judges must not make a distinction between bench and working types. Of course, anyone who works seriously with his Doberman has to do so regularly, which necessitates having sufficient time available, regardless of the weather. Also, it is important not to forget that even the perfectly trained dog will forget if he is not worked, and he must receive a review from time to time.

It is fifty years since the father of working dog trials, Herr Most, first arranged these classes. In the beginning they were for Dobermans only, because this was his favorite breed. It is too bad that Doberman fanciers did not continue along this line, instead of separating into two groups which worked at cross purposes. Had they done so, the Doberman might today stand in first place as the greatest working breed in Germany, instead of ranking only second.

SGT. IRVING CHERNUS AND HI-KI AT CANINE TRAINING
AREA, NEW CALEDONIA

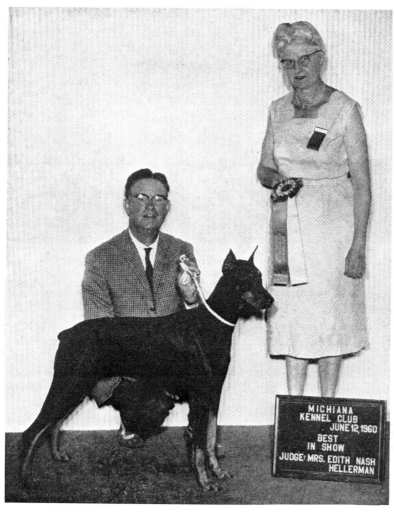

CH. MAR-BUD'S TUCKY MISS

At age of only two, one of the Top Ten Working Dogs of 1960. Owned by Bud and Mary Cosgrove of Jeffersonville, Ind., and handled by Phil Marsh.

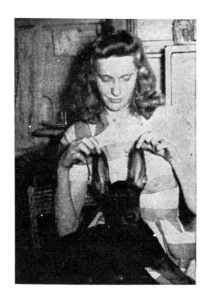

Margit Anderson's Doberman Puppy at 10 Weeks
(The day before ear cropping)

112

Ear and Tail Cropping

by

Anne Fitzgerald Paramoure

Publisher's Note: The inclusion of this article is not to be construed as advocating ear cropping at home. Surgery on dogs is the rightful province of the veterinarian, and that is where we firmly believe it belongs. However, for reasons economic or other, some readers will insist on doing their own, and for them we continue including this article—based on more than 25 years oj experience—in this edition.

HE cropping of ears is a deli-- cate subject and I realize that by giving instructions to the novice, I am treading on dangerous ground.

It has been the custom in states where anti-cropping laws exist for veterinarians to give a health certificate certifying that ear cropping was necessary on account of a dog's health and armed with such a certificate, exhibitors will not experience embarrassment at a dog show.

However, it has been my personal experience that although New York and Pennsylvania have ear cropping laws, no demand for a certificate has ever been made at the larger shows such as New York City or Philadelphia, although there are smaller shows in towns like Pittsburgh where the S. P. C. A. has been more active and health certificates have been demanded.

Hobday, who was a member of the Royal Academy of Veterinary Surgeons, tells us that previous to the revision of the rules of the Kennel Club in Great Britain on July 1, 1903, when ear cropping was abolished, the method used was to cut a piece of cardboard the required shape and lay it on the flap of the ear after the dog had been put under a complete anaesthetic. Strong scissors were then used to crop the right ear along the margins of the cardboard. When cropping the other ear the cardboard was reversed. Care must be taken to reverse the cardboard or the result will be very far from what is desired. Schmidt in his second edition of The Doberman Pinscher in America, advises the use of ear clamps. These clamps are supposed to give the correct shape to the trimmed ear and at the same time, shut off the circulation and prevent bleeding. Clamps are all very well if they are correctly placed. Otherwise the result is no better than the use of the cardboard pattern.

As the width of skull and length of head differ not only in breeds but in individuals of the same breed, a stereotyped pattern of cropping should not be used and the operator should learn from experience the type of cropping that will bring out the individual's expression. Dogs with short heads or thick skulls should have a longer ear crop, accentuating the length of head. This gives the over-all perspective of greater length.

I write the following from personal experience and while I do not claim to be ultra perfect in ear cropping, I did attain a semblance of perfection from experience as the result of numerous operations. The reader can take my suggestions for whatever they are worth and while I am aware that a very small percentage of the readers of this book will ever attempt to do their own ear cropping, if they are to make a financial success of raising a breed of dogs that require cropped ears by the dictates of fashion, they must curtail their overhead and thereby eliminate the expense of cropping. My experience was acquired on Standard, Miniature and Giant Schnauzers but cropping the ears of any breed is essentially the same.

As I did not believe in clamps or patterns, I wanted to learn the free-hand method. I therefore took cardboard cut in the shape of an uncropped ear and proceeded to cut the

114

CH. FEE V. OSTERSEE #17423
Blue with red markings
Sire: Artus v. Siegestor #7393 PH   Dam: Dodo v. Ostersee, #6173
An example of south German Dobermans of Roland v.d. Heide bloodlines
Excelled in chest, bone, forehead and hindquarters
Breeder: Mr. G. Trischler, Staltach, Oberbayern

cardboard as I would cut the dog's ear. I did this hundreds of times and became so proficient that I could actually cut out a perfect ear blind-folded.

I was then ready for the next exercise. I obtained a cloth sack about the size of a dog's head, stuffed it tightly with sawdust and pinned onto the dummy head, flexible cardboard the shape of an uncropped ear. I then proceeded to cut the cardboard and found that it was an entirely different matter when it was attached to the dummy head than when I could turn the cardboard around in my hands. Being right-handed, the left ear came easy but the right ear was a different matter: the shape was never the same. I seemed to get a narrower trim on the right ear than on the left. I overcame this difficulty by cropping the right ear first and then the left ear to match it.

After I had satisfied myself that I had gone as far as I could with the dummy, I took advantage of every dog that died at my kennel and before he was buried, his ears were cropped. Naturally as rigor mortis had set in, the ears would stand and the operation was not complicated by incorrect healing that sometimes occurs in live animals. However in several months I had become proficient in cropping free-hand and more than that, I had worked up a confidence in my own ability, which is the greater part of the battle.

My first endeavor was on a litter of Standard Schnauzers, most of which had ears like airplane wings, carrying them off to the side. I knew that with this type of ear carriage, the ears would be carried erect after cropping. First I put one puppy to sleep, using Abbott's Nembutal by hypodermic in the abdomen. The dosage is 1 c.c. to five pounds of body weight and the dog should go completely "out" within 15 minutes.

I did not crop the entire litter as a case of nerves on my part might have caused considerable damage. The next day I operated on two puppies and the following day, on four which was the balance of the litter. All operations were a success and the ears of each puppy stood by the time the tape was taken off.

Since that date which goes back to 1934, I have cropped

many dogs and can perform the operation with practically no loss of blood.

Care should be taken as to the amount of nembutal to be injected. The dosage is 1 c.c. for each five pounds of body weight, administered hypodermically for a dog of normal condition and correct weight. Should the dog be underweight or emaciated, it is far better to let the cropping go until it is put back into condition. However if the operation must be done immediately, a dosage of one c.c. to each 7 pounds of body weight is advisable and if the animal does not go completely "out", finish it up with an ether cone.

On an extra fat dog, do not attempt to give an additional dose of nembutal. It is better to give the correct amount and if insufficient to put it to sleep, finish up with an ether cone.

Should your hypodermic needle strike the bladder or the liver, the dog may not go to sleep but will merely stagger and wobble around, in which case under no consideration give it a second injection. Let it come out of the effects of the injection and a few days later try again.

The dosage of nembutal given in capsules by mouth is 2 c.c. for 5 pounds of body weight but I do not advise this method as the time required is too prolonged.

After you have had considerable experience you might try to give the nembutal intravenously. Shave the front leg above the first joint, put a tourniquet above the elbow and feel for the artery. Have the correct amount of nembutal in your syringe and when you are successful in puncturing the artery with the needle, a slight amount of blood will enter the syringe. Now inject the nembutal very slowly, and I mean very slowly, a fraction of a c.c. at a time, waiting a few seconds after each pressure of the plunger. Almost at the same moment when you have a sufficient quantity in the artery, the dog will go completely "out" and become limp. Any additional nembutal injected may cause death. The advantage of this method is that sleep is instantaneous. You do not inject too much or too little. There are no delays and no chance of the animal not going to sleep and the operation being delayed.

You should have in readiness a pair of sharp serrated scissors, to prevent slipping and at least two hemostats. These should have straight blades from two to three inches in length. Shorter blades or curved blades are not desirable. You may place these forceps on the ear about one-half inch back of where you intend to make the cut and thereby stop practically all bleeding. Now cut the ear and remove the lower hemostat near the base of the ear. Tie a knot in the cat-gut and start to sew, using the lace stitch pictured on an adjoining page. After you have stitched up as far as you can, remove a second forcep and continue sewing to the tip of the ear.

Do not pull your stitches too tightly, only enough to stop bleeding as otherwise you may cause the ear to pucker when healed. When you reach the tip of the ear, pull the cat-gut tight and tie a couple of knots in the end, about one-half inch from the ear. When released the slack will be taken up and the knot will hold the stitches from coming loose. If you do not pull the stitch tight before tying the knot, there will be too much slack in the cat-gut and the ear will bleed.

The use of the serrated scissors is necessary as otherwise the skin with hair on the outside of the ear which is loose and not attached to the cartilage, may either slip back or forward and you will have difficulty in sewing it evenly.

When ears are too heavy and inclined to flop, it is sometimes advisable to trim the skin that is covered with hair slightly back from the cartilage and draw it up to the edge of the cartilage when sewing. This tends to hold the cartilage erect.

There are just two arteries in the ear: one near the base and one about two-thirds of the way up, toward the tip. If you do not mind working in the blood, you may crop the ear before putting on the artery forcep and then merely clamp off these two arteries.

It is advisable to use cat-gut rather than surgeon's silk for the stitching as cat-gut will sluff off while silk has to be picked out and when left in too long, the ear will heal over the silk.

TAPING

There are many methods used to assist the cartilage to stand erect. With a dog that flies his ears out to the side, you need feel no alarm. The ears will stand of their own accord. But in the case of a dog where his ears flop like a hound, assistance should be given.

Tape must not be placed over the raw edges as this causes infection and a discharge of pus, retarding the healing. The ears can be taped over the head, the raw edges exposed to the air and dusted with BFI powder. If this method is used, the tape must extend not only over the ears but under the neck as well, otherwise it will not stay on. The dog will lose the hair where the tape has adhered. This of course is not a permanent injury as the hair will grow back in a few weeks but is unsightly until nature takes its course.

Another method is the use of collodion in conjunction with the tape, to insure adhesion and plaster many layers of tape on the outside of the hair part of the ear with the view to obtaining a stiff board- like effect which is rigid enough to hold the ear erect.

You could also insert a small piece of orangewood similar to a tongue depressor between the layers of tape to give more rigidity.

Another method is to place one layer of adhesive on the hair side of the ear and then coat the tape with water glass such as grandmother used to use to put her eggs down for the winter, only do not dilute the water glass with water. Use it as it comes from the can. This will become very rigid and the ears cannot possibly droop.

Each day grease the raw edges and pick off the surplus scabs. If there is any indication of puckering, stretch the edge and break the pucker. This is painful to the dog but it is unavoidable for if the edge heals in a pucker, the ear will never stand.

After the operation, put the dog in a small cage. While recovering from the effects of the anaesthetic, he will throw himself from side to side and unless confined in small quarters, may not only damage his ears but may do himself bodily harm.

119

It is well to be prepared and have on hand strychnine tablets of 1/120 grain. Should you through some error have administered an overdose of nembutal, you may be able to correct the damage and save your dog by the use of strychnine, a stimulant which counteracts the effects of the nembutal.

Dissolve 1/120 grain of strychnine in several teaspoonfuls of sterile water. Draw it into the hypodermic and administer half the contents of the syringe into the neck. If the dog does not show signs of recovering from the anaesthetic within 30 minutes, the remainder of the solution in the syringe may be administered. Be sure the water has been boiled and is sterile.

I want to warn the readers that while it is perfectly lawful to operate upon your own animals, under no conditions, practice on those belonging to a friend, either for a fee or gratis, as you are not a licensed veterinarian and if anything should go wrong, you can be held liable for damages for practicing without a license.

TAIL CROPPING

This is a minor operation when performed on puppies of from four to ten days of age. There is little pain and the wound is soon healed.

Have someone hold the puppy for you; push the skin of the tail back toward the body as far as it will go and cut off the tail with a pair of scissors to the proper length.

When released, the skin should cover the stump and if it does not, then cut off a small portion of the stump or bone so that the skin may be drawn over the end and stitched.

It is not necessary to use cat-gut or surgeon's silk, just borrow a piece of your wife's sewing cotton and one of her needles. It might be more convenient and would facilitate sewing if you could procure a curved surgical needle. Use two cross-stitches. This usually is sufficient but in severe cases of hemorrhage, put in as many stitches as are required to stop bleeding.

Some authorities advise the use of a tourniquet of cord at the base of the tail to shut off circulation. However this is not at all necessary or desirable, if you will squeeze the tail between the thumb and index finger, shutting off the circulation while you are making the cut and putting in the stitches.

The practice of using a tourniquet is, in my estimation, the wrong procedure. Should you forget to take off the tourniquet soon enough, the lack of circulation will kill the flesh between the tourniquet and the end of the tail and then a second operation will be necessary in order to remove the dead stump and you will have ruined your dog by causing him to have too short a tail.

Another reason for advocating sewing rather than a tourniquet is that it is always the liveliest pup that does the most moving around and consequently loses the most blood. He is more liable to break off a scab and start a fresh hemorrhage than a less active puppy. When tails are properly sewed, there is no danger of weakening an extra good puppy from excessive loss of blood.

It is well to touch the raw stumps with a little iodine but other than that, no medication is needed as the mother will lick the stump and keep it clean.

CROPPED EAR
LOOP STITCH

121

CH. JEM'S AMYTHEST V WARLOCK, C.D.
Many-time Best in Show winner, National Specialty winner, and one of
the Top Ten of all Breeds in 1964 Phillips System ratings. Amythest
is a daughter of famous Ch. Borong the Warlock, C.D.
Owned by Mrs. Henry Frampton, Miami, Fla.

Temperament

by
John T. Brueggeman

WHATEVER the source of the breed, the Doberman attained its modern form by intensive selection and inbreeding, plus some judicious crossing with Manchester Terrier blood. This was of prime importance in producing the color and coat which characterize the breed today, and also left its impress on temperament.

Between the Manchester crosses which were about six years apart, breed promoters crossed the Doberman with the Black English Greyhound with the intention of improving conformation.

While this cross restored some sharpness to the breed, it brought in new character traits such as aloofness and decreased affection towards master, poorer sense of smell but keener eye sight and greater speed. Generally, the Greyhound cross was less harmful to the Doberman's character than was the Manchester cross; but some of the original qualities of the Doberman were temporarily sacrificed. Dogs of the Greyhound type carry through to some of the present Dobermans that show aloofness and inferior sense of smell. The infusion of this Greyhound blood has unquestionably improved vision and speed, but this aloofness and lack of affection and respect toward his master should be bred out of our breed.

The Dobermans imported into this country after the first World War were for the most part extremely aggressive. Many of these dogs could be classified as rowdy and vicious, and proceeded to alienate the public against the Doberman Pinscher. There is a very close correlation between shyness and viciousness as a "fear biter" is the most dangerous type of dog; because such a dog will not hesitate to turn on his master if he becomes startled or frightened. It is dogs possessing these character faults that have given a black name to the Doberman Pinscher. Fortunately, lines emanating from these tyrants have practically disappeared from present day breeding stock. The favorable strains of correct Doberman character and temperament have survived to this day and have blended successfully with our imports just prior to the second World War. These more recent imports were of good character and temperament with the exception of a few.

The early undiluted Doberman possessed a keen mind, a fiery, shrewd disposition, was fearless and entirely loyal to his master and those he respected. These character traits should be rejuvenated and preserved for our breed.

Today, the temperament of the breed has been greatly improved, which is a tribute to our present responsible breeders. Improvement is still needed. True Doberman character and temperament should never be sacrificed for the sake of physical perfection.

What is the true character and temperament of the Doberman Pinscher? It can be described as follows: Circumspection of strangers, loyalty to and willingness to please master, shrewdness, uncanny intelligence, fear-

124

lessness, desire to protect master, his family, ability to cope with any emergency and general dignity.

Unfortunately there are many deviations from the true character and temperament which are primarily due to the cross breeding which had taken place. The present day tendencies lead toward a milder disposition but a general loss in intelligence. We should not permit him to become a mild breed but should keep him sharp, as he is intended to be, without being treacherous. His character and temperament should be improved or at least preserved in our present efforts for breed perfection. Shy or vicious dogs should never be propagated. Poor traits, especially viciousness and shyness which may have become dormant in individual dogs, sometimes reappear when the backgrounds of dogs to be bred have not been carefully studied. Some puppies show little or no signs of viciousness, however, upon reaching maturity, unfavorable hereditary traits appear. Authentic cases of this sort have been observed by those familiar with the breed. It is heartbreaking to an owner of a dog that has become vicious to have to put away his former friend and companion. While vicious dogs have been seen in other breeds, the public exaggerates unfavorable stories told of the Doberman.

To understand a Doberman is to know him. The entire breed should not be judged by the misdeeds of a few; until these few are eliminated, the Doberman Pinscher will be subject to repeated criticism. The adaptability of the Doberman is vast because of his temperament and character. His prowess as a protectorate for home and family is indisputable. Natural instinct to master emergencies and factors endangering lives or well being has been proven.

A typical account, illustrating the Doberman's protective instinct, was written in a Dayton, Ohio newspaper. A female Doberman had been boarded on a farm while his master was traveling. She quickly made friends with a four year old boy and assumed the responsibility of his welfare. Several days later the boy's life was threatened by a large rattlesnake, and the dog, sensing the danger, pulled him back by the seat of his trousers. The dog had to repeat this action several times as the small boy did not realize his peril. As a last resort the dog pushed the boy aside and killed the threatening snake. The Doberman jeopardized her life for the safety of the youngster.

Another Doberman hurled himself through a screen door to rescue his master's tiny daughter who was wandering toward a trash fire in the backyard. The dog kept the child away from the fire until his barking alerted the adults.

A Doberman that possessed extremely keen senses saved his owner's home from being destroyed by fire. The owner had left the dog in one part of the house while she went to another section and busied herself with housecleaning chores. She heard a commotion and tried to quiet the dog, but he persisted in whining and barking. Then he drew her attention to an adjoining room where faulty wiring had started a fire in the wall. Help was summoned in time to prevent a serious fire. It is interesting to note that the room where the dog had been, contained a fireplace in which a log fire was burning. Believe it or not, the Doberman had distinguished between the two fires and knew the smoke from the wall meant danger.

The Doberman Pinscher is one of the original police dogs of Germany and widely used for this purpose today. In this country, Dobermans are being used by the Berkeley, California Police Force with great success. His sharpness has been a great help in mob control and night sentry work.

There is no breed that surpasses him as an obedience dog. His willingness to please, attentiveness, lively disposition, and excellent memory make him outstanding among canines. He learns more readily than the average dog, and retains his training throughout his life.

His achievements as a tracking dog are exceptional. He is not hesitant when placed on a scent; is reliable, fast and intelligent. Quite a few years ago, a police trained Doberman in the East, followed a missing boy's scent over a day old trail through alleys, cross streets and busy sidewalks to a back alley. He led them up several flights of stairs to a rear landing and stopped in front of an old trunk containing the boy's body.

Another remarkable instance happened just recently. A Doberman female, who had never been trained to track, was given the scent of a small boy who was lost, and tracked him through a two mile wooded area in Chicago's Columbus Park. This was a fine achievement because the park was crowded with people and there were many distracting scents.

There is practically no use or purpose applicable to canines that cannot be mastered by the Doberman. He has proven his worth as a hunter, vermin killer, exhibition dog, farm dog and with all these attributes still makes a show dog of the highest order with unexcelled alertness and overall nobility of temperament.

The character and temperament of the Doberman Pinscher limits ownership. Prospective owners should be prepared to devote ample time to him from his puppyhood to old age. His spirited makeup demands that he receive much more exercise than the average dog. Extremely nervous people seldom make satisfactory masters, as Dobermans like all intelligent dogs are prone to reflect the disposition of their owners. He is not a good kennel dog because he requires individual attention and needs home life. The Doberman cannot be recommended as a dog for children unless he is intelligently handled and trained in their interest. Many dogs will resent the unintentional rough treatment by the average child. If a Doberman is raised with children, he is a fine protectorate and companion. It is interesting to note that he is gentle and careful while at play with small children and that he increases his degree of roughness according to the capacity and size of his playmate. He will not tolerate abuse. Dobermans that are owned by people of sadistic tendencies, are often unhappy and as a result may become shy or vicious. Prospective owners must realize that the Doberman is a dog of high calibre and therefore must be handled with care and intelligence. He demands and must be taught respect and enjoys uniformity in directed training. He has appropriately been called "The dog with the human brain."

A promising German-bred puppy, at 8 weeks.
IGON V. FORELL
Breeder-Owner: Ernst Wilking, Munster.

American Doberman Kennels

by

Kenton E. Smith

THE first Doberman champion in this country was Hertha Doberman, by Shill v. Dentz, out of Blanka v.d. Kieler Fohrde. The early Dobermans were imported mainly by persons who were familiar with the breed in Germany. Ringling Brothers Circus had a troupe of trained Dobes that caused much enthusiasm for the breed in this country.

Ludwig Gessner of Chicago, and Willy Necker of Wheeling, Illinois, have operated the outstanding training kennels specializing in Dobes in this country. Clyde Henderson was an outstanding amateur trainer and did a great deal to promote the breed.

The early kennels were located on the East Coast. Nothing of these early dogs remains in our bloodlines prior to importation of Helios' sons and Holland kennels to our

129

country. Much, however, was done by these dogs toward popularizing the breed in this country.

The history of Doberman kennels in this country is discontinuous, and the bloodlines show very little inbreeding. Not more than five people presently active in the Doberman Pinscher Club of America have been interested in Dobermans since Figaro v. Sigalsburg was imported. Fewer still can remember the disposition of Claus v.d. Spree, Troll v.d. Blankenburg, or Dietrich v.d. Barbarossahoehe. Some of the old timers have ceased to be active in the breed except for occasional judging assignments. Present breeders are fortunate in having some of these older breeders, who pioneered the breed in this country, present at our National Specialty show, sharing their past experiences and wisdom with present breeders.

Some of the best German dogs were imported by kennels whose interest in Dobermans lasted no longer than the fame of their import. By importing such dogs, they have been of great benefit to the breed, even though their interest was not lasting. Many kennels, both in this country and in Germany, have been made famous by a single bitch, but did no successful breeding without the bitch. Some have never been in the business of breeding dogs, but have profited by exploiting a few outstanding dogs and attaching their kennel name to the offspring.

Simbauer Kennels, in Chicago, is one of many little known kennels that has done a large amount for the breed. Mrs. Simbauer has maintained pure Holland bloodlines for six generations without showing any bad effects from inbreeding. It is interesting to note that these Holland breedings founded on such dogs as Benno v. Roemerhof, Martha v. Jaegerhof, Prinz Carlo's Lady, Urian v. Grammont, Nied of Randhof and Betty v. Jaegerhof, have never had, and still do not have, missing teeth. Where the Holland lines have been mixed with Blank v.d. Domstadt, Kurt v.d. Rheinperle-Rhinegold, Dewald v. Ludwigsburg, or Luz v. Roedeltal, missing teeth have appeared. It is hard now to find descendants of Favoriet v.d. Koningstadt, Angola of White Gate, or

130

Prinz Carlo v.d. Koningstadt unmixed with bloodlines that carry missing teeth.

The Holland bloodline originally had no missing teeth, and their outstanding quality was the beautiful head shape. Since they have not been maintained in anything like the original form, it is hard to find what the old Holland line looked like, outside of Chicago.

Mr. Bert Dow, of Iowa, past president of the D. P. C. A., is another that adopted a sound breeding program and stayed with it. The results achieved by Mr. Dow will be evidenced in our show rings for many years to come. The student of pedigrees has no need to investigate the background of any bitch whose name is prefixed with the famous Dow name, such as Dow's Cora v. Kienlesberg, Dow's Illena of Marien·land, and Dow's Dame of Kilburn.

Mr. Dow has observed the fame of many kennels built upon outstanding bitches and his own bitches are the foundations of many of our most successful kennels today. His program of breeding gave an emphasis to bitches in keeping with the exceedingly great influence which they, of necessity, have upon a discontinuous "system" of breeding such as is practiced in this country.

It is nothing new to find kennels "made" because they own an outstanding bitch. This was frequently the case in Germany, where Asta Voss made the great Blankenburg Kennels through her sons, Lux and Troll v.d. Blankenburg. Lotte v. Roeneckenstein did the same for the Sigalsburg kennels by giving the breed Lux's son, Alto v. Sigalsburg, and several other Siegers among Alto's full and half brothers.

In this country the same credit is due to outstanding bitches in being the basis of the breeding done by Mr. and Mrs. Brown in St. Louis, Mrs. Kilburn in Shanesville, Penna., and John T. Holliday, the owner of Edah v. Trail, in Los Angeles, California.

Dow's Dame of Kilburn produced seven champions out of her first two litters, and possibly more. None of her offspring has equalled her own great show record. Mr. and Mrs. Brown have used fine judgment in the breeding of this bitch.

Edah v. Trail is out of Lora v. Hays, a bitch inbred to Claus v. Sigalsburg through Redroof Exercist. More Sigalsburg blood enters her bloodline through both parents of her sire, Bubi v. Verstaame. Bubi is by Kanzler v. Sigalsburg, out of Lady Marta of Pontchartrain. Lora v. Hays was the first Doberman owned by Mr. Holliday. This, then, was the excellent foundation of the Von Trail kennels.

Among the older kennels were the Dawn Kennels of Mr. Hamilton Newsom, of Naperville, Illinois, and the Lawnwood Kennels of Mrs. Gibson in Hale's Corners, Wisconsin. Both of these kennels, at one time, had some of the best dogs in the country, but are now inactive.

Ferry v. Rauhfelsen was imported to this country by Giralda Kennels of New Jersey, owned by Mrs. M. Hartley Dodge. Ferry is out of Troll v. Engelsburg and Jessy v.d. Sonnenhoehe. All three of the above mentioned dogs had won the German Sieger title, and as both of Ferry's parents were imported, it is interesting to inquire why the mating was not repeated.

Mrs. Carpenter, of Jerry Run Kennels, has some present day descendants of Ferry, and the bloodline is still producing outstanding dogs.

Outstanding among the imported German descendants of Lux v.d. Blankenburg is Muck v. Brunia. Fortunately we had several Muck descendants imported to this country in addition to Muck. Muck was mated to Kora v.d. Ruppertsburg, both in this country and in Germany. The mating in this country produced the Lindenhof's famous "F" litter of Champions, Falka, Falk, Fritz, Fels, and Flammchen, full brothers to the German born Sieger Blank v.d. Domstadt, who was also imported.

Mr. Bornstein, of Peoria, Illinois, imported the Muck son, Troll v. Engelsburg and showed him extensively, but did not breed him extensively. The breed would be better off today if the reverse were true, that is, if Troll were bred more extensively in this country and shown less. Herr Gruenig, in his book, *The Doberman Pinscher,* is forced to give Troll credit for his German progeny and for his show record here,

132

TROLL V.D. ENGELSBURG
Champion German, American, Canadian
In United States and Canada: 95 Best of Breed, 78 Best
Working Dog, 48 Best in Show
Twice German Sieger, twice Wander Prize
Sire: Int. Ch. Muck v. Brunia   Dam: Adda v. Heek
Bred in Germany. Owner: E. Bornstein, Peoria, Illinois

though he does it grudgingly. Despite his very limited use as a stud dog in America, Troll produced many American Champions.

Mr. John Cholly, owner of the Glenhugel Kennels, of Canton, Ohio, and past president of the D. P. C. A., imported Troll's daughter, Ossi v. Stahlhelm, and mated her to Blank v.d. Domstadt, producing several litters of outstanding quality. It is these litters, bred by Mr. Cholly, that represent the backbone of the Muck line in present day Dobermans. Some of these dogs bear the kennel name of Marienland. Marienland Kennels, owned by Richard C. Webster of Baltimore, Maryland, was for a time very prominent in Dobe breeding, and Mr. Webster will always be remembered for his work recruiting dogs for World War II.

Mr. Kurt Nebel of Chicago, a director of the Chicago Dobe Club, had the interesting experience of observing a mongrel litter with only one Doberman parent containing several pups with naturally short tails. In the homozygous form this condition is lethal, which is why the early German breeders were forced to abandon attempts to produce a naturally short tailed strain.

The successor of Marienland Kennels was the Meadowmist Kennels, owned by Mrs. Wilhelm F. Knauer, of Philadelphia. Star of the kennel was Ch. Emperor of Marienland. (Mrs. Knauer, a woman of many talents and interests, is currently adviser on consumer affairs to President Nixon.)

There is a slight regional variation in the quality of Dobermans in this country. Although subject to many exceptions, it is possible to characterize the East Coast dogs centering in New Jersey, New York and New England as different from the dogs farther West.

Among prominent Eastern kennels were the training kennels of Mr. Elliott Blackiston; Pinckney Farms of Dr. and Mrs. Charles P. Horton, the owners of Ch. Pinckney Farm's Archon, and Adele v. Miegel, the dam of the late Ch. Favoriet v. Franzhof. Ch. Alcor v. Millsdod, Ch. Ardexter v.d. Valtheim, Ch. Jet v.d. Ravensburg and Alcor's brother, Ch. Merak, are representative of the Eastern type

134

dog. Dogs of the opposed type are Dictator v.d. Glenhugel, Ch. Saracen of Reklaw, and Ch. Komet of Pontchartrain. The bloodlines of Helios v. Siegestor, and the Holland dogs (with the previously noted exception of Simbauer) were predominant in Eastern United States. The bloodlines of Lux v.d. Blankenburg, and Muck v. Brunia are concentrated in the Midwest. In Hawaii, the older stock is of the Sigalsburg bloodlines (descendant from Lux), as the original Dobermans in Hawaii were imported from the Midwest. In Canada two major kennels have bred Dobermans. Von Blau Ture raised some excellent dogs based on the Marienland bloodline, but has since gone out of business. Mannerheim Kennels, owned by Dr. Shute, has had more than a score of champions, of which most were home-bred. He has exported dogs to South Africa and the United States. The bloodlines of Mannerheim Kennels are based upon Pontchartrain, Sigalsburg and Muck lines.

Noteworthy champion Dobermans were bred in Oklahoma by Torn Kennels of Oklahoma City, owners of the late Ch. Quo Schmerk of Marienland.

For purposes of this chapter, we could divide breeders into two indistinct classes designated as breeders and breed fanciers. The former are those who have had enough experience with the breed to be able successfully to breed dogs of top quality without consulting the judgment of anyone else. The breed fanciers are those who are unable to judge dogs and depend upon show results and public opinion to influence their selection of studs and breeding stock. The distinction is not a clear line, and it is difficult to say into which class many kennels belong.

It is not always true that those designated as breeders, those who have sufficient knowledge to breed dogs in accordance with the known principles of genetics, and to understand the reasons for the various requirements of the standard, are the most successful breeders in all cases. It is commonplace for persons who know nothing of genetics, and are not able to explain how a dog should gait, to produce Champions merely by careful observation of which studs

135

produce champions, and then breeding a bitch of good quality to those studs. I do not intend to imply that the above is not a good method, nor to say that they will not succeed in producing Champions by it. The fact is that every breeder began by use of this method before graduating into the class designated as true breeders rather than breed fanciers.

It is among those whom we shall call true breeders that dogs and personalities become mixed in such a way as to make it almost impossible to separate the two. It is here that the judging of dogs is not completely separate from the "politics" and opinions of people. It is here too, that my publisher and editor faces the difficult task of weighing historical accuracy against potential sales.

Let me define the issues that have become inseparable from personalities in this manner. We have on one side an ideal Doberman that stands in the ring like a beautiful statue. His hind feet are far apart and well behind the dog. The front feet face squarely to the front so that a plane drawn through the center of both left paws will be parallel to the vertical plane projected through the center of the dog lengthwise—that is, the front paws face the front as the standard describes them. The head is absolutely correct with the muzzle full and usually no deficiency of teeth. The general impression is one of beauty and staunchness. Here is a dog with ample rib spring, a large horizontal distance between his hocks and croup, and with good bone and substance.

On the other side, we have a type of dog that stands with his hind legs more directly underneath the dog. The back line is sloping and possibly a little steep at the croup, but not incapable of straightening, or even bending in the reverse direction when in motion. The front paws are in some cases a little inclined to toe out, and the chest is very deep, but not as broad as the dog described above. The hair is not as short as in some Dobermans. This dog has an alert and intelligent expression, but shows himself more favorably when in motion.

At the other end of the leash we have owners who are

DIAMOND OF PONTCHARTRAIN W66839
Breeder: Glenn S. Staines   Owner: Kenton Smith
Sire: Ch. Komet of Pontchartrain   Dam: Linda v. Nibelungenhort C.D.

137

sincere in the belief that the particular points in which their dogs differ from those of the opposite type are the points in which their particular dogs excel those of the opposite type. Judges give as reasons for placing one type of dog above the other exactly the points for which the losing exhibitor believes the decision should have been reversed. This does nothing to endear the judge to the exhibitor and places him clearly on one or the other side of the question at issue. It is well known that nothing succeeds like success. There is nothing that can be advertised in favor of a dog quite as effective as, "He won!" Nothing influences the breed fanciers as much as purple and gold ribbons. No argument concerning the merits of a stud dog is as good as, "My dog won the National Specialty."

It will be very hard for some to understand why and in what way politics influence show-ring results. It should be easier to understand why show results influence the quality of the breed. It is easy to understand that poor judging will directly influence the quality of dogs produced within a breed.

Suppose a judge is confronted with a large and small dog of the same breed. The question that the judge is asked to decide is not which dog is taller. The judge is not paid a hundred dollars to decide that one dog is twenty-seven inches high and another is twenty-eight inches high. The decision for the judge to make is "Which dog does the Standard say should win?" The judge is being asked in a practical way to interpret the Standard. Both he and the audience know which dog is taller. He is asked to describe his interpretation of the Standard in terms of *which dog*. The judge interpreted the Standard before be went into the ring. He decided before entering the ring—ten, twenty years before he entered the ring— what the ideal Doberman looked like. The persons who selected the judge may, or may not, have known beforehand exactly how the judge would interpret the Standard. It is possible that the people selecting the judge knew he would give the ribbon to the twenty-seven inch dog if the dogs were equal in other respects.

138

No one can say with certainty which dog will win before the show. I do not intend to tell the reader that dog shows are not honest. The judge may have been selected by the person with the twenty-seven inch dog, not because the person is dishonest, but because he believes a twenty-seven inch dog is better; not because his dog is twenty-seven inches tall, but the reverse—that is, he bought a twenty-seven inch dog because he thought a twenty-seven inch dog was ideal.

"I wouldn't own the dog that won today if you would give him to me!" "I wouldn't take that dog home if you paid me to!" These remarks are heard often enough at dog shows, but not because the winning dog was poor. The reason is that within the breed we have two different conceptions of what an ideal Doberman should look like.

The interpretation of the Standard is the issue over which people become quite heated. It is an honest issue that influences which dog wins, at which show, under which judge. It is an issue that influences which judge is selected to judge which show, who is elected chairman of the bench show committee, and who is president of the dog club.

This is very apparent in the case of the German Breed Clubs. The Doberman Pinscher Verein is a wonderful example of this point. The Doberman Verein has not the stabilizing influence of an organization of all breeds such as the American Kennel Club. The result is, whenever one party within the Verein is elected to office, the Standard is actually changed. Here again the question is one of interpretation of the Standard. In Germany, the two factions within the club actually advocate different standards. Thus a good dog today may not be a good dog after the election of officers.

Now, with the above in view, let's get down to cases. The two major parties within the D.P.C.A. have been centered around the two most famous kennels in this country, Westphalia Kennels and Pontchartrain Kennels. An experienced Doberman fancier can distinguish the Muck, Pontchartrain, and Westphalia bloodlines half a

139

block away without a catalog. Three different types of dogs have been typified by these bloodlines. The Muck bloodline, of course, is German and has not had a great influence in American Dobe politics, as both sides seem to agree that it is good. Mr. Glenn Staines could walk by the benches at a dog show and name the sires of sixty percent of the dogs without a catalog, and designate the bloodline of the remainder with wonderful accuracy.

The two factions within the D.P.C.A. have been centered around the two different types, or conceptions of the ideal Doberman that have been perfected by Westphalia and Pontchartrain Kennels respectively. There was a time, of course, when this dispute did not exist. Pontchartrain is the oldest existing kennel in this country. Although there are a few other pioneer kennels mentioned in the chapter *The Doberman in America,* Pontchartrain, owned by Mr. Staines of Detroit, Michigan, was always the largest and most prominent. Pontchartrain, to date, has produced thirty champions, and seventy other champions have at least one Pontchartrain parent. It has been charged, because it was so large, that it was a puppy factory. It was large because it contained not only Mr. Staines' breeding stock, but also dogs being trained for Pathfinder, a guide-dog school, founded in 1936 by Mr. Staines to train dogs for the blind. Another reason for its size was that Mr. Staines was never able to dispose of boarders who were behind in payments, stray Dobes that were given to him by "everyone and his brother" in Detroit, and special pets of no value, but who for some reason have a place in the large heart of Mr. Staines.

Mr. Staines' first Dobe was Judy of Detroit, a name that still appears in Pontchartrain pedigress. After this he bought several dogs through Mr. Fleitmann. Among these were Dyno v. Wiesengrund, a Troll v.d. Blankenburg son of fine quality, and Westphalia's Beda Armingardt v. Nibelungenhort. The last mentioned was bred to Claus v.d. Spree (the best dog imported and owned by Westphalia Kennels) and produced Ch. A. Hindo of Pontchartrain. Concerning Claus v.d. Spree Mr. Staines once wrote

140

me: "Claus was beautiful. His head was weak in muzzle and somewhat down-faced, but his body was superb. He defeated Lux v.d. Blankenburg at the Sieger show, but was deprived of the title because his head was weak. The Germans were afraid everyone would use him at stud and cause many bad heads, which are hard to outbreed. I had a few bad heads from him." This comment on Claus is quite a concession for Mr. Staines as he owned Sgr. Lux v.d. Blankenburg!

Among outstanding imports of Westphalia Kennels are the Holland dogs, Favoriet v.d. Koningstadt, and Prinz Carlo. White Gate Kennels, of the late Howard K. Mohr, through the efforts of Mr. Fleitmann, also imported some outstanding dogs from Holland with the Grammont Kennel name.

The immortal Jessy v.d. Sonnenhoehe is the greatest of the dogs imported by Westphalia Kennels, though she was not of the best temperament. Illisa of Westphalia and Illisa of Pontchartrain, two litter sisters, were raised by Mr. Staines. Both dogs were to have competed for the Sieger title in Germany, but Illisa of Pontchartrain was returned to Detroit at the last minute, from the port of embarkation.

Lux v.d. Blankenburg was born August 25, 1918 and imported to the United States by Mr. Staines in February 1927. He was a slow developer and his value was not recognized in Germany until he was four years old. It was not until 1923 that his best son, Alto v. Sigalsburg was whelped. He was, therefore, not used much at stud in Germany except for a period of about four years. During this time he improved the breed tremendously. It is practically impossible to find a dog of any quality now that is not a descendant of Lux v.d. Blankenburg. His descendants have built the breed both here and in Germany.

It was at the time Pontchartrain began to import dogs that Pontchartrain and Westphalia kennels began to favor two different types of dogs—both within the standard. I

141

do not wish in any way to imply that the two gentlemen, Mr. Staines and Mr. Fleitmann, who at this time ceased to be interested in the virtues of the other one's dogs, ceased to be gentlemen, nor ceased to be friends. Mr. Fleitmann has always supported Pathfinder and usually stayed at Mr. Staines' home in Detroit when attending dog shows there. Mr. Staines had a picture hanging in his office of Mr. Fleitmann judging one of his dogs. Both gentlemen had different conceptions of an ideal Doberman. Both were sporting enough to continue showing dogs where the other judged, even though this was done with the intent of showing the ringside, rather than the judge, the quality of the dogs being shown.

Of the two Doberman ideals, the variety favored by Mr. Fleitmann has been more favored by judges. Mr. Staines became more and more interested in the temperament of Dobermans and in the affairs of the D.P.C.A. He was an idealist, a politician and a hard worker. In the drug business, in the politics of Wayne county, Michigan, and in the politics of the D.P.C.A., Mr. Staines fought a continuous battle for the principles he thought right.

Mr. Staines began training Dobermans to guide blind people in 1936. At the time I met him, he had spent more money than he owned upon the project. At the same time, he refused to breed Pontchartrain dogs to prominent winners for fear of mixing into his bloodlines such undesirable qualities as insanity, shyness, and unsound temperaments, which some of these dogs were known to transmit to their progeny. Gradually he was *forced* to withdraw from the active showing of Dobermans. Within the D.P.C.A., however, he still managed to exert a major influence upon its elections, management, and affairs—an influence that was always of benefit to a club that has large numbers of members with only a short-lived interest in the breed, and a shifting desire for different types and styles of dogs.

In bringing this history up to date, it is my sad duty to record the death of Mr. Staines July 7, 1951. Many are the judges, the breeders, and Doberman owners who will continue to follow the sound principles of breeding first taught to them by Mr. Staines. The last three decades of Doberman breeding may well be improved upon by breeders able to profit from a study of the past.

MR. GLENN S. STAINES AND A PATH-FINDER DOG, RED LADY

CH. DICTATOR VON GLENHUGEL (Red) #A531251
Sire: Blank v.d. Domstadt   Dam: Ch. and Siegerin Ossi von Stahlhelm
Whelped August 9, 1941
Owners: Bob and Peggy Adamson, Roslyn Heights, New York
Breeder: John F. Cholley

Illena and the Seven Sires*

by
Mrs. Bob Adamson

N the history of the American Doberman, eight dogs produced more than ten American champions each These were: Ch. Westphalia's Rameses, Ch. Dow's Illena of Marienland, Ch. Favoriet von Franzhof, Ch. Westphalia's Uranus, Ch. Emperor of Marienland, Ch. Domossi of Marienland, Ch. Alcor von Millsdod, and Ch. Dictator von Glenhugel.

Rameses produced 11 American champions of record; Illena, 12; Favoriet, 13; Uranus, 14; Emperor, 18; Domossi, 20; Alcor, 26, and Dictator, 37.

These figures are recorded in the American Kennel Club as of July, 1951, and can probably be considered final for Domossi, Rameses, and Uranus, who have been dead for a number of years; also for Illena, who is alive but whose last litter was in 1946. Emperor died suddenly in 1949, Alcor and Favoriet in the spring of 1951. Of the

* This article, written in 1951, is presented as an "at-the-time" report of one of the most eventful decades in Doberman development. Dictator, the only one of the seven sires living at time of the article, died in 1952. The total of his champion progeny increased to 52.

145

Seven Sires, Dictator alone is living today, occasionally siring a litter but no longer at public stud. The number of champions by the latter four could therefore be increased appreciably.

The year 1941 was the golden year of the American Doberman. That year alone gave birth to Illena and the younger four of the Seven Sires: Emperor and Favoriet in the spring, and Alcor and Dictator in the fall, the latter two within a day of each other. All of the five were sired by the older three except Dictator, who was Domossi's younger brother. Rameses, the oldest, was whelped in 1938, Domossi and Uranus in 1939. Three of the Famous Seven died as the result of heart attacks: Domossi, at the age of 7; Emperor, at the age of 8; and Alcor shortly before his tenth birthday. Uranus, Rameses and Favoriet lived to the age of ten.

The Seven Sires were responsible for an era in American Dobermans which was as exciting and colorful as the dogs themselves. They towered over the Doberman world like mighty titans and the competition among them was brisk, awesome—and sometimes fierce. The dog magazines fattened on their advertising, the like of which the breed has not seen before or since. Their names were familiar to the veriest novice, and their offspring could be found in the remotest hinterlands. Each had his loyal partisans, and the legends concerning them were inexhaustible. With their passing, passes an era. History will not soon see the time when seven males of such stature live contemporarily again.

All of them lived on the Eastern seaboard, although Domossi and Dictator were bred in the Middle West. Five were kennel dogs, the exceptions being Alcor and Dictator, who were raised from puppyhood by their owners and valued by them primarily for their companionship.

These dogs were descendants of the best of the German imports. Domossi and Dictator were line-bred to Ch. and Sieger Muck v. Brunia through his two imported sons, Ch. Blank v.d. Domstadt, their sire, and Ch. and Sg. Troll v.d. Engelsburg, their dam's sire. Their dam, the red

Ch. and Siegerin Ossi v. Stahlhelm, was a granddaughter of Helios v. Siegestor through Kleopatra v. Burgund. Rameses and Uranus were line-bred to Helios v. Siegestor. Both were sons of the imported Ch. and Siegerin Jessy v.d. Sonnenhoehe, Rameses by the imported Ch. Kurt v.d. Rheinperle-Rhinegold, and Uranus by Kurt's American son, Pericles of Westphalia. Illena's dam, Ch. Dow's Cora v. Kienlesberg, was also by Kurt out of the imported Ch. Gretl v. Kienlesberg, a half sister to Jessy through Cherloc v. Rauhfelson.

Domossi and Dictator were full brothers, Dictator being the younger by two years. Emperor was the son of Domossi, Illena was the daughter of Rameses, and Alcor and Favoriet were the sons of Uranus. Uranus and Rameses were half-brothers, as were Alcor and Favoriet. Emperor's dam, Ch. Westphalia's Rembha, was a litter sister of Rameses. Favoriet's dam, Adele v. Miegel, was a daughter of Rameses' litter brother, Ch. Westphalia's Rajah. Alcor's dam, Ch. Maida v. Coldod, was a daughter of Inka v. Lindenhof, a full sister to the sire of Dictator and Domossi.

Dictator, Domossi and Favoriet were reds. Almost half (17) of the Dictator champions were red; three of the Domossi champions were red; and five of the Favoriet champions were red. Prior to Dictator's time, the only stud producing as many as seven red champions had been Dictator's sire, Blank, who was a black.

Alcor, Rameses and Illena were dominant black and all their champions were therefore black. Emperor and Uranus were black recessive. Two of the Emperor champions were red, and three of the Uranus champions were red.

There is no subject in dog breeding so cloaked in mystery, glamour and fable as that which surrounds the great stud dogs. The layman is convinced that great studs become great simply because the breed's best bitches all flock to them for breeding. Yet the records of the American Kennel Club show that of the total number of litters registered with Favoriet as the sire, only one-twelfth had

147

CHAMPION DOW'S ILLENA OF MARIENLAND
Mother of twelve champions from three sires. Five won
Best in Show all breeds

148

the assistance of bitches who were, or ever did become, champions! Of the total number of litters sired by Dictator, only one-fifth had dams who were, or ever became, champions; of the total number by Uranus, only one-fourth, and by Emperor or Rameses, one-thrid. Of the total number of litters by Domossi or Alcor, approximately half had dams who were, or later became, champions.

Although it has long been recognized that the better the bitch, the better the stud's opportunity to produce high-type progeny, the Seven Sires were able to produce an amazing number of champion offspring from bitches who never became champions themselves and in many cases could not even be considered show quality.

The records of Favoriet and Dictator were particularly impressive in this respect. Of the 13 champions by Favoriet, less than one-third (4) came from champion bitches. Of the 37 by Dictator, less than one-half (17) were from champion bitches. Of 14 by Uranus, 8 were from champions, and of 11 by Rameses, 7. Of 18 by Emperor, all but 3 were from champions; of 20 by Domossi, all but 2; and of 26 by Alcor, all but one were from champions.

A high proportion of the champions produced by several of these studs came from daughters of other studs included in the Famous Seven. Twelve of the 18 champions sired by Emperor were from daughters of the Seven Sires, with over half the Emperor champions from Rameses daughters alone.

One-half the 26 Alcor champions were from daughters of Dictator, Emperor and Favoriet. One-half the 20 Domossi champions were out of daughters of Emperor, Uranus and Rameses. Fourteen of the 37 Dictator champions came from daughters of Emperor, Alcor and Domossi, with ten of them from Domossi daughters only. Two of the 13 Favoriet champions were from a Uranus daughter and an Alcor daughter. One of the Uranus champions came from a Rameses daughter.

Rameses alone was never bred to any daughters of the Seven Sires, although fifteen of the champions sired by the others were produced by his daughters. Ch. Dow's Illena of Marienland was not only the greatest of his offspring, but the greatest producing bitch in the history of American Dobermans. From a total of five litters by three different sires, she produced the remarkable total of 12 champions. The three sires were Domossi and his two sons, Emperor, and Ch. Dow's Dusty v. Kienlesberg. There were five champions in the two Emperor litters, four in the one Domossi litter, and three in the two Dusty litters. No other American bitch even approximated this record.

Rameses was the only one of the seven who sired more female champions than males, producing 7 female champions as against 4 males. Domossi sired 10 champions of each sex, and Illena produced 6 of each sex. Favoriet and Uranus each sired 6 female champions, with 7 male champions for Favoriet and 8 male champions for Uranus. Emperor and Alcor each sired 7 female champions, with Emperor siring 11 male champions and Alcor 19 male champions. Dictator sired 14 female and 23 male champions.

As individual specimens, Alcor, the black, and Dictator, the red, outshone all others, a fact which was reflected in their spectacular show careers. Of the other five, Favoriet was little known as a showdog, but Emperor, Domossi, Rameses and Uranus attained notable prestige both in breed and group competition.

Five of the Seven Sires were between 27½ and 28 inches in height, Rameses being slightly over 28 and Domossi slightly under 27. All had scissors bites, and six had complete sets of teeth, the exception being Domossi who lacked one premolar. In gait and strength of quarters, Dictator and Alcor excelled the others, Dictator being noted for the strongest pasterns and Alcor for the best turn of stifle. Uranus had the more rear angulation and Domossi, the less. The family line from which the brothers Dictator and Domossi were descended was strong in pasterns and quarters, but frequently lacked sufficient angulation. The family from which the brothers Rameses and Uranus came was often weak in pasterns and tended to have too much

150

CH. DOW'S DAME OF KILBURN

Sire: Dictator v. Glenhugel   Dam: Ch. Dow's Dodie v. Kienlesberg
Breeder: Bert Dow   Owner: Eleanor Brown

angulation. In Alcor and in Emperor, the two families were combined, for both of them were outcrosses.

Although none of the seven were faulty in ribspring or depth of brisket, the chests of Rameses and Dictator were the deepest, while the other five possessed greater spring of rib. Alcor had the strongest back, Dictator the highest withers, and Favoriet the most pronounced forechest. Uranus, though not the largest, was the most powerful of them all, but did not have their elegance and length of neck. The four black dogs had eyes which were various shades of brown, in the case of Rameses two-toned. Dictator, alone of the seven, had a truly dark eye, the deep shade of brown for a red dog being comparable to a black eye in a black.

Alcor, Dictator, Domossi and Emperor had excellent tail-sets. Those of the other three could have been higher. The tails of Domossi and Dictator, which were always carried gaily, had a characteristic triangular shape, thick at the base and tapering to a point. The only one of the seven which could be described as a really compact short-bodied dog was Domossi. While Alcor and Dictator measured square, their backs were of medium length, and those of the other four were slightly longer.

If a composite Doberman could be made, using only one of the many qualities which each of the Seven Sires was known to possess and transmit, it might have Dictator's temperament, Favoriet's front, Rameses' chest, Uranus' ribspring, Alcor's rear quarters, Domossi's tail, and Emperor's elegance. But it would require the head of Illena, for her head was closer to perfection than any of the Seven Sires.

Not only was Illena famed for the beauty of her head and expression, but for her superb neck, shoulders and front, and the wine-red color of her markings. Her mouth was beyond criticism. She had a deep chest and excellent ribspring, but was too rounded in croup and rarely carried her tail up. Her greatest liability was a lack of showmanship and animation which often caused her assets not to be fully appreciated on first impression.

152

Only two studs have come within reaching distance of the Seven Sires. These are a black Emperor son, Ch. Roxanna's Emperor v. Reemon, and a black Uranus son, Ch. Kama of Westphalia. Both were whelped in 1943 and are still living. Roxanna's Emperor has sired 9 black champions from six different bitches, only two of which were champions. His dam, Ch. Westphalia's Roxanna, was a litter sister of Rameses. Kama has sired 7 champions (6 black and 1 blue) from four different bitches, only one of which was a champion. His dam, Alma v. Molnar, was a daughter of Rameses' litter brother, Rajah.

Among the younger sires, only three as yet have produced more than two champions: Favoriet's black son, Ch. Christie's Barrier, who died in 1951 at the age of six; Dictator's red son, Ch. Saracen of Reklaw; and Alcor's black son, Ch. Rancho Dobe's Presto. Barrier and Saracen were both whelped in 1945. Barrier has produced four champions from four different bitches, Saracen three champions from two different bitches. Neither of Saracen's mates were champions, and only one of Barrier's. Presto, whelped in 1947, has produced three champions from one champion bitch. Two of the Saracen champions were red. The Barrier and Presto champions were black. Saracen was out of an Emperor daughter, Kay of Reklaw; Presto was from a daughter of Roxanna's Emperor, Ch. Rancho Dobe's Kashmir; Barrier's dam, Ch. Christie v. Klosterholz, was a daughter of Rameses' litter brother, Rajah.

Of the younger Dobermans, male or female, the greatest producer to date is the red Dictator daughter, Ch. Dow's Dame of Kilburn, whose dam was the Domossi daughter, Ch. Dow's Dodie v. Kienlesberg. She was whelped in 1945, the same year as Saracen and Barrier, and in her first two litters produced seven champions (five males and two females). From the first litter, which was sired by Alcor, five became champions. From the second litter, sired by Emperor and whelped just after his death in 1949, two have already completed their championship. Her third litter, by her grandson, Ch. Berger's Bluebeard, and her fourth litter, by her own sire Dictator, are not yet of show-

153

ing age. The Alcor and Emperor champions were black, the Bluebeard litter is black, and the Dictator litter is red.

Here, indeed, is an interesting fact: the six Dobermans mentioned above—Roxanna's Emperor, Kama, Barrier, Saracen, Presto, and Dame—are all sons and a daughter of the Seven Sires!

In other lands also they have enriched the breed, many of the exports being Dictator or Emperor offspring out of daughters of the Seven Sires. In 1948, the Siamese Prince Bhanuband Yukol imported a Dictator son and daughter for the purpose of establishing the line in Siam. The red male, Damasyn The Shawn, was out of a daughter of Emperor. In Tokyo, Damasyn The Bat, who is by Dictator from a Domossi-Illena daughter, produced a litter sired by the Kama son, Ch. Dacki v.d. Elbe, whose dam was a Domossi daughter out of a Uranus daughter. One of these was awarded the 1951 title, Grand Champion of Japan. The Cuban Champion Damasyn Venture and his half-brother, Damasyn The Blade, have sired a number of litters in Havana. Both are by Dictator, Blade being a full brother of Damasyn The Bat. In Germany in 1950, Arda Lark of Inverness produced a litter by the Red Sieger Artus v. Wertachbrucke. She is a red Dictator daughter out of a Domossi-Emperor granddaughter.

The most famous of all the exports is probably Ch. Kilburn Escort, the Emperor-Illena son recently sold to Hawaii. Escort is one of the few Dobermans ever to leave America after completing his championship, most Dobermans being exported as puppies. Meadowmist Barrister, by Emperor out of a Rameses daughter, has established himself as a stud in Brazil.

The Seven Sires were the backbone of the American show Doberman. Through their intermarriages with the daughters, not only of each other but of the brothers and sisters of their families, they have transmitted a productive power that makes itself evident from generation to generation. During the ten years prior to August, 1951, a total of 416 Dobermans completed their championships in the United States. One-half of these were the descendants in the first,

154

second, or third generation of the Seven Sires. One-third of the total number were their own sons and daughters (139), sixty-two were their grandchildren, and seven were great grandchildren. Many, of course, could have fallen into several categories, but in considering these figures no dog was counted more than once.

CH. HARDING'S FAUST
Owned by Clair Stille, N. Hollywood, Calif.
A Best in Show winner, Faust was one of the Top Ten Working Dogs
of 1956.

156

Color in the Doberman

by

Gerda M. Umlauff

VERY slight acquaintance with the different breeds of dogs makes it clear that the variations in color are enormous, and in many cases entirely a matter of taste. Some breed standards almost completely disregard color. The Whippet standard, for instance, states that all colors are allowed except black and tan (the predominant color in Dobermans). On the other hand, some breeds put such a premium on correct color and markings that a slight variation is enough to disqualify a dog completely. Other breeds come in between, with a moderately wide choice of colors but definite limits set to the permissible variations.

Color can play an important part in the popularity of a breed. To the experienced fancier, it is a part of breed history. Any radical departure from accepted colors means a break with tradition, perhaps even an infusion of outside blood. Color may be the principal distinction between breeds, as in the case of Setters, where color is the characteristic by which the layman recognizes an Irish or a Gordon in contrast to an English Setter. Or color may be largely a matter of fashion, perhaps because it gives a flashy appearance in the ring, thereby catching the eye of judge or ringside; perhaps because some outstanding winner has made it popular. There was a time when Scotties were predominantly brindle, but with no change in the standard blacks have now become almost universal.

Since individual tastes do differ, it would seem that a considerable variety of colors should help sales, by appealing to a wider variety of possible buyers. On the other hand, if a limited color range has become definitely associated with a certain breed, it is likely that the customer to whom the breed appeals will unconsciously desire the color which he mentally associates with it.

In the case of the Doberman, the standard stipulates four possible colors: black, red, blue and fawn (isabella). The markings are to be a clear rust, sharply defined and not too large, appearing above each eye and on the muzzle, throat and forechest, on all legs and feet, and below the tail. The nose should be solid black on black dogs, dark brown on reds, dark gray on blues, and dark tan on fawns. A very small white spot on the chest is permissible, but must not exceed one-half inch square.

The first German standard of 1899 permitted gray undercoat on the neck, behind the ears and the top of the head, and also black spots on the toes. It called for dark brown eyes, but did not stress light ones as a major fault. In the case of reds, blues and fawns, the modern standard states that the eyes should blend with the color of the coat.

The fawn or so-called isabella color, newly permitted by the present standard, does not appear to have been common at any time. The name is said to be derived from Latin through the French word "sable" which means sand. A literal translation would therefore be "sand colored." Dogs of this color are said to show a general loss of pigmentation,

CH. DAMASYN THE SONNET (Red) #W97660

with light eyes and noses, which is believed to accompany or indicate weakness and deterioration of body and temperament. In the German studbooks there are only 25 registrations of isabella-colored Dobermans among the nine thousand entries between numbers 5,001 and 14,000, but it is, of course, possible that an additional number may have been culled at birth and never registered.

The matter of eye color is one in which the majority of breeds seem to agree to a large extent. Dark eyes are generally preferred with a few exceptions, such as Weimaraners, Chesapeakes, and a few others. However, both breed standards and popular preference may vary from a simple brown or dark eye to an insistence on a decided black. In Dobermans, the original standard called merely for a dark brown eye of medium size, with no stipulation as to shape. Now a dark eye, of medium size and almond-shaped, is demanded. The tendency has been to breed for a darker eye than was originally required, per-

159

haps because the average was lighter in the early days. It is not uncommon for breeders to admire and aim for a quality which is not sufficiently general to be made an absolute requirement. With selection over a period of years, the desired characteristic becomes more widespread. Dogs which lack it are penalized accordingly, and eventually the standard itself is revised to accord with the change in the breed.

It required much time and effort for serious Doberman breeders to establish the dark eye. Although attempts were made to utilize rules of inheritance, there were many failures and throwbacks to earlier types. This common occurrence is said to have caused an Australian scientist, a certain Dr. Parl, to do research in the hope of discovering a remedy. A few years before World War II he reported that he had spent many years in developing a substance which should be completely harmless but have the ability to change light eyes to dark, and at the same time make such dark eyes hereditary. This would certainly be an extremely difficult task, and one which conflicts sharply with modern theories of inheritance. Dr. Parl's experiments were claimed to have resulted in a substance which could only be used by veterinarians, with the proviso that neither dogs nor bitches could be used for breeding for a period of three months after its administration. German breeders have heard nothing further of the matter since the War.

A white spot on the chest appears to have been fairly common in the early days, since the original standard mentions it as permissible and gives no restriction on its size. However, it seems to have been frowned upon from the start. One well-known judge is quoted as having said that in the case of two dogs which were otherwise equal, one of which had a white spot on the chest and the other a light eye, the latter is to be preferred. The reason for this was that all the spectators would notice the white spot, while many would overlook the light eye! This is not an attitude which would be likely to be taken today, when the white spot is seldom seen and has been proved

160

comparatively easy to get rid of. However, it is of course true that in the descendants of dogs which had white spots this fault may sometimes recur. This is especially likely if a large white spot has been dyed (which is, of course, against the rules). Sometimes the white hairs, if not too numerous, have been pulled out, or even a small piece of skin removed from a puppy, so that when he is grown the defect is not apparent. Such illegal measures will not, however, prevent the dog from passing on the fault to his puppies.

White leg markings sometimes occurred also, and possibly still do occasionally. However, the fact that such markings are evident at birth, while it may be worth noting as a warning for future breeding operations, does not necessarily mean that the puppy in question will have white feet when he is grown. They are likely to disappear more or less completely, according to the original amount. One breeder is said to have destroyed a whole litter except for a single pup which he kept to nurse the dam, because they all had white feet and legs almost to the elbow. After a few weeks he was surprised to observe that the surviving puppy had entirely lost these white markings and was entirely normal in color.

The importance of understanding the color standard and the normal development at various stages is illustrated by the experience of a novice fancier just starting breeding operations. He reported that he had disposed of four puppies out of a litter of six because they were mouse grey at birth. He was unaware that this was the normal appearance for puppies which would mature into the blue color, which is one of those recognized by the standard, although it is comparatively rare. Not having studied the pedigrees of his stock, this breeder did not learn until too late that the sire of his litter was by a blue dog, thus explaining the appearance of this color in the puppies.

The original standard of 1899 recognizes only one color, black and tan, but as early as 1901 two others were recognized, namely red and tan, and blue and tan. It is said that Otto Goeller believed that the blue and tan variety resulted from the introduction of blue Great Danes, while other authorities favor the theory that the Weimaraner was responsible. Considering the size of the Great Dane, the use of this breed seems rather improbable. That the English Manchester Terrier was used to improve the black and tan color and markings and refine the appearance of the Doberman is generally accepted by breed authorities. In the early days of the breed the markings were frequently a light straw or yellowish color rather than the desired rust red, which was often difficult to produce.

To return to the blue Dobermans, the color is actually, of course, a gray rather than a real blue, and is claimed to be recessive to black. A study of the studbooks, volumes IV to VIII, and inquiries of a number of Doberman breeders indicate that the blues may result from the mating of two black and tans, but apparently only if both parents carry this color. It is reported that the mating of two red and tans results only in red puppies, whereas two blues produce black, blue, and red puppies in the proportion of 1:2:1. This would indicate that the blues are intermediate between black and red and can never be bred true. In this they would be comparable to roan Shorthorns in cattle, which are produced by breeding reds and white together. This casts doubt on the statement that the mating of blue and red dogs will produce black, blue, and red puppies in the proportion of 1:1:2. According to the Mendelian law, blues and reds should produce approximately equal numbers of blues and reds, but no blacks. On the other hand, blacks and blues should produce approximately equal numbers of blacks and blues but no reds.

In the period before World War I, a large number of blues of high quality were shown. A judge's report for 1910 speaks of the imposing picture made by the Dobermans of both the blue and red colors, which delighted both judges and spectators because of the entry of first-class animals. At that time these colors seem to have surpassed the black and tans in quality, showing greater symmetry and elegance. Some of these early browns, in particular, were not only excellent in themselves but

162

played an important part in the development of the breed and appear in the pedigrees of first-class black and tan Dobermans of later generations.

During the interval between the wars and since, up to the present time, the high standard of the earlier blues has not been reached again, but attempts are now being made to do so once more. The well-known German Doberman judge, Herr Wilhelm Kloth of Aachen, has recently offered a challenge cup for the breeder of the best blue Doberman. This trophy will be awarded each year at the championship show of the German Doberman club, beginning with 1950. It will be won outright by any breeder or owner winning three times. The trophy is offered for the best blue of either sex, and contenders must be registered and at least nine months old. The breeder or owner competing must be a member of the German Club. Breeders and owners of the winners will receive certificates. Undoubtedly this trophy will help to stimulate interest in the blue dogs. Increased competition will doubtless lead to improvement in the quality of coat, which is sometimes thin behind the ears and appears to be a characteristic in which this color is sometimes inferior. In regard to teeth, however, the blues are reported to excel. It is said that missing teeth are unknown among them, and it is even claimed that a couple of extra ones have been noted!

After World War I there was a great falling off in the number of high-quality red Dobermans, although now and then an outstanding class of this color would appear. However, in the course of twenty years there was such a pronounced falling off in their number that it was actually proposed to eliminate all classes except for the black and tans. This, however, was not done. It seems probable that the reason for the small number of reds was that no systematic attempt was made to breed them, but the matter was left entirely to chance. However, voices were gradually raised in their favor, since there are always individuals who prefer to be able to exhibit something out of the common run. It is also claimed that the blues and reds are better adapted to life in a hot climate and hence for export to the tropics, since black always absorbs the heat. Black and tan is unquestionably easier to breed, and the average breeder of this color has been little interested in any other. However, in Germany today there is a revival of both reds and blues, and very good specimens are to be found there. The reds, in particular, are making good progress and seem well on their way to regaining their old popularity. In the 1950 Sieger Show in Germany there are said to have been 109 Dobermans benched, of which 31 were reds, but only one blue. Sixty per cent of the red males and 56 per cent of the red bitches were rated "excellent," while of the black and tans only 30 per cent of the males and 45 percent of the females attained that distinction.

INT. CH. BROWN'S ARMAND
Sire: Ch. Alcor von Millsdod   Dam: Ch. Dow's Dame of Kilburn
Breeder: J. O. Brown, St. Charles, Missouri
Owner: Dr. W. E. Shute, London, Canada

164

A Short Explanation of German Grammar

by
Anne FitzGerald Paramoure

THE translation of foreign pedigrees and show reports is not easy, even for one who is well acquainted with the language in its everyday form. Just as the novice finds many English words used in an unfamiliar sense, so there is a special vocabulary employed by German-speaking breeders and exhibitors. To translate them it may be necessary to plow through ten or twenty variations of meaning in the unabridged dictionary, with no certainty that one will select the correct equivalent, even if it is included, while the ordinary abridged dictionary is likely to be no help whatever. Abbreviations are very frequently used, and may be fully as puzzling as an unfamiliar use of a familiar word.

All German nouns are capitalized, not merely proper names. Adjectives are not capitalized, even though they may form part of a kennel name, unless actually used in place of a noun. The formal second person "Sie" (meaning YOU) is also regularly capitalized. When an adjective is attached to the front of a noun so as to make a single word, however, it is capitalized instead of the noun to which it is attached, as in *Kleintierzuchter,* meaning small animal breeder.

CH. ROARK'S ABIGAIL VON PIA

Daughter of Ch. Steb's Top Skipper, Abigail is pictured being handled by Dick Salter to win of 1961 Best in Show at Lexington KC under judge Percy Roberts.

German plurals are not formed by adding *S*, but in most cases by adding *er, e* or *en* to the root of the noun. Sometimes the root vowel is changed by the addition of an umlaut (..) over a, o or u, making it ä, ö, or ü. This may be the only change or it may be in addition to the plural endings already mentioned. The umlaut stands for an *e* which is not written. In proper names or in a word beginning with a capital the *e* is often written in place of the umlaut, and where printing is done with type which does not include the umlauts the *e* itself may likewise be used. The umlaut can be important for three reasons: it changes the pronunciation, it may be the only sign that a word is plural and not singular; in a German dictionary or index all names or words which contain an umlaut will be alphabetized as though the letter *e* were printed after the vowel over which it is used. This may mean that a name or word will be found several lines or even pages away from the same name or word without the umlaut. Moreover, the presence or absence of the umlaut may completely change the meaning of a word. For instance, *Mucke* means a whim, while *Mücke* is a gnat. Finally, the feminine of many nouns is formed by adding an umlaut to the vowel and the suffix *in* to the end of the word, so Hund, dog (general or masculine) becomes Hündin, bitch.

Other peculiarities which may confuse those not familiar with the language are: nouns have four cases, nominative, genitive (usually ending in *s* or *es* but sometimes in *e, en* or *ens*), dative and accusative. There are three genders, masculine, feminine and neuter. Adjectives and pronouns also change their endings.

Another peculiarity is that the perfect participle of verbs is formed by adding *ge* to the *front* of the verb in most cases. Thus the participle of *decken* (meaning to breed) is *gedeckt* (bred) and the word will be found in a dictionary under *d* and not *g*. Compound verbs with *inseparable* prefixes do not add the augment *ge* for the participle, however. On the other hand, compound verbs with *separable* prefixes insert the *ge* between the prefix and the verb root, the participle of *anfangen* (to begin) being *angefangen*. In certain other tenses the separable prefix of the verb in the main clause comes at the end of the phrase or sentence, as for instance, *ich fang an* (I begin) is a form of *anfangen*. As a compound verb may have quite a different meaning from the simple one from which it is formed, non-Germans unaccustomed to this usage find it extremely confusing to discover at the end of a sentence a prefix which may unexpectedly change the whole meaning. The Teutonic word order which frequently puts the verb at the end of the sentence instead of where other people would expect it is also confusing.

The names of German dogs, which are likely to appear dauntingly long and formidable to those who do not understand the language are much easier to remember if they are broken down into their separate parts. Most of them consist of an individual name, a preposition with or without an article, and a kennel name. Most if not all German breeds require litter registration, all puppies carrying the breeder's registered kennel name, while it is usual for all of a single litter to have individual names beginning with the same letter. Kennels' names often refer to the town, village or local area in which the breeder lives. Sometimes they are related to the name of the breed or the breeder, and puns are not uncommon. Thus Herr Berger, breeder of German Shepherds, used the kennel name *Bergerslust,* meaning "Shepherd's Delight" or "Berger's Delight" as one prefers. The impressive-sounding "Fiffi v. Rhein-Herne-Kanal" is only Fiffi of the Rhine Canal at Herne, where her breeder lived. Wilhelm Schwaneberg took the kennel name "v.d. Schwanburg," meaning "of or from the Swan Castle." The owners of "Neckarlust," "Neckarstadt" and "Neckartal" all live along the Neckar River. "Zwergschnauzerheim" is nothing but "Home of Miniature Schnauzers."

CH. STORM'S POGO NIP OF KIA ORA

Pogo Nip, a son of immortal Ch. Rancho Dobe's Storm, was one of the
Top Ten Working Dogs of 1957. Owned by Mrs. Dora Sayers Caro,
and handled by A. Peter Knoop.

AM. CAN. & CUB. CH. BORONG THE WARLOCK, C.D.
Bred, owned, and handled by Mr. and Mrs. Henry G. Frampton
Borong, three-time winner of the National Specialty, scored 230 Best of
Breed wins. He was one of America's Top Ten Working Dogs from
1958 through 1961, and sired 38 champion offspring.

Official Breed Standard of the Doberman Pinscher

Submitted by the Doberman Pinscher Club of America, and approved by the American Kennel Club, October, 1969.

General Conformation and Appearance—The appearance is that of a dog of medium size, with a body that is square; the height, measured vertically from the ground to the highest point of the withers, equalling the length measured horizontally from the fore-chest to the rear projection of the upper thigh. *Height* at the withers—*Dogs* 26 to 28 inches, ideal about 27½ inches; *Bitches* 24 to 26 inches, ideal about 25½ inches. Length of head, neck and legs in proportion to length and depth of body. Compactly built, muscular and powerful, for great endurance and speed. Elegant in appearance, of proud carriage, reflecting great nobility and temperament. Energetic, watchful, determined, alert, fearless, loyal and obedient.

The judge shall dismiss from the ring any shy or vicious Doberman.

Shyness—A dog shall be judged fundamentally shy if, refusing to stand for examination, it shrinks away from the judge; if it fears an approach from the rear; if it shies at sudden and unusual noises to a marked degree.

Viciousness—A dog that attacks or attempts to attack either the judge or its handler, is definitely vicious. An aggressive or belligerent attitude towards other dogs shall not be deemed viciousness.

Head—Long and dry, resembling a blunt wedge in both frontal and profile views. When seen from the front, the head widens gradually toward the base of the ears in a practically unbroken line. Top of skull flat, turning with slight stop to bridge of muzzle, with muzzle line extending parallel to top line of skull. Cheeks flat and muscular. Lips, lying close to jaws. Jaws full and powerful, well filled under the eyes.

Eyes—Almond shaped, moderately deep set, with vigorous, energetic expression. Iris, of uniform color, ranging from medium to darkest brown in black dogs; in reds, blues, and fawns the color of the iris blends with that of the markings, the darkest shade being preferable in every case.

Teeth—Strongly developed and white. Lower incisors upright and touching inside of upper incisors—a true scissors bite. *42 correctly placed teeth*, 22 in the lower, 20 in the upper jaw. Distemper teeth shall not be penalized.

Disqualifying Faults—Overshot more than $\frac{3}{16}$ of an inch. Undershot more than $\frac{1}{8}$ of an inch. Four or more missing teeth.

Ears—Normally cropped and carried erect. The upper attachment of the ear, when held erect, is on the level with the top of the skull.

Neck—Proudly carried, well muscled and dry. Well arched, with nape of neck widening gradually toward body. Length of neck proportioned to body and head.

172

Body—Back short, firm, of sufficient width, and muscular at the loins, extending in a straight line from withers to the *slightly* rounded croup. *Withers* pronounced and forming the highest point of the body. *Brisket* reaching deep to the elbow. *Chest* broad with forechest well defined. *Ribs* well sprung from the spine, but flattened in lower end to permit elbow clearance. *Belly* well tucked up, extending in a curved line from the brisket. *Loins* wide and muscled. *Hips* broad and in proportion to body, breadth of hips being approximately equal to breadth of body at rib cage and shoulders. *Tail* docked at approximately second joint, appears to be a continuation of the spine, and is carried only slightly above the horizontal when the dog is alert.

Forequarters—Shoulder Blade sloping forward and downward at a 45 degree angle to the ground, meets the upper arm at an angle of 90 degrees. Length of shoulder blade and upper arm are equal. Height from elbow to withers approximately equals height from ground to elbow. *Legs,* seen from front and side, perfectly straight and parallel to each other from elbow to pastern; muscled and sinewy, with heavy bone. In normal pose and when gaiting, the elbows lie close to the brisket. *Pasterns* firm and almost perpendicular to the ground. *Feet* well arched, compact, and catlike, turning neither in nor out. Dew claws may be removed.

Hindquarters—The angulation of the hindquarters balances that of the forequarters. *Hip Bone* falls away from spinal column at an angle of about 30 degrees, producing a slightly rounded, well-filled-out croup. *Upper Shanks,* at right angles to the hip bones, are long, wide, and well muscled on both sides of thigh, with clearly defined stifles. Upper and lower shanks are of equal length. While the dog is at rest, hock to heel is perpendicular to the ground. Viewed from the rear, the legs are straight, parallel to each other, and wide enough apart to fit in with a properly built body. *Cat Feet,* as on front legs, turning neither in nor out. Dew claws, if any, are generally removed.

Gait—Free, balanced, and vigorous, with good reach in the fore-quarters and good driving power in the hindquarters. When trotting, there is strong rear-action drive. Each rear leg moves in line with the foreleg on the same side. Rear and front legs are thrown neither in nor out. Back remains strong and firm. When moving at a fast trot, a properly built dog will singletrack.

Coat, Color, Markings—*Coat,* smooth-haired, short, hard, thick and close lying. Invisible gray undercoat on neck permissible. *Allowed Colors*—Black, red, blue, and fawn (Isabella). *Markings*—rust, sharply defined, appearing above each eye and on muzzle, throat and forechest, on all legs and feet, and below tail. *Nose* solid black on black dogs, dark brown on red ones, dark gray on blue ones, dark tan on fawns. White patch on chest, not exceeding ½ square inch, permissible.

Faults—The foregoing description is that of the ideal Doberman Pinscher. Any deviation from the above described dog must be penalized to the extent of the deviation.

DISQUALIFICATIONS

Overshot more than ³⁄₁₆ of an inch; undershot more than ⅛ of an inch. Four or more missing teeth.

AGITATOR OF DOBERLAND (Red) #W162677
Breeder-Owner: Ivan Wolff, Forest Hills, New York

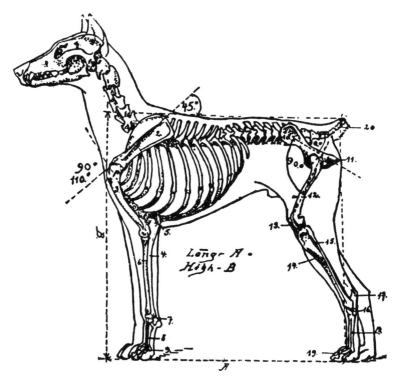

A Length —B Height
1. Head—2. Shoulder blade—3. Upper arm—4. Forearm
—5. Elbow—6. Radius bone—7. Front ankle—8. Pastern
—9. Toes—10. Hip—11. Haunch—12. Upper thigh—
13. Stifle—14. Lower thigh—15. Fibula—16. Heel—17.
Hock—18. Rear pastern—19. Toes—20. Tail.

The Blueprint of the Doberman Pinscher

HIS is no place to assert that the judging of dogs (or their evaluation, a better term) is an exact science. It partakes more of the nature of an art. Try as we may to make it objective, the personal equation of the judge must needs enter into the process. The judge's attitudes, preconceptions, and predilections, however they may have been produced or arrived at, must influence, even if they do not determine his decisions and awards.

Knowingly or not, a given judge may have a particular antipathy for a given fault in a dog, a light eye, an undershot mouth, or cow hocked hindquarters, and may as a result attach a greater penalty to a small manifestation of that particular fault in a given dog than he would attach to some more intense manifestation of some other fault with which he is less concerned, in some other dog. He is forced to balance, let us say, a shallow chest in one

177

dog against an unsound back in another; not only the presence of the faults but their degree. Faults are not absolutes. There are to be found excellent depths of chest, adequate depths, slightly shallow, and intolerably shallow chests, just as there are thoroughly sound backs, just perceptible hints of unsoundness, slight give in the spine, and utterly swayed backs. It becomes necessary to determine not only which fault in one part of the dog is the most to be discouraged or some other fault in another part of another dog, but also the seriousness or degree of the respective faults in the respective dogs.

Nor is the judge of dogs concerned only with the faults to be found in the exhibits which come before him in the judging ring. It is his duty to recognize and reward the outstandingly good points of a dog as much as to disparage the bad points. Two dogs may be good all over and approximately equal, but one may possess superlatively good feet or a particularly fine lay-back of shoulder, which the judge accepts as the deciding factor.

No award is ever an absolute determinant of which dog is the best or better; it is only the reflection of the opinion of a single judge at the time, the hour and minute that he makes it, and the circumstances and conditions under which it is made. Another judge in some future show may reverse the placings of two exhibits of approximately equal merits, and indeed the same judge may see the exhibits differently at some subsequent event. While, by and large, the most consistent winner in a given competition may well be considered to be the best dog in it, there is no finality to be attached to the awards at dog shows as evidence of which is the best exhibit. The best dogs in the long run reach the top or the approximate top in the awards under the jurisdiction of expert judges, but just because a dog wins at one or two shows it is not to be assumed that he was the best dog present, or because a dog fails to win that he is a bad specimen of the respective breed he represents.

For these reasons, it becomes apparent why we have no absolute yardstick to apply to canine excellence. This chapter does not purport to teach the reader who may not already be familiar with the breed how to discriminate and distinguish between two or more Doberman Pinschers of approximately equal excellence. It will not make a dog-show judge out of a reader who has not from outside the ring looked at and compared the respective merits of many dogs, weighed them one against the other, and soaked himself in the lore of the breed under considera-tion. This chapter is only an interpretation of the stand-ard of perfection of the Doberman Pinscher, a standard that is clear enough a guide to persons who have worked with the breed and compared many dogs one against the others over many years, but which may be obscure in its implications to the novice and the amateur fancier. It is intended to aid the reader in the evaluation of his dog or dogs; to show him the qualities in his Dobermans which are to be sought for and which are to be avoided; to en-able him to recognize the outstandingly excellent from the mediocre, and mediocrity from the definitely bad; to help him to determine whether his Doberman is worthy to be exhibited in a dog show; and to enable him to watch the judging of Doberman classes in the shows with an awareness of what is going on.

Most judges are willing, if they can, to explain their decisions briefly after they are made. They are under no obligation to do so, however. They are frequently fatigued after a grueling task and their memories of two obscure dogs may have forsaken them. Moreover, between two exhibits of almost equal excellence, small points may have turned the scale in the favor of one of them, and the judge may fear the implication that because he liked one best he did not like the other, or because he considered the winner better in some particular attribute the defeated dogs were bad in that respect. It is to be remembered that all the dogs in a given competition may be good in a certain point, and yet one better than the others in respect to that point; or all the exhibits may fail in some particular respect and the judge may be forced to choose the best of a bad lot. That a dog wins does not necessarily mean that he is faultless any more than that he fails to win means that he is not good. The explanation of the judges' decisions, unless they are very explicit, are so much subject to misinterpretation that many judges are reluctant to express them.

There is no way for the onlooker to know which dog is the best unless he is able to evaluate them for himself. To him all Dobermans may look alike, but there are nuances of difference between all of them which an experienced scrutiny will reveal. He may be a crank about good hindquarters while the judge is an equal crank about good heads or some other points; but experience will teach him to balance the good attributes of dogs against the bad attributes. He will come to prefer a dog with many small and insignificant faults over another that is well nigh perfect except for a single glaring fault that overbalances all his ʻexcellent features and leaves him hopelessly outclassed.

It requires a considerable space in which to assess a dog of the size of a Doberman. The average living room may be big enough to enable the survey of the dog standing, but it requires a considerable open space to examine his gait. Moreover, the amateur is likely to examine a dog from a point too close to him to enable him to see the animal whole. It is not to be denied that it is necessary to go over the dog point by point at close quarters, but the examiner must have room also to stand away from the exhibit, to look at him as a single unit, and to ascertain how well the various parts, however good or ill they may be as parts, fit together to form a whole dog. It is to be remembered that it is not the mere parts that we are surveying, but rather their assemblage into a beautiful and efficient whole.

Therefore, though we may look at him in the living room, before we form any final estimate we must take the dog out of doors, out on the lawn or sidewalk or into the park for our inspection.

One of the pleasant things about the Doberman is that he can not be faked. Under his short, close fitting jacket, it is impossible to conceal his faults. The Chow, or the Collie, or the Poodle may have its coat so trimmed or adjusted to bring out its virtues and to hide its shortcomings. Not so with the Doberman. The Doberman is forthright for what he has and what he is. It is possible in the living dog to discern his skeleton and its articulation. There is nothing that can be covered up and hidden.

That such is the case, however, does not imply that a Doberman's condition has no bearing upon his excellence. A dog may be distorted by being hog fat or greyhound thin. He may lack style or dash from ill health, be flabby from want of exercise, or may be dirty and ill kempt. These faults may be more chargeable to the owner or keeper than to the dog himself, but it is the dog that suffers from them. Many a Doberman has gone down in the prize lists under others fundamentally better because of his condition.

It is certainly unwise to exhibit a dog in public competition unless he is in the best possible condition; and it is impossible to evaluate the merits of a dog in the private survey unless he is in shape to have whatever fundamental merits he may possess recognized.

First he must be in good flesh and that flesh must be firm and hard. The dog must have been exercised rigorously until his muscles ripple and until he is capable of manifesting all the power that his skeletal structure declares to be possible. To show a dog or to seek to evaluate one that is either flabby with unexpended fat or thin to the point of emaciation is unfair to what might be otherwise a fine animal.

Secondly, a dog must be freed from intestinal parasites in order to bring him into top condition. This is best done after a microscopic examination of his feces which will determine whether he has worms and, if so, what kind. If there is no evidence of worms, the dog should not be treated for them. Vermifuges are irritants, and when they are not indicated may do more harm than good. On the other hand, the presence of worms may so affect the animal systemically as to render him listless and phleg-

181

matic and unfit for exhibition. The particular kinds of worms (or their eggs) found in the microscopic examination of the feces should be treated and not merely a shotgun dose of vermifuge administered. This is not to be done the very day or even the week before the dog is to be exhibited or examined at home. The worms have begun the depletion of his system the very day he acquired the first of them, and it may require weeks, or even months if the infestation has been severe, for the system to recover from their ravages. Tapeworm very often does not show in fecal examination.

Thirdly, the nails of a Doberman Pinscher should be blunted. Some dogs with sufficient exercise keep their nails worn and shortened and for such dogs no attention need be given to the nails. But such dogs are exceptions. Most dogs, without attention, grow nails that require being filed back to enable the feet to appear their neatest, most compact, and shortest. Caution must be used in the operation never, never to file into and injure the quick of the nails. This quick is very sensitive and a dog that has been injured by having it touched is very prone forever afterward to resent having his feet handled at all. It is much better to file back the horn of the nail that is exposed, weekly if need be, waiting between operations for the quick to recede, and filing down the rough edges, than to go at the job in a spirit of wanton butchery.

If time does not permit the gradual process of bringing the feet and nails into condition and it is determined to amputate the nails to the very toes in one fell swoop, at least have the humanity to give the animal a general anesthetic before the operation. The toes will remain tender a few hours after the dog comes out from under the anesthetic, but there is little danger of infection. Normal gait may be expected quickly to reestablish itself.

A fourth requisite is that the dog shall be clean and free from external vermin. This may be accomplished either with a dry bath with fuller's earth, corn meal or some such substance thoroughly rubbed into the coat and subsequently as thoroughly brushed out; or it may be done,

182

usually more satisfactorily, handily, and thoroughly with bland soap and warm (but never hot) water. The soap should be completely rinsed from the dog's coat, and he should be rubbed and massaged until he is entirely dry. Special attention should be given to the cleansing and drying of the interior of the ears. This is not the place to discuss the simple technique of giving a bath to a short haired dog like a Doberman Pinscher; it is only to say that in order to look his best and to feel his best, a dog must be clean inside and outside. A man too squeamish to introduce his dog into his bathtub does not deserve to own a fine dog.

A fifth detail that is too frequently overlooked before exhibition is the condition of the dog's teeth. To present before a judge a dog whose teeth are coated with slime or tartar is an insult. Sound teeth may be kept sound by occasional, weekly or oftener, scouring with a small dampened cloth dipped into powdered bicarbonate of soda (common kitchen soda). Small deposits of tartar can often be removed with a small pointed instrument, such as a nut pick. A dog whose teeth are heavily incrusted with tartar should be taken to a veterinary dentist. After the teeth are cleaned they should be kept clean by frequent attention.

The muzzle will appear neater by cutting back the dog's "whiskers" or "feelers" as short as possible before his exhibition. This is by no means obligatory and most judges will take no cognizance that it has not been done. It is, however, a convention usually observed. It is not likely to make the difference between victory anl defeat.

More than the things here set down the Doberman does not require. These things should be habitual and routine kennel procedure, but it is to be feared that haphazardness and negligence is the way of most kennels until it is determined that a dog is to be exhibited. The poor fellow is then subjected to a regimen of fast preparation that is mere makeshift and that does not enhance his chances of winning.

It may seem that in an amateur survey, allowance can

well be made for fatness or thinness, flabby muscles, ill health, long nails, and dirtiness. It is not true. They all affect even the owner's appreciation of the beauty of a dog and will impair any fair evaluation. Give the poor dog a chance to be seen at his best.

In a private survey, as in a public one in a dog show, it is best to have somebody to control the dog, to pose him for examination, to steady him, to lead him from or toward the surveyor at command. This person need not be a professional handler, but may well be the owner, his wife, child, or a friend. It is not intended that this amateur handler try to conceal the dog's faults, but that he allow the dog to stand naturally so that the faults will be apparent. Poor handling can overemphasize faults, cause a dog to move badly, even make it difficult to see many of the dog's better qualities. Without attempting to conceal faults, it must be remembered that a *show* dog must *show*. All that is required is that the person showing the dog shall be strong enough to manage the dog on a leather lead, and intelligent enough to accept simple directions.

The first requirement of a Doberman Pinscher is that he shall be a terrier. In saying this it is recognized that the Doberman is now, under dog show rules, included in the Working Group of breeds. Until a few years ago he was shown in the Terrier Group, which grew unwieldly large—the cause of the transfer. However, the Doberman remains a terrier, to whatever purpose he may be put. In the German language the very word *pinscher* means terrier; and however much the earlier German dogs fell short of terrier characteristics, such was the ideal.

The English word *terrier* was derived from the Latin word *terre* or earth, and a terrier is literally a dog that "goes to earth" in search of his game, dragging it or driving it from its holes, dens, or lairs. Admittedly the Doberman Pinscher is too big for this purpose, but so too is the Airedale Terrier, whose classification as a terrier nobody denies. The Bullterrier and the Staffordshire Terrier do not strictly belong to the category of earth dogs, any more than does the Boston Terrier, which is in the Non-Sporting Group.

184

To define a terrier is not too simple. It is in large measure a matter of character, a devil-may-care readiness for action, a jaunty good nature with a chip on its shoulder, a glint of daring in the eye, an alertness not found in other than terrier breeds, a happy insouciance, a fight-or-frolic elan, that is unmistakable. A terrier is tense and shows his tension. On the physical side, the terrier is characterized by a straight, narrow front, a compactly short body and especially loin, and a high and alert carriage of head. His jaw structure is very firm and even, enabling him to grapple and hold.

The Doberman is a dog of good middle size without being tall or stilted. The requirements for height are such that a person of normal height can hold his dog by the collar without stooping. Height of shoulder of males is given as 26 to 28 inches, of bitches 24 to 26 inches. This range of height will give a weight of between 60 and 80 pounds. While "undersized or oversized" is mentioned in the Standard as faults, and while 24 inches at shoulder is an approximate minimum, an excess of size that does not include coarseness or clumsiness is hardly to be deemed reprehensible. It is only the coarseness and clumsiness that too often are found in oversized Dobermans that is to be penalized—and those qualities are to be avoided in Dobermans of any size whatever.

A svelte elegance is the hallmark of the Doberman. He must have grace and dignity, a recognition of his own beauty and importance. Your good Doberman is something of an egoist. He must appear to strut. This was not always true. The pictures we see of the earlier Dobermans indicate that they were most commonplace dogs without the dash and grace and finish of structure that we have since come to demand. The same shortcomings were evident in the earlier Dobermans that were brought to America.

The Doberman was a made breed, concocted in the late nineteenth century from crosses of Manchester Terriers, German shorthaired shepherds, Rottweilers, and later perhaps a dash of other bloods. Just what kind of breed of dogs Herr Louis Dobermann had in his mind to produce we have no idea and doubt that he had. Dobermann (the final "n" has since been dropped in the name of the breed) was a dog catcher in the small town of Apolda in Thueringen, Germany, and it is likely that he employed in the potpourri that bears his name any dog that was at hand and that he believed would contribute something to the mixture. There is no evidence that Dobermann was in any sense a scientist. It is doubtful that he ever considered elegance as a requisite attribute of the breed upon which he was working. Be that as it may, the Doberman Pinscher has developed an elegance and refinement, without which he has little claim to excellence.

This elegance is by no means a decadence; it does not imply any sacrifice of strength and power. On the contrary, it is an expression of the dog's sureness of his superabundance of power. The Doberman has become an aristocrat among the breeds of dogs. Power is evidenced in the animal's structure; elegance penetrates to both his structure and his bearing.

The Standard provides the Doberman Pinscher shall be "elegant in appearance, of proud carriage, reflecting great nobility and temperament." Nobility is, of course, a part of the dog's elegance. However, the Standard does not say what kind of temperament the dog should possess, even if it were possible for a judge in the show ring to determine what a dog's temperament actually is. In a sentence without a verb, the Standard says, "energetic, watchful, determined, alert, fearless, loyal, and obedient." These adjectives are possibly presented to define "temperament," but they fail to do so; and in any event the qualities implied by them are impossible to evaluate without living with the dog.

"Shyness and viciousness" are set down in the Standard as "disqualifying faults," as they should be in the standards of all breeds. These attributes are definitely evident in the show ring, although it is necessary for a judge to exhibit discretion about just how much shyness or viciousness

186

is intolerable to the extent of warranting the disqualification of an otherwise good dog. A dog may display his dissatisfaction with being handled by a stranger without being either shy or vicious. The Standard is specific in the declaration that "an aggressive or belligerent attitude toward other dogs shall not be deemed viciousness." It is an interesting commentary that the Doberman Pinscher that won Best in Show at the Westminster Kennel Club show in Madison Square Garden, New York, in 1939 was so vicious that the judge of Best Dog in Show was forestalled from placing his hands upon the exhibit. Such a dog would of necessity be disqualified under the terms of the current Standard.

Before undertaking the assessment of the individual parts of the Doberman, it is well to stand away from him by some fifteen or twenty feet to consider him as a whole. No matter how excellent the parts may be as parts, they must form a whole organism which is pleasing. You are, of course, familiar with your dog and could pick him out from an assemblage of a thousand, but have you ever looked at him intently or critically? Set aside your personal liking for him and your bias in his behalf as well as you are able, and scrutinize him objectively, as if you had never before set eyes on him. And do not permit your fears and misgivings that he may not be perfect deter you from looking at him honestly. The perfect Doberman has not yet been whelped, and it is no disgrace for the owner to be compelled to admit the faults of his dog. Walk around him, see him from all angles, have your handler move him for you. Keep your eyes glued upon him. Observe his every stance and how he handles himself.

Does he appear to be too high on the leg? Squatty? Is his head in correct proportion to his body, too big or too small and peanut-like? Is his body longer than his height at shoulder? Is his back level? Does his brisket extend to his elbow? Is his neck long enough and strong enough? Is his bone structure adequate? Do his shoulders or his hindquarters appear as mere props and without sufficient angulation? Are his feet thin or splayed? Does he as a whole impress you as excellent enough animal to justify the trouble of analyzing his parts?

The experienced judge requires only a little more than a glance to spot the glaring defects a dog may have and to know whether he demands further careful consideration. The amateur, however, may require a good deal of looking to see that something is wrong and to determine just what is it. An aesthetic sense, a feeling for proportion, an awareness of symmetry may be of aid. The Doberman is first of all an efficient machine, and his beauty is in his apparent efficiency. If the dog as a complete unit is unpleasing, it is useless to pursue the examination further; the animal may as well be discarded as a worthy example of excellence in his breed.

On the other hand, if he survives this preliminary survey, it is well to approach him closer and to go over him part by part, with an assurance that if the parts are correct they will fit together into a typical dog of the Doberman Pinscher breed.

The head of the Doberman is not his most important attribute, but, as in other breeds, it may be considered as the index of the breed. A good Doberman can not have a bad head, but neither can excellence of head compensate for shortcomings in the other parts of the animal.

The ideal head is one of moderate length. The Standard says it shall be "long and dry." It must not be attenuated or otherwise freakish. The skull is flat on its top and without noticeable occipital protuberance. The stop or step-down between skull and muzzle is only moderate and hardly noticeable. The top-skull is rather narrow, but not to the point of weakness; it is rounded sharply to the cheeks which should be as flat and free from bulge as possible. The Standard says, "Cheeks flat and muscular." In fact, their muscularity does not show, and the power of the grasp of the muzzle does not depend upon the bulge of the muscles of the cheeks.

The Standard describes the head as "resembling a blunt

188

wedge," which is true also of many other breeds of dogs. The top of the Doberman muzzle is as nearly parallel as possible with the top of the skull, although a slight downward curve near the tip of the nose is permissible. The permissible downward curve does not mean a ram's head or a Roman nose, which is a serious malformation. The dishface, which is seldom seen, is equally reprehensible.

The muzzle should be deep and well filled up under the eye, but not so much as to produce an oriental slant of the eyes such as is seen in the Bullterrier. The skin of the whole head is close fitting and there should be no surplus anywhere. The lips are dry and just sufficiently ample to cover the teeth thoroughly; certainly there should be no pendant flews.

The correct length of head is impossible to state, since it must depend upon the size and proportion of the entire dog, an attentuated head being as wrong on a dog with an inclination to cloddiness as a stubby head on a racily made dog. The head should balance length of top skull and length of muzzle; a head half as wide as its length over all would probably appear coarse. Rather than indulge in any exact measurements of the head, let us say that it should be narrow rather than thick, that the muzzle should be well filled below the eye, and that the head should fit the dog.

The eyes, despite the description in the Standard, should be very dark, the darker the better, no matter what the body color of the dog. It is true that "medium brown" eyes are not quite so offensive in a red dog as in a black-and-tan; light eyes in a Doberman are, however, abominations. The Standard says that "in reds, blues and fawns, the color of the iris blends with that of the markings, the darkest shade being preferable in every case." This statement means, in simple truth, that in red dogs, and even more in blue dogs, dark eyes are difficult to find, and that lighter eyes in dogs of such colors are to be tolerated (not encouraged) because dark eyes are rarely to be found.

The eyes are rather on the small side, without being piercing shoe buttons. They are "almond-shaped" or

189

triangular, but not narrow or cut into the skull at such an angle as to make the expression sinister. They should be set in the front of the brow but not so close together as to produce a sharp or a quizzical expression. If the muzzle is wide enough the eyes will not appear too close together.

The bite should be even, the teeth large, clean, and well developed. By an even bite is meant one in which the inner surface of the upper incisors overlaps and plays upon the outer surfaces of the lower incisors.

The former Standard, now superceded, listed among mouth "faults" teeth which are "overshot or undershot exceeding one-quarter inch." This has been revised in the present Standard to read: "Disqualifying Faults.—overshot more than 3/16 of an inch. Undershot more than 1/8 of an inch." This is a distinct improvement from a mere "fault" of a badly overshot or undershot mouth to a disqualification for a slight divergence of the incisors. Most judges are not inclined to be lenient with incorrect occlusion of the incisors, and the penalty of disqualification should rapidly and rightly weed such faults from the breed.

The Standard specifies "42 teeth—(22 in lower jaw, 20 in upper jaw)." While it is true that a dog should possess a full complement of teeth, there are other faults more grievous than a missing pre-molar. This is said with full knowledge that in Germany no Doberman may be awarded a prize if any teeth are missing. Some judges become cranks about missing teeth and spend much of the time allotted to them searching in the mouths of exhibits. Woe betide the dog with a vacant space in his mouth who comes under the jurisdiction of such a dentist! Other judges, while demanding even bites, pay scant attention to the teeth behind the canines. It is well to know how much consideration a judge gives to missing teeth before making an entry under him. It has been said that only judges who do not know dogs fall back upon the counting of teeth.

Nostrils are large and noses blunt. The nose color corresponds to the coat color of the dog, and is seldom wrong. It is defined at greater length in the Standard.

190

The ears are set well up on the top skull, trimmed to a long point and carried symmetrically erect. An expert trimmer of ears tempers their length to the length of the dog's head, since long, ribbon ears accentuate the shortness of a stubby head. The tendency is as longer and more refined heads are produced to leave the ears longer. While it is stated in the Standard that the requirement of trimmed ears is waived in states where ear trimming is prohibited or where dogs with cropped ears cannot be shown, it is too much to ask of an untrimmed Doberman that he shall compete against one with conventionally altered ears. This should not be true, since there is nothing in the rules that provides that the ears of any dog of any breed shall be trimmed. But the fact remains that the untrimmed Doberman Pinscher, for all his admitted beauty and virtues, has never attained great popularity in the British Isles, where a humane people prevent by law the cropping of dogs' ears—and make their laws stick.

The neck should be, above all, muscular and rather long than short. It should be long enough to enable the animal to feed and to pick up small objects with his mouth from the floor without stooping or trussing his front legs. The throttle should be dry, which is to say that there should be no surplusage of skin under the throat to spoil the clean line.

The neck should taper considerably and gradually from the shoulders to the set-on of the head. Judges will agree that they have seldom if ever seen a Doberman neck with an excess of arch. The male Doberman usually displays a greater crest than the bitch, upon which an equal demand cannot be made. The neck, it may be said categorically should not be straight. As for a concavity of the neck, a ewe neck, it is highly reprehensible, not only for its ugly outline but because it argues an uprightness of shoulder which will almost invariably be found with it.

The neck is to be considered as something more than a connection between body and head. It is a support for the head. No matter how great the grasping power of the jaw, it is of no effect without the aid of the neck in the

191

manipulation of the thing grasped. The Standard states that the neck should be "proudly carried, well-muscled and dry." The dog should be high-headedly alert, which means that the neck should be set firmly into sloping shoulders to support the head with ease.

Under the subject of "body," it will be noted that the "back" is declared to be "short." This is literal; it is the back from the withers to the pelvis that is short and not the whole body. An abnormally short body is prone to lack forechest and to have narrow and weak hams. The power of the dog is developed in the hindquarters and transmitted through the back to the fore quarters, and the longer the back the greater the likelihood of a loss of that power, or of a part of it, in transmission. A body may be too short, but not likely a back.

The back should be strong throughout its entire length. The top line from the withers to pelvis should be level, without the constriction which produces a hump or roach, and without a sway or depression that evinces weakness of spine.

There must be ample room to accommodate a large heart and a vast breathing apparatus. But the ribs must not be rounded or barrel-like. Rather, they must broaden out from their junction with the spine, and taper downward almost flat to the depth of the brisket.

Fanciers often speak enthusiastically of a dog's having a "barrel rib." Such men are either ignorant or are not literal, for a rounded rib impedes the action of the elbows and forces the dog which possesses it to totter from side to side in his action, throwing the weight of his body first on one side and then on the other.

The brisket extends downward at least as far as the elbows. It may possibly go farther without any penalty. The deeper it may be, the better. As for the "belly well tucked up," it can be too much tucked up. The belly should be firm and moderately tucked. There is no semblance of a Greyhound curve to it, which would imply a roach to the back which should not be.

"The slightly rounded croup" should be arched as little

192

as possible. The croup does not slope from the pelvis to the set on of the tail if such a slope can be avoided. The tail ideally should be set directly upon the back and carried well-nigh upright. A low-set tail is deemed by most good judges of the breed to be a positive fault. The standard says, "tail docked at approximately second joint;" the tail length is really immaterial. What counts is its set-on and upright carriage.

The upper arm and the shoulder blade, of approximately equal length, should be joined at an angle of as little more than ninety degrees as is possible. The "not more than one hundred and ten degrees" specified in the Standard provides for an extremely open and upright shoulder which is hardly to be tolerated in a good Doberman. It is to be admitted that Dobermans formerly won with insufficient angulation of shoulder, but now a dog with a shoulder of one hundred and ten degrees would receive short shrift in any competition where really good dogs are found. The matter of correct shoulder assembly is one that is too frequently overlooked by the novice fancier, but is very important in the evaluation of the modern type of dog.

The shoulder must not only be bent, but its musculature must be long and flat. Bulging shoulder muscles are inefficient for the articulation of the joint and are unpleasant to the eye. The double faults of bulging shoulder muscles and bulging cheek muscles are usually found together in the same dog. The owner's excuse that the dog was given bones to chew and that he was handled by the shoulders as a puppy just will not go down, since it is known that neither is responsible for the muscular malformation.

The front legs should drop straight and plumblike from the elbows to the feet. There may be a just perceptible "give" of the pastern joint, but the less the better. Any semblance of a dog being "down on his pasterns" is an unpleasant fault and argues weakness.

The correct Doberman front should be neither wide enough to suggest coarseness and clumsiness, nor narrow to the point that would eliminate power, lung and heart room. The Doberman front is a terrier front, which does not

193

mean that both front legs shall appear to "come out at the same hole," but even worse is the Bulldog formation which may cause a dog to waddle in coming toward one. The term "terrier front" can be most misleading, especially in view of the fact that so many terrier standards are very vague in describing this very important part of the terrier's anatomy.

"French front, bow-legged front" are both mentioned as faults in the now superceded Standard and italicized. The omission of these faults from the present Standard is unfortunate, since they are still faults as much as ever they were. By French front is meant literally one in which the legs turn outward below the pasterns, a German conception of the French dancing master. Just as much to be avoided, however, is the front in which the entire leg below the elbow turns outward, and that formation is perhaps to be included in the French front which the old standard warns against. The bowlegged front, on the other hand, is due to a malformation of the bones of the lower leg, usually the result of earlier rickets. It is too often confused with the equally unpleasant fault of loose shoulders which cause the elbows to turn outward. With this latter fault, it is usually found that the front feet toe inward, which they should not do.

The forechest should be full enough to be obvious when viewed in profile. It should, when viewed from the front or from the side, appear convex.

Brisket should be deep, the ribs moderately sprung, loin powerful—though neatly tucked. This type of structure allows not only the essential speed but the staying power required for police work, guard duty or war work.

The bone structure of the Doberman is usually judged by the girth of the bone of the lower arm, which should be substantial. It is possible, but unlikely, that the bone may be too great, in which case the dog will probably have a cloddy appearance, the head be thick and common, and the neck too short. Unless it is accompanied by the other faults enumerated, the bone can hardly be too large, and it is certainly better somewhat too great than too small.

194

The standard advises that dew claws are generally removed. All dogs normally carry dew claws on the front legs and most breeders remove them artificially from young puppies. There is no obligation to do so, however; and the dog cannot be penalized for retaining them. Dew claws on the rear legs are abnormalities which frequently impair the dog's action. They should be removed in puppyhood if they are present. Even when left on the front legs, dew claws are given to catching upon random objects, tearing loose, and causing trouble. They are a good riddance when removed in early puppyhood.

Doberman feet are short, thick, with well arched toes and firm thick pads. They are terrier-like and usually characterized as "cat feet." The nails are short, heavy, and blunt. They may be artificially shortened and blunted, but a thoroughly good foot will blunt its nails with sufficient exercise.

Hindquarters are big, well angled, and muscular, but not beefy. Hams are thick as well as broad. The thighs, which the standard refers to as the "upper shanks" should be long, the bone inserted at approximately ninety degrees to the pelvis. The bones of the lower leg or stifle should also be long and should meet the upper leg at an approximate right angle. They are attached to the hocks, which should be short and low, with a powerful and distinct Achilles tendon. The hocks, when the dog is standing, should be quite upright; they should neither angle forward into what is known as "saber hocks," nor should they be a mere linear continuation of the lower leg, which is known as "rubber hocks."

Such a formation provides a pair of hindquarters with ample angulation. A dog may not possess sufficient musculature to support the angulation that he has; but with adequate muscles, excessive angulation would be found only on a deformed monster. Insufficient angulation is a much more frequently found fault. Indeed it is as rare as it is pleasant to see a Doberman with enough angulation both in his shoulders and in his hindquarters.

Especially to be avoided is a dog with mere props for

hindquarters, with no bend at the stifle joint. Such dogs seldom have adequate thigh muscles, and would have nothing to use them for even if they were present. The angulated quarters enable the dog to step out with a long, springy, easy motion that is impossible with a straight rear leg, which produces a stilt-like action. It is to be remembered that the hindquarters are the source of the dog's power. He is pushed, not pulled. This is the reason why the frequently overlooked and neglected hindquarters are so important a part of the dog's structure.

The rear feet, made in the same thick closely knit formation as the front feet, must point directly forward, toe neither outward or inward.

The whole hindquarters are laterally symmetrical, the hocks upright and parallel moving forward in parallel planes. Cow hocks (the hocks converging) are only worse faults than bandy legs with their divergent hocks.

It may well be said that in truth the less the arch in the croup the better. The straight and level line of the back may well continue absolutely straight to the set-on of the tail. Otherwise the tail will be low set, and the entire conformation of the rear assembly thrown out of gear. While the very, very slightly arched croup can not be penalized, the less the arch, other things being equal, the better the propulsion.

The length, texture, and density of the coat require but little discussion here. The healthy coat is seldom inadequate. It suffices to say that the entire dog is covered with short, firm hair, which will be found somewhat longer on the neck and body than on the head and legs.

Nor need too much attention be devoted to color and markings of the dog, since most pure bred Dobermans are reasonably orthodox in those respects. The most prevalent body colors are black or puce brown with deep rich red-tan (what the Standard refers to as "rust-red") markings on each of the lower legs, forechest, muzzle, throat, vent, and forehead. The distribution is that of the conventional black-and-tan pattern. The most likely to be found in the way of faulty coloration is in the fading or light

196

color of the tan, which should be of a vivid reddish shade. On a dog of correct structure, a weak tan is only a minor fault at worst.

Dogs with steel blue body color and conventional tan markings are rare but acceptable. The objection that is to be found to blue dogs is not in their hair color but in the unpleasantness of their light yellow eyes, which are almost universally found in blue dogs.

Fawn body color, called "isabella" had been a cause for disqualification in some former standards, but the latest standard revision—adopted in 1969—now lists it as acceptable.

A small spot of white, small enough to be covered by a coin, is undesirable but tolerable and is not a cause for any penalty. Larger white spots on the chests of adult Dobermans are deemed to be faults. A whole white shirtfront simply spoils an otherwise good dog. However, it is to be noted that white spots on the chests of puppies tend to grow smaller as the animal develops and often a narrow streak of white will entirely disappear by the time the animal is fully mature.

Having surveyed the individual features of the Doberman, it is well again to stand away from him and consider him as a whole animal. The examiner in the course of his examination may have found some point or points not exactly to his liking. He must now determine whether and to what extent these minor "outs" impair the efficiency or the symmetry of the whole dog. It may be very little. However, it is to be remembered that a dog with many minute faults is to be preferred to another dog with a single major fault of one particular part.

And it is not only the faults that are to be noted and penalized, but dogs must be given credit for their outstanding virtues. While a single bad fault may ruin the whole dog and some obvious virtue may not cancel it out, an all-over good dog must be particularly admired for those attributes in which he exhibits excellence in a notable degree.

197

A dog may win consistently, may even become a champion, upon the basis of his freedom from serious faults, but he can not be considered as a great specimen of his breed unless he have some point or points in which he is notably superior not only to his competitors but to the other members of his breed as a whole. The amateur examiner is prone to look for faults and to accept particular excellences for granted. A beautiful skull-structure, a superlative shoulder, or a superb front may make a dog famous, but only if he is reasonably acceptable in other respects.

The difference between the good judge and the mediocre judge is that the former recognizes and appreciates these outstanding virtues when he finds them and the latter looks only for faults in the exhibits.

There remains the gait to be examined. In it lies the test of structure. A dog standing may be as correct as you please, but if he fails in action he cannot be considered as a good dog.

He is first to be led away from the examiner at a walk and returned toward him at the same gait. Once may be enough, or it may be repeated until the examiner is satisfied. In going away, the rear feet should track exactly forward with no deviation either inward or outward. The hocks should move in planes absolutely parallel with ample clearance between those planes that there shall be no interference nor semblance of it. There should not be so much distance between the hind legs that the dog appears to waddle from one side to the other, but there is less likelihood that this will be found than that the rear tracks will be too close together. The turning inward or convergence of the hocks at their tops, known as cow hocks, is a prevalent evil and a bad fault. Their turning outward, while less often seen, is just as bad.

In the return of the dog toward the examiner, the "trueness" of the front should be noted, the forward tracking of the feet and the movement of the front legs in planes perpendicular to the floor and parallel to each other. "Weaving" of the front legs, the tendency to cross the front feet in action, denotes ordinarily a looseness of the attachment

198

of the shoulder. "Paddling," the throwing of the feet outward, denotes a constriction of the shoulder. Both are to be avoided.

The walk will determine soundness. Now the dog should be thrown into a slow trot and should be examined in that gait from the rear, the front, and from the side. Occasionally a Doberman is found whose natural fast gait is a pace, which is harmless provided he can also be made to trot. Although it may require some effort and patience to change the gait, most dogs can be taught. From the rear and from the front the same trueness of gait is demanded as in the walk.

When trotting the dog, observe the back from a side view to see whether it retains its straightness and levelness, or whether on the one hand, it humps or constricts or, on the other hand, sags or sways. It should remain level.

Another thing is the length of stride. The rear leg should reach well forward, straighten out and transmit power through the back, and then follow through with vigor. The step should be long and show ample driving power. The shoulder should open to permit the front step to be as long as the rear step. It is for this purpose that great angulation both fore and aft is demanded. Correct angulation at the shoulder without enough at the rear is wasted, just as sufficient propulsion is wasted if the shoulder can not be opened to absorb it. No power is developed in the front, which serves only as a suspension to keep the dog from falling forward upon its head.

At the trot the dog should not slouch or drag its feet. The feet should be lifted smartly to clear the floor freely. However, high dancing or prancing action is a waste of power. The rear step should be long rather than high, and it cannot be both. High, hackney-like action with the front legs is frequently much admired by an enthusiastic gallery which considers it a mark of "style." It may be spectacular, but it is not good Doberman gait; it is effort thrown away.

We cannot look for or expect perfection in a dog. The most we can hope for is an absence of glaring faults. How

199

much each of such faults shall be penalized when it is found no man can say.

In the 1969 revision of the Standard, the "Scale of Points" has been wisely dropped from the standard. Judging dogs in accordance with scales of points has been long abandoned as impracticable; and to evaluate dogs by any point system all too frequently leads to the placing of a dog with some very gross individual fault over another dog that has numerous minor faults but is on the whole well balanced and excellent throughout. All judges do not look with the same blame at a given fault. One may censure a yellow eye more than an undershot mouth, or vice versa, but he should consider how yellow the eye, and how much undershot the mouth. A judge may be a crank about shoulders or backs or hindquarters or some other part, and we may disagree with his placements, but he is within his rights to make them as he sees fit.

This is not designed to tell the reader how to make an exact evaluation of his dog's merits or demerits, since no exact evaluation is possible, but it is hoped that a study of the standard followed by a perusal of this elaboration and discussion of its terms will enable the reader to classify his Doberman as excellent, good or bad. It is the same animal with which we began, and our survey has done him no harm.

The Doberman Pinscher
in a Nutshell

What to Look For and What to Avoid

Look For:	Avoid:
A dog of medium size, square as viewed from the side, fine, compact, muscular, powerful, of great elegance and grace.	Undersize, excessive size, excess length, coarseness, flabbiness, commonness, awkwardness.
Length and leanness of head, bluntly wedge shaped. Narrow, flat topskull. Minute offset (stop) between skull and muzzle. Powerful muzzle, well filled under the eyes. Top line of muzzle in profile parallel to top line of skull. Cheeks flat and lean. Lips dry and close fitting. Nostrils generous.	Head, too short or too wide. Deep stop. Weak, snippy muzzle, or one scooped out under the eyes. Ramshead. Dishface or downface. Bulging cheek muscles. Heavy, thick, or drooping lips. Nostrils pinched or stingy.
A complete set of sound, large, white, even teeth, with canines well spread apart. Scissors bite, with upper incisors just covering and playing upon outer surface of lower incisors.	Missing teeth. Pitted, discolored, uneven, or crowded teeth. Jaw too narrow. Pincers bite. Undershot or overshot bite.

Look For:	Avoid:
Eyes, only moderately small, almond shaped, set obliquely in head with moderate distance between them. Eyes dark as possible in black-and-tans; slightly lighter eyes tolerable but not desirable in red and blue dogs.	Large, bulging, or round eyes, too close together or too much spread. Eyes, small and stingy. Light or yellow eyes.
Ears set high on head, neatly cropped to a point and carried erect.	Ears low on head, carried sidewise, too short, badly cropped, shrivelled, wrinkled, or folded.
Neck, long, strong, muscular and arched. Dry and clean in the throttle.	Short, weak, straight, or ewe shaped neck. Dewalp or throatiness.
Back, short, firm, straight and level from withers to pelvis.	Back, long, undulant, swayed, roached, or sloping.
Chest, well developed, capacious and extending at least to the elbow. Ribs well sprung but never round. Well ribbed back.	Shallow chest without large capacity. Narrow or barrel-shaped ribs. Short thorax.
Loin, short, muscular, and well knit. Moderately tucked up.	Loin, long and slack, or with greyhound-like tuck up.
Shoulder blades, long, flat, and laid back at an angle of ninety degrees to bones of upper arm. Withers high and distinct, with small space between tops of shoulder blades.	Short shoulder blades, steep and upright. Low withers with wide space between shoulder blades.
	Front, wide or pinched, loose or constricted. Lower arms bowed or trussed. Inadequate or spongy bone.

202

Look For:	Avoid:
Front, moderately narrow—terrier-like. Lower arms, straight, vertical, and parallel. Bone, hard, strong, copious, and substantial.	Shallow, thin, splayed, long, or open feet. Nails, frail, long, sharp, or pointed. Feet turned in (pigeon-toed) or turned out (slew-footed).
Feet, compact, deep, well knuckled, and catlike. Nails, large, short, and blunt. Feet directed forward.	Hindquarters inadequate in breadth, thickness or depth. Narrow or thin hams. Stifle joint not well defined.
Hindquarters, broad, thick, and deep. Hams and buttocks large. Ample angulation; ninety degree angle at stifle joint. Long lower thigh. Hock joints set low. Hocks moving in parallel planes.	Straight and stilty stifles. Short lower leg. Long hocks. Hocks turned together (cow hocks) or turned outward (bandy legs).
Tail, substantial, docked, set on high. Croup a continuation of back line.	Pipe stopper tail, set on low. Diagonal or rounded croup.
Coat, short, hard, fine, and lying flat.	Coat, soft, wooly, long, wavy, staring.
Color and markings, black, red, blue, and fawn (Isabella), with well-defined rust markings. White thumb mark on chest tolerated but not desired.	Faded or straw colored markings. White mark on chest larger than five-cent piece.
Gait, supple, easy, free. Movement, straightforward. without weaving or fanning in front, or deviations in rear. Back without undulation in action. Great style.	Sloppy or constricted gait. Tied or loose shoulders and elbows. Hocks turned inward or outward in action. Weaving, flopping, swaying or undulating back line.
Character, proud, alert, gay, confident, and devil-may-care; reserved but friendly.	Sullen, cowed, shy, cringing, vicious, or aggressive.

CH. HAYDENHILL'S HURRAH
with handler Corky Vroom
Hurrah, many-time Best in Show winner, was designated Best Western
Showdog by Kennel Review, 1962. Bred by Haydenhill Kennels (Calif.),
and owned by R. E. Souders.

Gait of the Doberman

by

Curtice W. Sloan

DOBERMAN TROTTING

BAYERN V.D. HEIDE

John T. Brueggeman, Chicago, Illinois, Owner

THIS SERIES of thirteen pictures was selected from a strip of movie film taken in slow motion at the rate of sixty-four pictures per second. They show the extreme accuracy of the movements of a properly angulated Doberman while trotting.

Although it cannot be seen in these pictures, as they are all taken from the side, the dog is single tracking; that is, all four feet, when placed on the ground during trotting, are placed on a single line the same as the dog would have to do if he was trotting along a tight rope suspended above the ground.

The time interval of the pictures has been given in 64ths of a second and it should be noted that each full step required 17/64ths of a second or a total of 34/64ths of a second for the dog to take two full steps and return his legs to the starting position as shown in Picture # 1.

205

Inasmuch as all of this action takes place in just a little over one-half second, it is not surprising that many of our owners and even some judges do not know exactly what a dog does do with his feet because the movement takes place entirely too rapidly for the eye to follow.

There are, however, other means than the slow motion camera for checking the proper movement of a dog and that is to observe the tracks he leaves behind him when trotting. A properly angulated dog, carrying himself in good balance, will leave behind him a single line of tracks which are in a straight line.

EXAMPLES

Front Foot—O   Hind Foot—H

\# 1   Ⓗ   Ⓗ   Ⓗ   Ⓗ   Ⓗ   Ⓗ   Ⓗ   Ⓗ

This is the correct gait when single tracking. Notice the hind foot print is directly on top of the front foot print.

\# 2   O H   O H   O H   O H   O H   O H

Correct gait flying trot—also single tracking. Notice that the tracks are still on a straight line but that the dog's body moved forward in the air in that split second between the front foot movement and the hind foot placement so that the hind foot places in front of the front foot track. However, the tracks are still on a straight line.

\# 3   O   O   O   O   O   O   O   O
       H   H   H   H   H   H   H   H

The dog is side gaiting and although he makes a straight line of tracks with both his front feet and his hind feet, they are in two different planes. Some people, without distinguishing between front foot prints and hind foot prints, have concluded that the dog is gaiting with his right hand legs in one vertical plane and his left hand legs in a parallel vertical plane.

4

The dog is still single tracking independently with his front and hind legs but is side gaiting to prevent his hind feet hitting his front feet because he is over-stepping. This dog probably has too much angulation in the rear to match his front angulation.

5

Some dogs actually do move with the right hand legs in one vertical plane and the left hand legs in a parallel vertical plane separated by the full width of the dog. These dogs leave tracks behind them as shown above.

6

O   O   O   O   O
H   H   H   H   H   H   H   H   H
   O   O   O   O

This dog is single tracking with the hind feet but moving the two front feet directly fore and aft in two parallel vertical planes.

7

H   H   H   H   H
O   O   O   O   O   O   O   O   O
   H   H   H   H

This dog is single tracking with its front feet and moving its hind feet in two parallel vertical planes.

PICTURE SERIES OF EXAMPLE # 1

Picture # 1—The series starts at the point where the right front foot and left hind foot have been just put down on the ground and where the left front foot and right hind foot have just completed their turn of carrying the weight of the dog.

Picture # 2, taken 2/64ths of a second after picture # 1, illustrates the follow through of the hind

PICTURE # 1

PICTURE # 2

208

PICTURE # 3

PICTURE # 4

209

feet. The right hind foot has continued backward after leaving the ground and at this point is at its farthest rearward position. Follow through is as important a factor in dog movement as it is in a golf stroke.

Picture # 3, taken 6/64ths of a second after picture # 2, shows the right hind hock lifted well up to pass the right hind foot over the left hind foot as is necessary when a dog is single tracking.

Picture # 4, taken 3/64ths of a second after picture # 3, shows the start of the reach forward of the left front foot and the right hind foot.

Picture # 5, taken 3/64ths of a second after picture # 4, shows the feet approaching the maximum reaching position.

Picture # 6, taken 2/64ths of a second after picture # 5, shows the feet in the maximum reaching position. Please observe that the feet are just barely above the ground in this position so that the feet meet the ground at exactly the end of the reach without shock. This is especially important in the front feet. Pictures of dogs with too much rear angulation show that the hind legs have driven the dog's body forward further than he can step with his front legs and at the end of his front reach the front foot is still two or three inches above the ground so that he lands on the front feet with a shock at each step. Please note that the right front foot is moving just a split second ahead of the right hind foot which is moving forward to be put down exactly in the track of the right front foot as shown in Picture # 7.

Picture # 7, taken 1/64th of a second after picture # 6, shows the reach completed and the left front

210

foot and the right hind foot now on the ground carrying the weight of the dog. Please observe that in this picture a line drawn through the left front foot and the center line of the shoulder blade makes a 45° angle with the ground. Also, that a line drawn through the right hind foot and the ball and socket hip joint of the hind leg also makes a 45° angle with the ground. These angles represent any dog's maximum possible forward reach which reach is controlled by the angle of the shoulder blade.

It is anatomically impossible for the shoulder blade to be laid back any farther than a 45° angle to the ground. It is possible, however, for a dog to be over-angulated in the hind legs so that he could reach considerably farther with his hind legs than with his front legs. Consequently, when over-angulated in the rear, he has to stilt the movement of his hind legs in order to keep his hindquarters from trying to go faster than his forequarters.

This is the main reason why dogs that are too well angulated in the rear have poor gaits since it is anatomically impossible to put a matching angulation in the forequarters.

The dog shown in these pictures has a rear angulation which matches his front angulation. If this dog had any more rear angulation he would not be able to gait with the extreme accuracy shown in these pictures. Everyone should study carefully the skeleton drawing of the Doberman standard which is so drawn as to give the dog maximum possible front angulation and a rear angulation which exactly matches the front. Dogs with more rear angulation than the one in the

PICTURE # 5

PICTURE # 6

PICTURE # 7

PICTURE # 8

213

standard are, of necessity, over-angulated as it is impossible to put more angulation in front. Most Dobermans do not have as well laid back shoulder blades as the one in the drawing and, therefore, should have steep or slightly angulated hind legs to match their steep fronts so they can move in balance. It is always better to have matching angulation fore and aft, be it much or little, than to have different angulation at each end of the dog. Any dog with matching angulation fore and aft will move better than one whose angulations do not match. Naturally, the optimum anatomical construction for a dog is to have the full front angulation and the matching rear angulation as called for in the drawing of the skeleton in the Doberman standard.

Picture # 8, taken 2/64ths of a second after picture # 7, shows the follow through of the left hind foot in its farthest back position.

Picture # 9, taken 6/64ths of a second after picture # 8, shows the left hind hock up to carry the left hind foot over the right hind foot which is on the ground.

Picture # 10, taken 3/64ths of a second after picture # 9, shows the start of the reach and is comparable to picture # 4 only this time it is the right front leg and the left hind leg that are doing the reaching.

Picture # 11, taken 3/64ths of a second after picture # 10, is comparable to picture # 5 where the left front and right hind feet are approaching maximum reach.

Picture # 12, taken 2/64ths of a second after picture # 11, is comparable to picture # 6 wherein again

214

PICTURE # 9

PICTURE # 10

215

Picture # 11

Picture # 12

216

the front foot is moving a split second ahead of the oncoming hind foot so that it may be placed on the ground in the left front foot track. This is the maximum reaching position of the right front and left hind legs.

Picture # 13, taken 1/64th cf a second after picture # 12, shows the dog's feet again returned to the same position they were in picture # 1; that is, the right front foot and left hind foot have been just placed on the ground to carry the weight of the dog.

PICTURE # 13

PICTURE # 1

PICTURE # 2

218

Doberman Galloping

DIAMOND OF PONCHARTRAIN
Kenton E. Smith, Chicago, Illinois, Owner

The high speed gait of a Doberman is the double suspension gallop as shown in the following series of sixteen
pictures. These pictures were also taken at the rate of
sixty-four pictures per second with the slow motion camera.
So that you may be able to follow the pictures more closely,
below is a diagram of the tracks made by the dog during
galloping.

EXAMPLES

1—Full Gallop—Top Speed

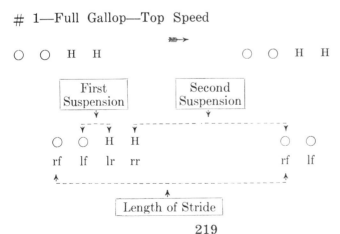

219

This shows the full stride tracks left by the dog at his maximum speed. It will be noted that the tracks appear in groups of four and that the hind foot tracks are in front of the front foot tracks in the direction in which the dog is going. This shows what is called the double suspension or that the dog has all four feet off the ground twice during the complete cycle of his galloping stride, the first suspension taking place between the front foot tracks and the hind foot tracks of a group of tracks and the second taking place between the two groups of four tracks which complete the cycle. The letter notations on the last group (rf— lf—lr—rr) indicate the placement of the right and left front and hind feet.

2—Starting the Gallop

This shows the tracks that are quite likely to be left behind by a Doberman getting up to speed on his gallop. You will notice that in the first few strides the tracks are not on a line as he is using the power of both hind legs simultaneously to overcome the inertia of the weight of his body and get him under way. As his speed increases, the feet are placed more nearly on a straight line.

Some dogs will continue to gallop moderately with their feet placed as shown in the last group of tracks; that is, with the left rear foot a little off the line. It will be noted, however, that the two front feet and the right rear foot are on a line inasmuch as the dog is right galloping and using his right hind leg primarily in his spring forward which he carefully places on the center line of his travel forward.

Picture # 1 shows the right front foot about to touch the ground at the end of one stride and the beginning of another.

Picture # 2, taken 3/64ths of a second after picture # 1, shows the full weight of the dog now on the right front foot with the pastern bent back to cushion the shock of landing.

Picture # 3, taken 1/64th of a second after picture # 2, shows the left front foot just touching the ground directly in front of the right front foot as the dog moves forward.

Picture # 4, taken 1/64th of a second after picture # 3, shows the left front foot now taking the load.

Picture # 5, taken 3/64ths of a second after picture # 4, shows the left front foot now carrying the full load and the pastern fully bent to cushion the shock. The loin is arching and the hind feet are coming forward.

Picture # 6, taken 1/64th of a second after picture # 5, shows the left front pastern now completely straightened out and ready to leave the ground for the first suspension.

Picture # 7, taken 2/64ths of a second after picture # 6, shows all four feet off the ground with the hind feet moving forward to meet the ground. The dog is now in the first or minor suspension of the galloping stride.

Picture # 8, taken 2/64ths of a second after picture # 7, shows the front feet picked up out of the way of the hind feet, the left hind foot just about to touch the ground ahead of where the front feet were. This is the end of the first suspension. It is interesting to note here that the cross relation of leg action maintains in the gallop as well as in the trot; that is, the right front foot was placed down first (pictures # 1 and # 2) and now it is the diagonal or left hind leg which is being put down first.

221

PICTURE # 3

PICTURE # 4

PICTURE # 5

PICTURE # 6

PICTURE # 7

PICTURE # 8

224

PICTURE # 9

PICTURE # 10

225

PICTURE # 11

PICTURE # 12

226

PICTURE # 13

PICTURE # 14

227

Picture # 9, taken 2/64ths of a second after picture # 8, shows the left hind leg now carrying the full weight of the dog with the hock nearly touching the ground.

Picture # 10, taken 1/64th of a second after picture # 9, shows the right hind foot now about to touch the ground ahead of the left hind foot and directly in front of it. Notice that the loin is fully arched ready for the rearing action to get the forequarters of the dog up and contribute to the next spring forward by the hind legs.

Picture # 11, taken 1/64th of a second after picture # 10, shows both hind feet on the ground and the start of the rearing action. Notice the front legs by this time have moved forward, starting to get into position for a landing at the end of the next suspension.

Picture # 12, taken 1/64th of a second after picture # 11, shows the beginning of the spring forward.

Picture # 13, taken 2/64ths of a second after picture # 12, shows the left hind foot off the ground and the right hind foot completing the forward spring action. Notice that the loin has straightened out considerably but this movement is not yet complete.

Picture # 14, taken 3/64ths of a second after picture # 13, shows the completion of the hind leg thrust in giving the spring forward on the second or major suspension. Notice that the loin is now nearly completely straightened out.

Picture # 15, taken 1/64th of a second after picture # 14, shows the dog in the second or major suspension period with all four feet off the ground and the loin completely straightened out as a result of the hind leg follow through.

PICTURE # 15

PICTURE # 16

229

Picture # 16, taken 1/64th of a second after picture # 15, shows the end of the major suspension period and the end of the stride. Picture # 16 is comparable to the starting picture # 1.

Just in case you find it hard to visualize a dog's ability to place his feet on a line one in front of the other, Pictures # 17 and # 18 have been added showing first the dog's two front feet placed on the ground one in front of the other followed by the two hind feet on the ground one in front of the other.

The entire sequence from picture # 1 to picture # 16 required 25/64ths of a second. Inasmuch as the dog's length of stride (that is, from one right front foot paw print to the next) is a distance of fourteen feet, the rate of speed can be calculated at twenty-four and one-half miles per hour. With the dog going by at this rate of speed and the foot sequences requiring from 1/64th to 3/64ths of a second, it is impossible for the naked eye to see exactly what the dog did with his feet. Here again, however, one may check his dog by observing footprints in light snow at a full gallop.

In order to do this one must first learn to distinguish between front foot tracks and hind foot tracks which can easily be done due to the fact that the front feet are considerably larger than the hind feet and make a correspondingly larger print.

PICTURE # 17

PICTURE # 18

231

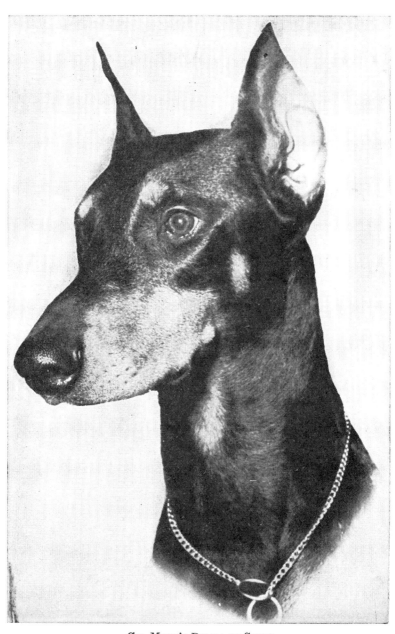

CH. MARC'S DIANA OF SOLBO

The Doberman in America

by

Anne F. Paramoure

HERE is no means of knowing who first brought Dobermans to this country. The earliest importation may have arrived with his European master, come to settle here, or may have been brought home by some American traveling abroad. The former is perhaps more probable, since the oldest animals entered in the German *Stud Book* were not whelped until 1893 and 1894 nor the first volume of the *Stud* issued until 1906. It is not very likely that a casual traveler would know anything about the breed.

However, recorded history of the Doberman begins in 1908 and has continued without a break since that time. In that year the kennel name "Doberman" was granted to Theodore F. Jager. The following year it was listed under the joint names of T. F. Jager and W. Doberman, the latter said to have been a relative of Louis Dobermann of Apolda.

The "Doberman Kennels" were located at Pittsford, N. Y., and later at Schenectady. Of course, today no one would be allowed to register the name of a breed as a kennel name. The rules for changing the names of imported dogs are also much more strict. Pedigrees are also more carefully checked for errors in spelling, dates of birth and names of breeders. It would no longer be possible to find litter mates entered in the *Stud Book* with two different breeders— for instance, two individuals whelped the same day from the same dam with apparently different sires because the latter was known under two names.

The first and only Doberman registered in 1908 was bred and owned by Doberman Kennels, which led in promotion of the breed for a number of years. This dog, black and tan in color, was Doberman Intellectus 122650, whelped June 20, 1908. He was owned by Carl Schuylheiss of New Haven, Conn., but seems to have left no mark upon the future of the breed either as show dog or sire. However, though Intellectus himself is of interest solely because he was the first Doberman registered by the AKC, his sire and dam both played important parts in the early days, and their descendants are still winning at the present time.

Among the 13 dogs and 15 bitches registered in 1909 all but two were bred or owned by Doberman Kennels. The patriarch of the breed was Bertel von Hohenstein, bred by Ammon & Bender of Bleicherode, Germany, whelped September 26, 1905, and probably imported soon after he was two years old, since his first American litter was whelped June 20, 1908. Registered in this country as Bertel Doberman, he left at least one litter behind him in Germany, for a son, Primus v. Koburg, appears as the sire of Doberman Teddy AKC 140815, whelped in 1909. Neither Primus nor Teddy, however, are known to have left any champion descendants.

Primus' litter brother, Prinz v. Koburg, however, sired the imported Minca v. Koburg, dam of Koenig v. Grunland and Prince v.d. Eichthal. The dam of Prinz v. Koburg was Jungfer Anna, a sister to Freya v. Thüringen (the granddam

234

of Hellegraf). Prinz v. Koburg was mated to Jenny v. Schlegel, whose dam was a sister of Junker Slenz.

Bertel v. Hohenstein, called in the United States Bertel Doberman had the following pedigree:

Lux v. Groenland
Greif v. Groenland
Tilly v. Groenland

Bertel v. Hohenstein

Busso v. Michelhorst
Helmtrude v. Hohenstein
Otrud v. Thüringen

Busso v. Michelhorst was sired by Junker Slenz v. Thüringen. Otrud v. Thüringen was sired by Greif's brother, Belling v. Groenland.

On the basis of pedigree, Bertel v. Hohenstein might have gone far had he remained in Germany, but he was exported too young to leave many get behind him and may have sired no more than the one litter there. Whether he was shown in Germany, and how he would have ranked as a show dog had he remained there it is impossible to tell. As Bertel Doberman he was shown fairly extensively in this country, going Winners eight times and Reserves Winners once in 1910, when he was defeated only by Grandduke Kimo de Doberman, Winners at the classes sponsored by the Pinscher Club of America at Charlotte, N. Y. He never went to the top at Westminster, and does not seem to have been shown extensively after 1910, but, mysteriously enough, he suddenly reappears in the September 1920 issue of the AKC Stud Book in the list of champions for that year. Search of the show wins announced in the Gazette for several months back does not reveal him among the winners. One wonders, therefore, whether previous omission in publication was not suddenly rectified at this late date, when the dog was fifteen years old!

In Bertel, then, we have a dog of excellent breeding in his day, a winner eight out of nine times shown in 1910, and an AKC champion, used considerably at stud in the Doberman Kennels for several years, with probably as good a chance to prove his breeding worth as was possible in America at that time. The result was one champion son, Graf Rupert, plus five sons and two daughters three of which produced champions, the remaining four becoming the ancestors of champions. Bertel's male line continued for five generations. His daughter, Doberman Irene, was the dam of Ch. Doberman Dix, the first male and first American-bred Doberman to complete the title. In addition, he sired Doberman Intellectus, the first of the breed registered by the AKC. All his American-bred get but Ch. Graf Rupert were out of the bitch Hertha v. Hohenstein, registered with the AKC as Hertha Doberman. Hertha was by Schill v. Deutz (making her a half-sister of the blue Siegerin Jenny v. Deutz, the dam of Sieger Prinz Carlo Viktoria) out of Blanka v.d. Kieler Fohrde, a bitch whose pedigree shows no notable names for two generations back. Hertha herself was whelped April 26, 1907, and registered in 1909, but must have been imported before the birth of her first litter by Bertel, on June 20, 1908. She was the first Doberman to make an AKC championship in 1912 and her winnings include nine Reserve Winners and two Winners in 1910, when she once defeated Duchess Chica de Doberman to whom she was Reserve at the 1910 Charlotte, N. Y., show in which classes were sponsored by the Pinscher Club of America. Hertha was also Winners at New York and Boston in 1911. She was bred regularly, producing in addition to her 1908 litter by Bertel—containing Doberman Intellectus, Doberman Irene (dam of Ch. Doberman Dix) and Doberman Arena and Doberman Veracity—two further litters by him in 1909 which contained the producers Doberman Dorussia (Dog), Doberman Prinz Eitel, and the non-producing blue Doberman Prinz Heinrich. In 1910 she whelped the producing Doberman Graf Robert and Prinz Wallie Doberman II, likewise by Ch. Bertel. Hertha whelped at least two more litters, one by Doberman O.K. in 1911 (containing Doberman Conqueror who was registered as "black, white and tan"), and one by Weddo v. Eichtal in 1912, but her seven producers were all by Bertel.

This may not seem a remarkable record by modern standards, but it was excellent for its day and no other prewar dog or bitch did as well. Bertel can be traced from one to several times in the pedigrees of fifty-one champions which completed their titles during the period from 1946 to 1950. This is almost one-fourth of the total!

There were only eleven imported bitches whelped before 1920, which left champion descendants; all but one of them were whelped during the years 1905 to 1909. Easily the most important was Ch. Hertha Doberman already mentioned. Her sons included Doberman Graf Robert, whose line stopped with Ch. Frieda v.d. Wildenbach, the second American-bred bitch champion; Doberman Dorussia, Doberman Veracity and Prinz Walli Doberman II, with the less important Doberman Prinz Eitel; and her daughters were Doberman Irene, the first American-bred bitch to produce a champion (Doberman Dix) and Doberman Arena. Irene's daughter Hilda II v. Everfaithful was the dam of Ch. Walden v. Everfaithful. This line from Ch. Bertel Doberman and Ch. Hertha Doberman through Doberman Irene was reinforced by the mating of Ch. Walden v. Everfaithful to Gretal v. Steubenfield, a bitch tracing three times to Bertel and Hertha (via Prince Wallie, Dorussia and Veracity). It produced two bitches, Countess Gisela v. Walden and Judy of Steubenfield, each carrying four lines to Bertel and Hertha. Gretal also had another daughter, Thelma of Steubenfield, by the imported Prinz v. Nibelungenhort, while Gretal's brother Hensel of Steubenfield likewise carries down to present day champions.

The oldest Doberman bitch registered with the AKC, though she was not entered first, was the imported Gerta Doberman 128449, whelped April 11, 1905, by Puck II v. Thüringen out of Lily v. Hessen. Puck was a son of Graf Belling v. Thüringen and Freya v. Thüringen, being thus a full brother to Graf Wedigo v. Thüringen, an important early sire, while Belling was a half brother to Bertel v. Hohenstein (otherwise Ch. Bertel Doberman). Before being im-

237

ported Gerta was bred to Sieger Prinz Carlo Viktoria, an outstanding show dog and popular stud of the day whose male line seems to have completely died out, though his female descendants are still found far back in some modern pedigrees. Two producing daughters resulted from this mating and the line through Doberman Brunette can be traced to at least eleven dogs and bitches which have completed their championships in the last half dozen years, some of them tracing more than once.

Actually the first Doberman bitch registered with the AKC would appear to have been Annagret II v. Thüringen 127476, whose number indicates that she was entered before Ch. Hertha Doberman. Whelped March 1, 1908, she was bred by Otto Goeller of Apolda and owned by Max Donath. Annagret's dam was Carmen v. Thüringen (full sister to Gerta Doberman's sire) and Annagret's sire was Carmen's own son by the great Hellegraf v. Thüringen, named Hellegraf v. Thüringen II. Along with Annagret, Donath imported a stud dog, also of Goeller's breeding, whelped February 2, 1907, and named Claudius v. Thüringen 127475. Claudius was by Nikodemus v. Thüringen, on his sire's side a grandson of Hellegraf's sire Landgraf Sighart v. Thüringen and on his dam's of Sieger Graf Wedigo v. Thüringen (full brother to Annagret's dam Carmen). Claudius' dam, Irmgart v. Thüringen, was (like Bertel v. Hohenstein) by Greif v. Grönland, and her dam, Elalia v. Thüringen, seems to have been a full sister to the prepotent Betti I v. Ilm Athen (dam of Sturmfried v. Ilm Athen). Despite this excellent pedigree, however, the mating of Claudius and Annagret led to nothing more than two bitches, Ilka 156831, (whose line failed after her son Ch. Tristan and a great grandson Ch. Knight of Tidewater) and Diana 153311. Diana carries down via Stella III, Boulevard Queen and Reins v. Rennstieg to Mary Lou v. Rutsen, dam of Max v. Haugaard and Echo v. Weis, through each of which dogs the line appears twice (on her dam's side) in Ch. Colleen of Archwood, 1948 champion. Max v. Haugaard was also found once in the third generation of

238

the pedigree of Lady Leda v. Smet, dam of the 1949 champion Ventura Gypsy.

Ch. Flora v. Königshof, whelped in 1908, was by Rolf v. Königshof, a son of Prinz v. Ilm Athen, out of the Prinz v. Ilm Athen granddaughter Norma v. Grönland. Flora apparently was imported in whelp during the summer of 1910, and finished her championship in 1914. In that year, owned by Mrs. H. F. Meyer, she was Reserve Winners at Philadelphia with her daughter Flora II v. Geholz taking Winners. Flora v. Königshof's daughters Flora II and Gretchen v. Geholz were from her first American litter, by Vito v.d. Wumme. Vito was by Orgetorix v. Thüringen, a Prinz v. Ilm Athen grandson, out of Walda v. Thüringen, the latter a full sister to Annagret v. Thüringen's sire Hellegraf II. The mating of Flora to Vito before her importation thus produced a litter with Prinz v. Ilm Athen three times in the first four generations. It contained no champions but two daughters who carried on. Flora II v. Geholz appears in the pedigree of Puquette's Nina, dam of three champions, Hans, Horst and Karla v. Koch, which all finished in 1948. Ch. Asta's Ace has two lines through Flora v. Geholz and a third through her litter sister Gretchen v. Geholz. Asta's Ora, sister to Ace, was the dam of Ch. Diva of Blue Top. Another line from Flora is to be found in the pedigree of Mary Lou v. Rutsen mentioned above and consequently appears in the latter's champion descendants Ch. Colleen of Archwood and Ch. Ventura Gypsy. Still another line from Ch. Flora v. Königshof and Flora II v. Geholz comes directly from dam to daughter in tail female for eight generations through Trail'em Velvet Queen (a bitch whelped in 1922 when her dam was twelve years old), Schnuppe v. Rhodenbach I, Schnuppe v. Rhodenbach II, Schnuppe v. Octorara and Rusty Lady to Rusty's Trina v. Domstadt, dam of Ch. Admiral of Preakness Hills, a champion in 1947.

Bred at least twice more, Ch. Flora v. Königshof produced Ch. Graf Carlo v. Köenigshof, a dog who failed to carry on, by Carlo v. Oslebshausen, and the unregistered daughter Trixie v. Geholz by Titus v. Rolandsmarkt. Trixie mated to Pascha v. Geholz (son of her half-sister Flora and

239

imported Pascha v. Adrianopel), produced Prince v.d. Norris. Ch. Kana of Pontchartrain, finished in 1948, and Ch. Komet of Pontchartrain in 1949 each trace twice to Lady Katche of Pontchartrain who has three lines to Ch. Flora v. Königshof through Trail'em Queen. Ch. Wittland's Black Knight (finished 1947) traces to Prince v.d. Norris through his dam, Duchess Beauty v. Zeider.

A number of other current champions are descended from Ch. Flora v. Koenigshof and Flora II v. Geholz through the latter's daughter Fürstin Sophie v. Fern Felsen, who was by Carlo v. Oslebshausen. Sophie was the dam of Judy of Detroit, from whom the von Kochs trace, as already stated, and of three sons, Buddy, Daddy and Ch. Joffre of White Gate. From Buddy descends Ch. Kloe v. Elblac, Ch. Kyde v. Elblac, Ch. Klovelt Kristin, Ch. Elblac's Electra, Ch. Ximenes of Elblac and Ch. Elblac's Blitz. From Daddy of White Gate comes Ch. Gessner's Scarlet. Ch. Joffre, whelped in 1917, had a notable show career in the early twenty's under the name of Joffre of Heart's Haven and was not registered under the White Gate name (then owned by Miss Mary E. Fryling) until 1922. He was Winners at Westminster in 1920 and 1921, both being 5 point shows. So far as the stud books reveal, however, he never sired a puppy and left no permanent impress on the breed.

Another early imported bitch of some importance was Duchess Chica de Doberman, a Prinz Carlo Viktoria daughter who went Winners 11 times and Reserve once in 1910, but appears never to have completed her championship. Her wins included the classes sponsored by the Pinscher Club of America at Charlotte, N.Y., where she defeated Ch. Hertha Doberman. Duchess was the dam of Ch. Lucie Doberman, whelped in 1911, by the imported Weddo v. Eichtal who was her half-brother, by Prinz Carlo Viktoria. Wiltrude Bertilda, whelped in 1912, was a daughter of Doberman Dorussia (by Ch. Bertel Doberman out of Ch. Hertha Doberman). A grandson of Wiltrude mated to a granddaughter of Ch. Lucie produced Elizabeth v. Waldhaus Wedon, who appears in the pedigrees of all the Elblac champions mentioned above in connection with Ch. Flora v. Koenigshof. Ch. Lucie's daughter, Nina v. Waldhaus Dober, is also to be found in the pedigrees of Ch. Damasyn the Virginian, Ch. Princess Patricia Spegal and Ch. Wittland's Black Knight. Duchess Chica's line through Ch. Lucie was perhaps strengthened by the inbreeding to Prinz Carlo Viktoria, although this excellent dog failed to carry on strongly in Germany. Or perhaps it was due to the fact that Nina Waldhaus Dober's sire was Claudius v. Thüringen and that Claudius and Duchess Chica were both grandchildren of Freundsberg v. Thüringen, a son of two outstanding producers, Landgraf Sighart v. Thüringen and Ullrich's Glocke v. Thüringen, making Freundsberg a little-known full brother to the great Hellegraf. In addition to the line from Duchess Chica already discussed, two further lines coming down from Nina Waldhaus Dober through her daughter Ch. Countess v. Rupert appear in Ch. Elblac's Blitz already mentioned, and also in Ch. Elblac's Dorcas (who does not have the line through Elizabeth).

Duchess Chica's line through Wiltrude runs to Gretal of Stuebenfield, a daughter of Shelly v. Marychel (son of Wiltrude's blue son Harro v. Marychel) out of Lona v. Steinenfeld II. Lona was the only producing get of the imported bitch Laura v. Steinenfeld (by a son of Leporello v.d. Nidda out of a granddaughter of Graf Wedigo v. Thüringen) who was mated to Doberman Veracity, one of the sons of Ch. Bertel and Ch. Hertha. Although Gretal produced no champions, she must have been a bitch of considerable prepotency, for no less than five of her daughters carried on into the 1940s. Four of these bitches, Peggy of Stuebenfield, Thelma of Stuebenfield, Judy of Stuebenfield and Countess Gisela v. Walden, appear in the pedigrees of twenty-three champions of the past five years, while the line from Arna v. Avonthal seems to have terminated with Ch. Kyack v. Wagner, who finished in 1940-41.

Gretel v. Römercastle seems to have been completely unrelated to any of the other early importations. Whatever the stock behind her, for three generations not only the individuals but even the kennels in her pedigree are un-

241

familiar names. Whelped in 1913, she was not registered with the AKC until 1919, but as her daughter by Lord v. Spichernberg, Wanda v. Marychel, was whelped in 1916 she must have been imported some time earlier. Gretel was also the dam of the non-producing champion Knight of Tidewater, by Peppo of Marychel, at the age of seven, and also of the dog Shelly of Marychel by Harro v. Marychel. Both Peppo and Harro were blues, and this color seems to have been extraordinarily prevalent in the early days. Gerta Doberman (imported in whelp in 1909 as previously described), was a brown and was sired by a full brother to Gunzo v. Thüringen. Her litter by Prinz Carlo Viktoria, whelped July 2, 1909 after her arrival in this country, contained the blue Doberman Sultana, who failed to carry on but appears to have been the first of her color on record in this country. Gerta seems to have had and earlier litter by Prinz Carlo on Dec. 24, 1908, before leaving Germany, which contained Duchess Elsie de Doberman. Since Prinz Carlo Viktoria's dam was the blue Siegerin Jenny v. Deutz it is scarcely surprising that the mating of his daughter Duchess Elsie (full sister to the blue Sultana), with Weddo v. Eichtal should produce the blue Winkle Belshazzar, as Weddo was not only a Prinz Carlo son but out of a Schill v. Deutz granddaughter as well. The blue Winkle was mated to another blue in producing Peppo v. Marychel, whose sire Prinz Carlo v. Parthengrund was the son of still another blue, Harras II v. Parthengrund. This blue line, however, ended completely with Peppo's son Ch. Knight of Tidewater, a black and tan like his dam, Gretel v. Römercastle. It is an odd fact that Gretel v. Römercastle should have been bred to two different blue dogs, and suggests an attempt on the part of her owner to produce a strain of this color. If so, it failed.

Harro v. Marychel, a blue sire who carried on to the present day, was out of Wiltrude Bertilde, whose dam was the Prinz Carlo Viktoria daughter Duchess Chica de Doberman and whose sire was Doberman Dorussia. Harro's sire was Prinz Wallie Doberman II, a full brother to Dorussia.

242

FOLLY OF PONTCHARTRAIN W227715

Sire: Masterpiece of Pontchartrain   Dam: Duchess of Logenhauer
Breeder: Robert F. Scott   Owner: Mrs. Stella Lee

They were sons of Ch. Bertel and Ch. Hertha, both black and tan, but their parents had produced at least one blue, Doberman Prinz Heinrich, although he did not prove to be a producing sire. Harro carried on the male line of Ch. Bertel Doberman, being the only grandson to do so. His producing get were both sons, Shelly v. Marychel out of Gretel v. Römercastle, and Ch. Prinz Eitel v. Wedon out of Gretel's daughter Wanda v. Marychel, so whatever strain was behind her must have formed a satisfactory combination with Harro. Shelly v. Marychel bred to Lona v. Steinenfeld II carried the Ch. Bertel male line a generation further to Hensel of Stuebenfield, who is still represented through descendants of his daughter Wilhelmina in Ch. Gwyn of Von Kay, while Hensel's sister Gretal of Stuenbenfield is found through all the descendants of Ch. Duke Troll of Spanway, a most successful sire of the early 1940s who carried a substantial number of the early lines. Harro's other son, Ch. Prinz Eitel v. Wedon, whelped in 1917 out of Wanda v. Marychel, was the sire of two champions—Swa-Kop-Mund (a daughter out of Ch. Kamerun Fraulein) who did not carry on, and Ch. Kamerun Nasanakang, whose son Whistling Rufus, whelped in 1922, was the last descendant in male line of Ch. Bertel Doberman with descendants still to be found in today's champions. Rufus carried on through his daughter Fritzi Ritz to all the Elblac champions derived from Berta v. Bassewitz. Berta has additional lines through Princess Patricia, a daughter of Ch. Nasanakang, and through one of the three producing daughters of Ch. Prinz Eitel, Elizabeth v. Waldaus Wedon. Prinz Eitel also sired another son, Doherty's Bimbo (a full brother to Ch. Nasanakang), whose line ended with the non-producing Ch. Riesa v. Wittenberg. Both Prinz Eitel's champions and two of his producers were out of Kamerun Fraulein, while the other two daughters, Kootsch v. Wedon and Elizabeth v. Waldhaus Wedon, were out of Elizabeth v. Waldhaus Dober. Ch. Swa-Kop-Mund finished in 1921 and her brother Ch. Nasanakang in 1922. Their dam was Ch. Kamerun Fraulein whose sire Armin v. Wildenbach also sired Ch. Gretchen v. Wilden-

244

bach. Gretchen's dam, Hertha II, was the granddam of Fraulein, who was out of Kindry by Rolf v. Thüringen.

Among the other early sires who have left descendants among recent champions (the imported dogs of the pre-war era, about 20 in number, were more numerous than the bitches) we ought not to forget Doberman Lump, whelped in 1907, who sired Ch. Doberman Dix, the first male of the breed to win an American Kennel Club championship, in 1912, and also the first American-bred. Lump also sired Doberman Hottentot, apparently the first American-bred blue. Misprints are frequent in the early registration, indicating a small knowledge of German, not to mention the probability of handwritten pedigrees in German script. Lump's sire, variously rendered as Linka or Tunk, was perhaps Junker v. Grammont, by Graf Isalan v. Elbthal, a son of Freundsberg v. Thüringen the brother of Hellegraf. Lump's dam was Lotte v. Grammont, and the Grammont Kennels were located at the Hague in Holland, although the stud book records Lump's breeder as August Scharf of Apolda. Doberman Lump and Claudius v. Thüringen were related through Freundsberg, who was the great grandsire of Lump and the grandsire of Claudius.

The prominent position occupied by Prinz Carlo Viktoria in the early importations deserves notice. Duchess Chica de Doberman, Duchess Elsie de Doberman (apparently imported), and Doberman Brunette, her full sister whelped in this country, were his daughters. Carlo v. Oslaben, Grandduke Kimo de Doberman and Weddo v. Eichtal were all his sons. In addition, Ch. Hertha Doberman was sired by his maternal grandsire, and Harras II v. Parthengrund was his grandson. No other dog had such a representation among the early importations who contributed to the formation of the breed in America, yet it is surprising to observe that not one of his sons or daughters became a champion. However, Grandduke Kimo de Doberman was winners at what may be considered the first Doberman specialty show, the classes sponsored by the Pinscher Club of America at Charlotte, N.Y. in 1910. Kimo was of slight importance as a sire, but the other two sons, Carlo v. Oslebshausen and Weddo v. Eichtal, sired five champions and six additional producers between them.

Carlo v. Oslebshausen was owned by the Herman F. Meyers of Philadelphia, who also owned Ch. Flora v. Koenigshof and used the kennel name of Geholz. His son Ch. Graf Carlo v. Koenigshof, out of Ch. Flora, did not carry on, but from her daughter Flora II v. Geholz he sired Ch. Lady II v. Fern Felsen, Ch. Rolf der Geheim Polizist, Carlo v. Geholz and Fürstin Sophie v. Fern Felsen (all from different litters). Still another daughter, Flora v.d. Norris, was out of Flora III v. Geholz, by Titus v. Rolandsmarkt out of Flora II v. Geholz. Titus (who also sired Trixie v. Geholz and Jeff v. Geholz out of Ch. Flora v. Koenigshof), was sired by a full brother to Prinz Carlo Viktoria, while his dam was a half-sister to Ch. Flora's dam, Ch. Rolf. Carlo v. Geholz and Flora v.d. Norris carried on to only a limited extent. Fürstin Sophie, however, was the dam of Ch. Joffre of White Gate, the first Doberman to go winners at Westminster in two successive years, and of three others who carried on as Joffre failed to do— Buddy of White Gate, Daddy of White Gate, and Judy of Detroit. Sophie will be found today in the pedigree of a dozen or so recent champions. His mating to Ch. Tisch v. Eichtal, by the Prinz Carlo Viktoria son Weddo v. Eichtal out of Weddo's own daughter, though (or because) it involved strong inbreeding to Prinz Carlo Viktoria, led to no results of value.

Grandduke Kimo de Doberman was a Prinz Carlo Viktoria son good enough to win the Doberman specialty in 1910 and Westminster in 1911. His champion great granddaughter Tisch v. Eichtal, result of a sire and daughter mating to Weddo v. Eichtal, was outcrossed to the Danish Rolf fra Bornholm, and can be traced down to Ch. Acho and Ch. Berta v. Gesellschaft.

Pascha v. Adrianopel, mentioned in connection with the descendants of Ch. Flora v. Koenigshof, was linebred to Schill v. Deutz (the maternal grandsire of Prinz Carlo Viktoria) and was also a grandson of Flora v.d. Nidda, the

CH. FELLOW BOY V. LEE W81037

Sire: Ch. Brahms v. Del Acres
First Hawaiian bred champion

Dam: Gypsy of Polynesia
Owner: Lt. Cdr. Arve Lee

dam of Leporello v.d. Nidda (otherwise Leporello v. Main). He sired two producing sons, Pascha v. Geholz out of Flora v. Geholz, and Otto of Penn Lynn out of Pascha's sister Gretchen v. Geholz. Pascha v. Geholz carried the male line a generation farther through his son Prince v.d. Norris. Prince, through a daughter, Bessie v. Heimbach mated to Otto of Penn Lynn, carried down eventually to Ch. Wittland's Black Knight. Otto was also mated to Bessie v. Rheinland, daughter of his half-brother Pascha v. Geholz, and sired Trail'em Queen. Two daughters of Queen carried on, both from her mating to Ch. Lord v.d. Horstburg (who was also bred to the Otto daughter, Bessie of Maple Shade, from whom Wittland's Black Knight descended). It is thus apparent that Pascha v. Adrianopel carried on only through descendants linebred to him and to Ch. Flora v. Koenigshof, with Flora more strongly represented (four times in Bessie of Maple Shade and three times in Trail'em Queen), and only when these linebred descendants were mated to Lord v.d. Horstburg. Queen's daughters by Lord, the litter sisters Trail'em Lady and Trail'em Nora, each appear in several recent champions. From Lady come Ch. Asta's Ace, Ch. Diva of Blue Top, Ch. Komet of Pontchartrain and Ch. Kana of Pontchartrain. Komet and Kana trace to Lady through both sire and dam. From Nora come five champions, Assault v. Aleck (twice over), Cunningham's Baron Award, Franchon of Erline, Sonya v. Clarehof, and Asta v. Loefelstelz. All five trace from Nora's great great granddaughter, Melba v. Eckert, the dam of Ch. Boby v. Eckert. Boby v. Eckert's sire Ch. Boby v. Hohenzollernpark was also the sire of Ch. Carlo v. Bassewitz. Boby v. Hohenzollernpark was a son of Ch. Figaro v. Sigalsburg the best imported son of Alto v. Sigalsburg. Boby himself had no champions but five producing daughters. Two were the dams of champions, Frieda v. Aleck, bred back to her sire, was granddam of one and great granddam of another, while the other two were granddam and great granddam.

Ch. Treu v. Grunau was the first imported male to finish his championship, in 1913. His pedigree for three genera-

248

tions on both sides contains no familiar name and he carried on solely through a blue son, Siegfried from Sternhof, whelped in 1911 out of Doberman Brunette (whose dam was Gerta Doberman). In 1920, just before his tenth birthday, Siegfried was bred to a young bitch, Kunigunde v. Stolzenfels, whose parents, Maxim and Princess Bella v. Edelweis were full brother and sister (by Jeff v. Geholz out of Bella v. Sternhof, daughter of Satan v. Rosenplatz and Gundula v. Rosenplatz). From this mating of Siegfried and Kunigunde came five bitches who between them have carried down to a round dozen of the champions of the past five years. One of the five, Witch Hexe v. Stolzenfels, was a blue like her sire, but with her this color seems to have disappeared.

Weddo v. Eichthal was the sire of two champions, Tisch v. Eichtal and Lucie Doberman, and of two other daughters, Doberman Appleblossom (the dam of Tisch) and Winkle Belshazzar. He also sired Prince v.d. Eichthal and Koenig v. Grönland out of Minca v. Koburg, the imported granddaughter of Ch. Bertel. Koenig carried on through a daughter, Guarda v. Marychel. Weddo is remarkable in that he appears in the pedigree of champions of the past five years more often than any other early sire except Ch. Bertel Doberman. Weddo is found in no less than forty-two of these champions—sometimes several times over, and his six get which carried on were out of five different dams. His own pedigree is interesting, for he was sired by Prinz Carlo Viktoria, while his dam, Irma v. Eichtal, was by Prinz Carlo's paternal grandsire, Peter v. Thüringen (or v. Ilm Athen) out of a daughter of Prinz Carlo's maternal grandsire. Peter was a double grandson of Greif v. Grönland, while his sire, Prinz v. Ilm Athen, was also the sire of the great Sturmfried. The dam of Prinz, Lady v. Ilm Athen, was a bitch of unrecorded pedigree but reliably declared to have been part Manchester Terrier. It may well have been the line breeding to Peter which gave Weddo v. Eichthal his value as a sire. Of his two champion daughters, Tisch v. Eichthal was the result of a sire-daughter mating, while Lucie Doberman was out of

249

his half-sister, Duchess Chica de Doberman, who was likewise sired by Prinz Carlo Viktoria out of a granddaughter of Greif v. Grönland's litter sister.

Titus v. Rolandsmarkt was sired by a younger full brother to Prinz Carlo Viktoria (Titus v.d. Oden Wumme) out of a daughter of Peter v. Ilm Athen. Although his breeding was so similar to Weddo v. Eichtal's he was much less successful and carried on only through his mating to Ch. Flora v. Koenigshof and one of her daughters. Flora was by Prinz v. Ilm Athen out of a Peter v. Ilm Athen daughter. Flora's daughter by Titus was bred to the Flora grandson Pascha v. Geholz and their son Prince v.d. Norris mated back to a granddaughter of Titus out of another Flora daughter. After one more generation of inbreeding the line was outcrossed and apparently lost its force, although there are still a few descendants, including Chs. Komet and Kana of Pontchartrain, Wittland's Black Knight, Asta's Ace and Diva of Blue Top.

Jeff v. Geholz, by Titus out of Ch. Flora v. Koenigshof, sired a son and daughter, Maxim 264142 and Princess Bella v. Edelweiss, both out of Bella v. Sternhoff (by Satan v. Rosenplatz out of Gundula v. Rosenplatz) From the brother-sister mating of Maxim to Princess Bella came Kunigunde v. Stolzenfels, whelped in 1919, who has already been mentioned as the dam of five producing daughters all by Siegfried from Sternhoff.

The remaining sires of the early period included Arnim v. Wildenbach, son of a sieger and siegerin, Armin v. Hochheim and Hertha v. Wildenbach. Arnim himself sired two champion daughters, Kamerun Fraulein and Gretchen v.d. Wildenbach. Each left four progeny which carried on. Ch. Fraulein's were all from her mating to Ch. Prince Eitel v. Wedon and included two champions. Ch. Gretchen's only champion was by Doberman Graf Robert, a son of Bertel and Hertha Doberman. Two of her three producers, Gretchen II and Odessa v. Marychel, were by Ch. Lord v. Spichernberg, a double grandson of Marco v. Hoernsheim, who was identical with S. Marko v. Luetzellinden. Whelped in 1912, Ch. Lord did not complete his championship until 1918. He sired another producing daughter out of Gretel v. Römercastle, Wanda v. Marychel, dam of Ch. Prince Eitel v. Wedon. Ch. Lord's sire, Lord v. Nesselrode, was also imported, but carried on only through his imported descendants which besides Ch. Lord included Rolf fra Bornholm, a grandson of Lord v. Nesselrode's son Traf who was imported during the 1920's.

Lord v. Lilienkron was a son of Theo v.d. Funkenburg, a handsome brown dog who failed to make his mark as a sire except through his daughter Senta v. Jaegerheim, the dam of Asta Voss. Since Asta was the dam of Sieger Lux v.d. Blankenburg, among others, Theo certainly cannot be rated a complete failure.

Two other minor sires were Hans v. Franken, a son of Prinz Modern v. Ilm Athen, and Lux v. München, a great grandson in direct male line of Graf Benno v. Thüringen and out of a Sturmfried-Wand v. Burgwall granddaughter. These two, in combination with Doberman Veracity (one of the Bertel-Hertha sons) come down over a single line from Boulevard Queen and her daughter Reina v. Rennstieg which extends to Ch. Ventura Gypsy.

Prinz v. Pfalzerland, who sired two producers out of Ch. Lord's daughter Odessa v. Marychel, was out of a Sieger Lord v. Ried daughter and by Sieger Adelfried v.d. Wendenberg, a grandson of Hellegraf. Satan v. Rosenplatz, a Landgraf v. Thüringen son out of a daughter of Hopsa Hinz, carried on solely through his mating to the Hopsa Hinz daughter Gundula v. Rosenplatz which produced Bella v. Sternhof. Tasso v. Bult, whose dam was a half-sister to Prinz Carlo Viktoria and was the granddam of Prinz v. Pfalzerland, was sired by a son of Hellegraf, Sydow v. Deutz, whose maternal granddam, Chica v. Deutz, was the granddam of Prinz Carlo. Tasso left two daughters, whelped when he was eight and a half, out of Guarda v. Marychel, daughter of Koenig v. Grönland and Ch. Gretchen v. Wildenbach.

Two additional dogs, Hans v. Franken and Ch. Montwitz v. Eckhardstein, are of interest as being sons of Sieger Prinz Modern v. Ilm Athen. It is through Modern, one of

251

the great sires of the breed, that the male line to Lux v.d. Blankenburg descends. Neither Hans nor Montwitz carried down except in a single line, but Montwitz, if the dates are correctly given in the stud book, established something of a record. Whelped in 1912, he was mated to Flora II v. Geholz, whelped in 1910, and their daughter, Trail'em's Velvet Queen, is registered as having been born in October 1922, when her parents were ten and a half and eleven. Queen was bred the following year to the seven year old Ch. Rolf der Geheim Polizist, her half-brother on her dam's side, and produced Schnuppe v. Rodenbach. The bitch line starting with Ch. Flora v. Koenigshof whelped in 1908 runs in only nine generations to Ch. Admiral of Preakness Hills, who finished his championship in 1947 at the age of two.

Ch. Harras II v. Parthengrund, a blue dog whelped in 1911 and completing his championship in 1915, was the first imported Doberman who left important get behind him in Germany. His American-bred descendants died out in a few generations.

His German bred descendants are mainly through Stopp v. Parthengrund whose progeny are as follows:

| F₁ | F₂ | F₃ | F₄ | F₅ |

F_1 F_2 F_3 F_4 F_5

Arnfried v. Brandis
    Zeus v. Parthengrund (brown)
        Burschel v. Coeln
            Hedda v. Margaretenhof
                Jockel v. Lobenstein
                Jessy v. Lobenstein
                Kasper v. Lobenstein
            Faust v.d. Pleisenburg
        Axel v. Hindendorff
            Axel v. Kirchenbuehl
                Emir Lentulus

Three other imported bitches from this early period deserve some mention—Gretel v. Römercastle, Gundula v. Rosenplatz and Minca v. Koburg. Minca was not registered and

INT. CH. ASTA V. DOMSTADT

Sire: Muck v. Brunia   Dam: Kora v.d. Ruppertsburg

Owner: E. Bornstein, Peoria, Illinois

CH. DUKE V.D. RAVENSBURG III

Sire: Ch. Alcor v. Millsdod   Dam: Ch. Flora of Collenburg II

Owner: Alonzo B. Reed

253

appears only through her son Koenig v. Grundland, by Weddo v. Eichtal. Through Koenig the line carried down to at least ten recent champions, Ventura Gypsy, Colleen of Archwood, Marc's Diana of Solbo, Hallwyre Hester, Hallwyre Heddaburg, Hallwyre Happy Kristine, Patroon v. Rensselaer, Clipper v. Falkenstein, La Belle v. Falkenstein, and Blitzen v. Schoeler. Minna is of interest because she was sired by Prinz v. Coburg, a son of Bertel v. Hohenstein, otherwise Ch. Bertel Doberman. Accordingly, in addition to his American get Bertel has carried on also through this imported granddaughter. Gundula v. Rosenplatz, whelped in 1905, was close to the beginnings of the breed, being by Hopsa Hinz out of Hopsa Gerda, the latter a daughter of Junker Slenz v. Thüringen. Hinz, by Graf Belling v. Thüringen out of Freya v. Thüringen, was full brother to Gunzo v. Thüringen, the first brown Doberman exhibited at any show. Gunzo is described as coarse and quite lacking in quality, but Hinz was a good dog; and as a litter brother to Ullrich's Glocke v. Thüringen, dam of the great Hellegraf (likewise a brown) he carried excellent lines. The mating of Ch. Bertel Doberman to Gundula v. Rosenplatz combined some of the best strains in the breed, with two lines to Graf Belling, one to his brother Greif v. Grönland, two to Junker Slenz v. Thüringen and one to Landgraf Sighart, the sire of Hellegraf. The result was Ch. Graf Rupert. Rupert's daughter, Ch. Countess v. Rupert, was the dam of two champions, Lucia and Mona v. Telless. Mona and a non-champion sister, Guda v. Telless (all three were by the Swiss Ch. Max Schuess) carried down over three lines each. Guda was the dam of Ch. Nero v. Telless, who in turn sired Ch. Carlo v. Belger, who sired two champions, Minka and Hans v. Ingehoven, who did not carry on, and two non-champions, Troll and Dely of Oxbo, who did. Thus the line from Bertel runs for seven generations with Guda v. Telless the only break in the succession of champions. After Ch. Carlo v. Belger there is a lapse of two generations on the line of Troll v. Oxbo and his daughter Duchess V. Then comes Ch. Duke Troll of Spanaway, who in turn sired two champions, Gwyn von Kay and Smoky Joe of Von Kay, while a

254

third daughter, not a champion, was Lady Lou of Von Kay, dam of Ch. Gretchen of Von Kay who finished in 1947. Through Duchess of American Lake and her daughter Mitzi v. Coblenz, neither of them champions, Ch. Duke Troll also carries down to Ch. Libra v.d. Luftwege. From Bertel to Gretchen of Von Kay is eleven generations, seven of which were champions, and this is, I think, the most consistently winning line from the beginnings of the breed in America. Out of the whole eleven, Troll v. Oxbo was the only one in the direct line who had no champion get, while three of them (Countess v. Rupert, Carlo v. Belger and Duke Troll of Spanaway) had two.

Besides his daughter Ch. Countess v. Rupert, Ch. Graf Rupert carried on through two other daughters, Elizabeth v. Waldhaus Dober, dam of Elizabeth v. Waldhaus Wedon (already mentioned under Duchess Chica), Princess Susana (who produced Ch. Riesa Wittenberg and four producers), and two sons, Prinz v. Kuckuck and Peter Pepper. Neither son carried on in male line, but Prinz v. Kuckuck is represented today in Ch. Wittland's Black Knight and Ch. Kitchawan's Acquila. Peter Pepper is of interest because he was the result of a mating of Graf Rupert to his daughter Princess Susana. Princess Susana's dam, Princess Gretel II, was by Prince v.d. Eichthal (Waddo v. Eichthal-Minca v. Koburg) out of Princess of Mystic Side (Doberman Prince Eitel-Doberman Pavlovna).

Peter was mated to Smarty Brunhilde v. Stolzenfels, a bitch not descended from Bertel and Hertha but carrying two lines to Gundula v. Rosenplatz, Graf Rupert's dam, but otherwise only distantly related. The resulting daughter, Clara v. Jaegerhof, who was whelped in 1923, is found in the fifth generation back of Ch. Birima's Gypsy and the ninth from Ch. Printz v. Schwaben. From Ch. Bertel Doberman (whelped in 1905) via Clara v. Jaegerhof to Ch. Birima's Gypsy whelped in 1948 is a matter of ten generations and forty-two years. The average of more than four years per generation is unusually long. Only one of the parents was less than three years old (Gypsy's dam, Willowcrest Ritz, was two and eight months) while Clara v. Jaegerhof was

255

actually eight years and three months when her daughter Schnitzel v. Rheinhof was whelped. Clara was apparently the last producer of the old pre-war stock uncrossed by the newer importations which began with the 1920's. A possible rival, Countess Gisela v. Walden, was sired by Ch. Walden v. Everfaithful, who was registered on wins and whose sire, Togo, is obscure. Clara was mated in 1925 to Artus v. Schlingelhof, an Edelblut v. Jaegerhof grandson, and six years later to Ch. Elmar v.d. Rheinperle. The bitch from this latter mating, Schnitzel v. Rheinhof, was mated to Ch. Hyde of Pontchartrain, and the line from their daughter, Chloe v. Surericht, is one of the few cases in which Hyde bred on. Chloe's son Troll of Strebor was by Ch. Muck v. Brunia, and Troll's daughter Willowcrest Ritz was strongly inbred to Muck, her dam, Freya v. Flodinheim, being by Ch. Carlo v. Fasanenheim (grandson of Muck and his litter sister Mona) out of Ch. Flaemmchen v. Lindenhof, a full sister to Carlo's sire, Ch. Blank v.d. Domstadt.

This early line was evidently vigorous and long-lived, for Peter Pepper was whelped when his sire, Ch. Graf Rupert, was eight and a half years old. Indeed, the latter sired at least one litter in 1923 when past twelve. Besides Peter Pepper, Princess Susana carried on through another son, Whistling Rufus, whelped in 1922, by Ch. Kamerun Nasanakang. Rufus, like Clara v. Jaegerhof, was of the old pre-war strain. His two litter sisters, Princess Patricia and Princess Rosa, likewise carried on, so this was evidently a successful mating. As Princess Susana carried three lines from Ch. Bertel and Kamerun Nasanakang had two the litter was definitely line-bred to him, but the force of this was lost in later generations when outside matings were repeatedly made. Princess Susana's daughter Ch. Riesa Wittenberg, by Doherty's Bimbo (a full brother to Ch. Kamerun Nasanakang), was the last champion of the old pre-war line, and she did not carry on.

This raises the question of what might have happened if the early strain had been carefully line-bred without being submerged by newer stock. The answer is not hard to guess. The new importations were sweeping the shows.

256

Those were the days when new importations equalled or exceeded the number of American-breds registered, when Dobermans were beginning to be known and recognized by the general public. Fashion plays a part in all breeds, directly in determining the public demand and hence the amount of breeding which can be undertaken successfully without leaving too great a surplus on the breeders' hands. Less directly, the fluctuating tastes of fanciers and judges determine the types which win, and which breeders will try to produce. In order to produce that type, many breeders, especially those without experience and lacking a knowledge of the individuals who are to them only names on a pedigree, will breed to stud dogs who are the fashion because of their show ring performance or their supposed ability to beget the type in demand at the moment, whether or not such dogs have the hereditary makeup which is suited to a given bitch or group of bitches. It was inevitable that the descendants of the pre-war stock should be bred with the later comers. Had the dogs of the older strain consistently defeated the newcomers in the show ring such interbreeding would still have taken place, though with a different emphasis and a different end in view. Since the newer dogs were superior in the show ring, attempts were made by the owners of the older stock to produce successful winners by combining the two. In some cases this was successful. Down through the years a number of champions resulting from such matings occurred. A few, such as Ch. Nero v. Telless, Ch. Carlo v. Belger, or Diecker v. Ulmeholz were reasonably successful sires (Diecker sired three champions, Trok, Hela and Teckla v. Ulmeholz, the first named good enough for Best in Show at Los Angeles in 1927 but left no champion descendants), but not one appears on the list of outstanding sires. And when they were bred back to bitches of similar breeding the results were even less. While it is true that some of the present day champions trace nearly a dozen times to the early dogs, they appear many generations back—scattered more or less at random—and largely neutralized by subsequent line breeding or inbreeding to dogs of later importation.

257

Why was this so? The fact that one champion out of four who finished during the past five years carried the older lines, speaks well for their quality and indicates how widespread this stock must be through the breed as a whole. Moreover, in analyzing the comparatively small group of dogs and bitches imported before the war, it was evident that nearly all of them carried the same general bloodlines as the contemporary ancestors of the later group. Many, indeed, were very close to the best of the dogs of their day.

The answer is probably twofold. First, no really outstanding dog or bitch was imported until after 1920, so far as appears on the record. It is a well known fact that brothers and sisters may differ widely in type and quality; that the get or grandget of a truly great dog are not always great themselves. Probably the early dogs were of the same general type as their relatives remaining in Germany, but lacking the outstanding show winners who stayed at home the average must have been somewhat less good. Then as Dobermans increased in number in Germany the type was refined and improved, so that when importations were resumed after the war the German-bred dogs had probably advanced to a point not yet reached in this country. The war not only cut off the supply for a time, but by sharply curtailing breeding operations in Germany itself, undoubtedly led to drastic culling there. When lack of food and other restrictions made it possible to keep and raise fewer dogs, only the most outstanding would have been generally used for breeding. While many excellent animals were undoubtedly lost through this cause, it is certain that many marginal animals were not allowed to reproduce. It is significant that judges were also imported! In brief not only dogs, but a new style in dogs was imported from Germany.

The comparatively small number of Dobermans imported before World War I and the long distances over which American breeders were scattered undoubtedly limited the choice of sires. Then the breed was new and little known in this country, while in Germany nearly twenty years of effort and experiment had begun to bear fruit. No wonder

258

CH. RU MAR'S TSUSHIMA, C.D.
"Tish", daughter of Ch. Rancho Dobe's Cello, was the top winning of all dogs, all breeds, in America for 1965 (Phillips System). Owned by Margaret and Rodney Carveth, Portola Valley, Calif. Handled by E. R. Hastings.

that when importation was resumed in the early 1920's the older bloodlines faced a severe handicap.

The spread of the Doberman during the period before World War I was amazingly rapid. The earliest breeders and exhibitors included Max Donath of New Jersey; Theodore F. Jager of Rochester and Schenectady, N. Y. (Doberman Kennels) ; Mr. and Mrs. Meyer of Philadelphia (Fern Felsen Kennels) ; Mr. and Mrs. Vucassovitch of Wellesley, Mass. (St. Marychel Kennels). However, by 1914 the stud books record breeders in Connecticut, New Hampshire, Idaho, Iowa and Washington State. Wanda v. Marychel, the dam of Ch. Prinz Eitel v. Wedon, was bred in Iowa but owned near Boston, Mass., indicating that fanciers were in touch with those outside their own locality.

In 1910 there were Dobermans exhibited in Chicago, in 1911 in St. Louis, and in 1912 in Maryland, Rhode Island, Wisconsin and Washington, D. C., and Georgia. In 1914 Vermont was added to the list, and Duchess Chica de Doberman was exhibited by David Whitcomb of Seattle at the local show, where she went winners.

Very little seems to be known about the earliest breed club in the United States. It is not mentioned in the section on the early history of the breed in America which was written in 1929 for the second edition of W. S. Schmidt's *The Doberman Pinscher* by the late Howard K. Mohr of White Gate Kennels. However, the American Kennel Club stud book for 1910 notes that the Pinscher Club of America sponsored classes in that year at a show at Charlotte, N. Y. This was near Rochester, where the Doberman Kennels of T. F. Jager were then located, so no doubt he was one of the promoters. Search of the available volumes of the American Kennel Gazette indicates that this club was not a member of the AKC, but during the years from 1913 to 1919 the list of Specialty Club Secretaries includes S. Schneidam or Schneidman (it is spelled both ways) of Ithaca, N. Y., and later of New York City. When this list first appears, in November 1913, the name has become the Doberman Pinscher Club of America. Whether this organization disbanded or was reorganized is not clear. The statement that breeders and exhibitors of Dobermans at the Westminster Show of 1921 met and decided to cast their lot together by fostering the interests of the breed, the outcome being the Doberman Pinscher Club of America, suggests the founding of a new association, especially since it is declared that contact was made with the AKC to determine if any similar club held the charter as an AKC parent club. The D.P.C.A. seemingly dates its foundation from this time, for its tenth annual specialty show was held in 1931.

Mr. George H. Earle III, later U.S. Minister, and Governor of Pennsylvania, was asked to secure the official Doberman standard from Germany, and this was adopted by the D.P.C.A. on February 13, 1922. To secure a better knowledge of the breed it was decided to obtain a German authority for the 1923 Westminster Show, and the choice fell upon Herr Peter Umlauff of Hamburg.

Beginning about 1921 the breed in this country underwent tremendous changes. For the first time, outstanding German winners were imported and shown widely. Ch. Joffre of White Gate, winners at Westminster for two successive years in 1920 and 1921, was the last American-bred in years to do so. The first of the new invasion was Ch. Lord v.d. Horstburg, imported in 1921 by Earle's Red Roof Kennels. With his kennel mate, Ch. Centa v. Rinkenbuehl, he went to the top at Westminster in 1922. Lord was a son of Edelblut v. Jaegerhof, and has been described as an almost ideal Doberman except for a somewhat too heavy head. He was easily the best imported up to that time, and was very popular at stud. His dam, Werry v.d. Rolandsburg, was by Prinz Modern v. Ilm Athen, who was consequently Lord's double grandsire. Werry's dam was by Theo v. Funkenburg, the grandsire of Ch. Joffre, out of Hertha v. Hohenstein. (This was, presumably, Ch. Hertha Doberman, although the dates of birth of Hertha and her first litter by Ch. Bertel leave the matter slightly open to question.)

Whelped in 1919, Lord was scarcely two when imported and cannot have left many get in Germany. However, his son Brummer Hochwart sired a later importation, Ch.

261

Eva v. Essen, and Hektor v. Hindendorff, sire of imported Ch. Arno v. Maintor. Four Lord daughters, Alma v. Siegestor, Berta-Rota v.d. Nibelungenhort, Burga v. Scharflueck and Ida v. Hornegg, were themselves imported. In spite of his quality and his considerable opportunities, Lord sired only two American champions. Ch. Louis v. Arcald is today represented through one daughter and Ch. Red Roof Rowdy through two sons. In all, seventeen of Lord's sons and daughters can be found in the pedigrees of the 240 champions who have finished during the past five years. However, Lord's influence was probably most important through his imported daughter Berta-Rota v.d. Nibelungenhort, who was the double great granddam of Ch. Baroness Brenda v.d. Hoehen and her sister Ch. Baroness Blenda. Baroness Brenda was one of the few American-breds who has been shown in Europe. She won the Open brown class at the Cologne international Show, received V and first in the youth class at Recklinghausen, Westphalia, and was runner up there for Best of Breed, defeating Troll v.d. Engelsburg—the winner at the 1934 Berlin Sieger Show the following month, though he did not receive the title because he was under age. Brenda was the dam of three champions, Orama, Orissa and Orsova of Westphalia. Through the first two, and through a non-champion sister Ouida of Westphalia, Baroness Brenda has carried on to the present time. Ch. Elblac's Dorcas, Ch. Ximenes of Elblac, Ch. Adithkin O'Lon, and Ch. Barlyn's Brenda are descended from them. Berta-Rota also carried on through her imported son, Prinz v.d. Nibelungenhort.

Ch. Bella v. Stolzenberg, imported by Earle in 1922, was a six months younger full sister to the 1921 Siegerin Asta v. Stolzenberg, who was herself imported later on. Bella was a daughter of Ch. Troll v.d. Blankenburg and Lotte I v. Simmenau. She was bred first to Lord v.d. Horstburg, then to Ch. Benno v. Burgholz, and finally, at the age of seven and a half, to Ch. Claus v. Sigalsburg (the son of her sister Ch. Asta). By Lord she had Ch. Red Roof Rowdy and three other producing sons; by Benno she had a son and three daughters, one of them Ch. Red Roof

Rilda and another, Red Roof Hexie, the dam of three champions. Her litter by Claus contained Canadian Ch. Gilda of Leal's Farm, Ch. Bella of Thuringia and her most prepotent son, Red Roof Exorcist. Gilda was the dam of Ch. Asta of Oxbo and of Eddi v. Nibelungenring II, the grandsire of Ch. Duke Troll of Spanaway. Ch. Asta of Oxbo was the dam of Ch. King Adam v. Wagner, sire of Ch. Adam of Walgrove, whose son Ch. Ed's Bachelor Boy of Chadra sired two champions in the last five years, while King Adam's son Ch. Ames v. Sidlo sired three. Red Roof Exorcist, though not a champion himself, was the sire of three champions. Only one of them, Ch. Trail'em Lucinda, carried on, but through her and through Exorcist's son Buddy of Pinecrest this line carries down to Ch. Edah v. Trail, the dam of seven champions and a producer. Exorcist's daughter Toska v. Penfield, was the dam of two champions, one of which, Ch. Monterey v. Stahlhelm, was the dam of three.

The red bitch Centa v. Rinkenbuehl who was winners at Westminster along with Lord v.d. Hortsburg, in 1922, had won her title in Germany the previous year and seems to have been the first Siegerin imported. She left no champion get, but carried on to some extent through her mating to Lord v.d. Horstburg. However, her winning descendants were less numerous than those of Bella v. Stolzenburg.

By 1922 the breed in Germany had recovered from the effects of the war, and 223 Dobermans were benched at the Berlin Sieger Show. The Siegers that year were Benno v. Roemerhof (Dutch champion in 1923) and the red Benno v. Burgholz, both whelped in 1920. These two dogs soon found their way to America, where they headed the long list of imported Siegers and were much used at stud. The trend of the times was strongly shown in the 1923 Westminster classes. The previous year an American-bred puppy, Zepp v. Telless, later a champion (by the Swiss Ch. Max Schuess) had gone Reserve Winners to Lord, and three American-breds placed in the Open Dog class and two in Open Bitches. In 1923, under Umlauff, all four

263

places in both Open classes, both Winners, and both Reserves were imported. The Winners dog was Ch. Falko v.d. Sternallee, a son of Zeus v. Parthengrund, with Ch. Dyno v. Wiesengrund Reserve, while the winning bitch was Ch. Carola v.d. Combreshoehe. Dyno's win was the first important one by the Westphalia Kennels of Mr. F. F. H. Fleitman, which became one of the most important factors in the development of the breed.

Dyno v. Wiesengrund finished his championship in 1923 and was a popular sire for a number of years. He was a litter brother to Dora v. Wiesengrund, the dam of Lotte and Stolz v. Roeneckenstein, to one or both of whom nearly all present champions can be traced. Dyno, however, though he died at the age of ten in 1930, sired only one champion, the non-producing Arnold v. Minkelried, and although his line continued through two sons and five daughters he had no champion grandchildren.

Ch. Benno v. Burgholz, imported late in 1923, and the first known Sieger in this country, was a red dog by the 1921 red Sieger Salto v. Rottal, out of an Edelblut v. Jaegerhof daughter. Salto was the son of Roland v.d. Haide, one of the most controversial dogs the breed has ever produced. Roland was sired by Lord v. Ried out of the unregistered Stella. This bitch, whelped in 1908, at a time when various experimental crosses were being made in an effort to improve the breed, is conceded to have been the daughter of a Black English Greyhound sire and a Doberman dam. Stella's daughter Sybille v. Langen was mated to Prinz Modern v. Ilm Athen and produced Bayard, Heidi and Hispa v. Silberberg. It is through Bayard, his son Arno v.d. Gluecksburg, and grandson Burschel v. Simmenau that the male line of Lux v.d. Blankenburg descends. Heidi mated to her litter brother Bayard produced Sybille v. Silberberg, whose daughter Adele v. Oststern (by Artus v. Langerode) was mated to Bayard's grandson Burschel to produce Claus v.d. Spree. The other sister, Hispa v. Silberberg, was mated to Bodo v. Elfenfeld (by Moritz v. Burgwall) and produced two bitches, Borste and Brunhild v. Falkenhain. Borste's son, Alex v. Sim-

264

CH. DOBE ACRES CINNAMON

Cinnamon scored 5 all-breed Bests in Show in 1957 to place among the Top Ten Working. Bred by R. B. Hoover. Owned by Harley Plummer, Cleves, Ohio. Handled by Dick Salter.

menau, was the grandsire on the dam's side of Siegerin Asta v. Stolzenberg, Ch. Bella v. Stolzenberg, and Dilly v. Stolzenberg. Brunhild v. Falkenhain, the granddaughter of Sybille v. Langen, was mated to Sybille's litter brother, Roland v.d. Haide, to produce Ch. Benno v. Burgholz. Roland was severely critized and his progeny are said to have been narrow, deep-chested and coarse, with round eyes. Although Roland's son Salto v. Rottal became a Sieger, and two of Salto's sons, Harras v. Ostersee and Benno v. Burgholz, won the title in their turn, his influence upon the breed appears to have been of very questionable value. His sister Sybille, on the other hand, appears in some of the greatest dogs of the breed.

Benno v. Burgholz sired two American champions, Red Roof Rilda out of Ch. Bella v. Stolzenberg, and Wenham Goldemar, neither of which carried on. Of his ten producers, Red Roof Hexie produced three champions and Trail'em Memories one. Both Hexie and Memories were out of Ch. Bella and full sisters to Ch. Red Roof Rilda, therefore this mating may be said to have been his most successful. Memories' daughter, Ch. Lady Anna v. Seigrist, was mated back to her grandsire, Benno, when he was ten and a half years old, and produced a son, Wachter v. Glenhugel, who carried on down to Ch. King Peter v. Buchholz. Lady Anna mated to Ch. Toppe v. Sigalsburg likewise carried on to the present time, when her descendants include Ch. Adonis of Huffmanheim, Chs. Komet and Kana v. Pontchartrain, Ch. Elbojara's Flame, Chs. Jetona and Lona of Wallou, and Chs. Bron and Damson v. Ernharkenburg, Chs. Cantor and Cy of Dobe-Haven. Benno v. Burgholz survived until 1932, when he was almost twelve years old.

The Swiss Ch. Max Schuess, who finished in 1922, was by a grandson of Sturmfried out of a granddaughter of Prinz Modern. Max sired three champions, Zepp, Lucia and Mona v. Teless, Ch. Mona carried on via three daughters, while four other daughters have continued to the present day, and a son, Koppe v. Macwahoc, sired Diecker v. Ulmeholz out of Ch. Hela v. Goetterfelsen. Although

266

none of Diecker's three champions from Red Roof Hexie carried on, Ch. Trok v. Ulmehoz was good enough to be one of the first American-bred Dobermans to go Best in Show in 1927.

Ch. Bodo v. Musenbach, an Edelblut v. Jaegerhof grandson who finished in 1923, was another popular sire, whose best son was Ch. Nero v. Telless, the sire of Ch. Carlo v. Belger. He likewise carried on through six non-champion sons and daughters.

The year 1924 was another important one. Imported dogs continued to sweep the shows. Ch. Claus v.d. Spree, Ch. Prinzessin Elfrieda v.d. Koningstad, and Ch. Prinz Carlo v.d. Koningstad finished their titles. The first was bred in Germany, the other two, who were sire and daughter, in Holland. Carlo, whelped in 1919, survived until the last day of the year 1931. A dog of good, medium size, he was beautifully balanced and harmonious in build, while his pedigree contained all the great sires of the breed—Hellegraf, Lord v. Ried, Prinz Modern v. Ilm Athen, Moritz v. Burgwall and Edelblut v. Jaegerhof. Out of Angola v. Grammont, litter sister to his sire, Ajax v. Grammont, Carlo sired three champions before leaving Holland, and Sieger Apollo v. Schuetzeneck in Germany, all of which were later imported. Prinzessin Elfrieda, Prinzessin Ilisa, and Prinz Favoriet v.d. Koningstad (the two last became champions in 1925) together with their sire Carlo produced twenty-four champions, two out of Ilisa, five out of Elfrieda, and fifteen by Favoriet. This was by far the best record of any sire up to that time. Although none of Carlo's American-bred get became champions, two sons and five daughters carried on. One of the daughters, Carla v.d. Koningstad, was the dam of Ch. Carlo v. Belger. Another, Elodia v.d. Hoehen, was bred to her half-brother Prinz Favoriet v.d. Koningstad and produced Troll v.d. Hoehen, the sire of Chs. Orama, Orissa and Orsova of Westphalia. Even down to the present time Favorit's record of fifteen champions has been exceeded by few dogs, among which are S. Lux v.d. Blankenburg, Ch.

Kurt v.d. Rheinperle, Ch. Alcor v. Millsdod and Ch. Dictator v. Glenhugel.

Favoriet sired six champions out of a single bitch, and five out of another. The Lux v.d. Blankenburg daughter, Ch. Freya v. Stresow, produced Ch. Hyde of Pontchartrain and his sisters Chs. Hella, Hertha, Hesta, Hexie and Hilda. Hella and Hertha were the most successful as breeders. Pontchartrain Kennels had a fire during this period in which over twenty of its better dogs were lost. Ch. Hyde, although one of the outstanding American-breds of his day, sired only one champion, the unimportant Hans v. Dombachtal and his line has almost disappeared. However, Willowcrest Ritz, dam of the 1948 Ch. Birima's Gypsy, was sired by Hyde's grandson, Troll of Strebor, a son of Ch. Muck v. Brunia.

Favoriet's other most notable litter was out of imported Ch. Alli v. Goldgrund, daughter of Ch. Troll v.d. Blankenburg and Ch. Hela v. Götterfelsen. Both Troll and Hela were grandchildren of Edelblut v. Jaegerhof, who appears twice in Favoriet's pedigree, while Edelblut's sister Helga v. Jaegerhof is found twice also. It was doubtless this breeding to Edelblut which accounted for the quality of the Favoriet-Alli litter, while a similar combination, once to Edelblut and once again to his sire, Prinz Modern, appears in the mating to Freya v. Stresow. Favoriet's son, Ch. Carlo of Rhinegold, out of Ch. Alli v. Goldgrund, was probably the first American-bred Doberman to win Best in Show, while Carlo's litter sister, Ch. Alli of Rhinegold, was the dam of one champion and the granddam of three. Angola of White Gate, out of Bacchante of White Gate, a daughter of Favoriet's sister Elfrieda, was the dam of three champions by him. The Favoriet daughter, Ilisa v.d. Hoehen, was the granddam of Ch. Baroness Brenda v.d. Hoehen, previously mentioned, and another daughter, Ch. Princess Lita of Rhinegold (out of Ch. Alli v. Goldgrund) was the dam of Ch. Doddy of Rhinegold. Doddy was the dam of four champions and the granddam of eight more. Troll v.d. Hoehen, whelped in 1930 when his sire was nine years old, was one of the last sons of Favoriet. Though he does not seem to have become a champion and was little used at stud, the quality of his get is shown by his litter out of Ch. Baroness Brenda which contained Chs. Orama, Orissa and Orsova of Westphalia. Mated to the Swiss bitch Toni v.d. Baerenburg Troll sired Lona of Somerville, whose two daughters by Ch. Westphalia's Rajah are the dams of Ch. Gunther of Westphalia and Ch. Pinckney Farms Archon. Favoriet's daughter Ch. Lady Anna v. Seigrist has already been mentioned.

Prinzessin Elfrieda v.d. Köningstad was the dam of five champions and a producer of Ch. Claus v.d. Spree, who carried three lines to Edelblut's sire, Prinz Modern, all through his mating to Sybille v. Langen, and another to Edelblut through his daughter Siegerin Asta v. Starkenburg. In spite of its high level, this litter has carried on only through the non-champion Bacchante of White Gate and through her brother Ch. Big Boy of White Gate. Elfrieda's sister, Ch. Prinzessin Ilisa v.d. Köningstad, produced two champion daughters, also by Claus v.d. Spree. One of these, Ch. Ilisa of Pontchartrain, left four champion sons, three of them producers, and two non-champion daughters, Citi of Kettle Cove, the dam of three champions, and Norma of Pontchartrain, the granddam of two. Of Ilisa of Pontchartrain's sons, one was Ch. Navigator of Pontchartrain, sire of Ch. Countess of Navigator, who played an important part in developing the breed in Canada. A second son of Ilisa, Ch. Prince Claus of Pontchartrain, sired four champions and ten producers, while Ch. Prinz Noah of Pontchartrain, the third brother, sired four champions and eleven producers. Navigator, Prince Claus and Prinz Noah were by Ch. Lux v.d. Blankenburg. Through Prinz Noah the Lux male line is carried down to date via his sons Heidel v. Wagner, Peter the Great and Ch. King Adam v. Wagner. Prince Claus likewise carries on in male line through Siegert and Marko of Pontchartrain to Peck, sire of Ch. Komet of Pontchartrain who finished in 1949. This last line is intensified by the mating of Peck to Miss Black Magic, whose dam was a granddaughter of Siegert of Pontchartrain.

Prinzessin Ilisa v.d. Köningstad's other daughter of Claus v.d. Spree was Siegerin Ilisa of Westphalia. This bitch, registered with the AKC as Princess Ilisa of Westphalia,

269

has the unique distinction of being the only American-bred ever to have won a German Sieger title. Ilisa was a brown bitch of excellent type, whelped in 1926. Her one recorded litter, by Sieger Helios v. Siegestor, contained Astor and Asta of Westphalia. Asta was the dam of Ch. Ador v. Emschertal, whose descendants include Ch. Wittland's Black Knight, Ch. Chance Run's Town Talk, Ch. Asta's Ace, Ch. Diva of Blue Top and Ch. Baron of Lakewood (sire of four champions), whose dam, Westphalia's Valerie, was whelped when Ador was past seven.

Astor of Westphalia is a dog about whom it is interesting to speculate. He was of good medium size, with excellent body type and splendid substance. He died comparatively young and sired only a few litters. What he might have accomplished with longer life and greater opportunities at stud can only be conjectured. Astor was mated in Germany at the age of two years to Siegerin Anita zur Immermannhoehe, a brown. From this litter came Karlo, Kriemhilde, Ch. Kora, and Ch. Kurt v.d. Rheinperle. In 1934 Astor sired two more litters. From Rogerschmidt's Orphan Ann, by Ch. Adonis of Pontchartrain, came Barbara of Garry Glen, dam of Ch. Kurt of Dawn II. From Bajadere of High Larches, by Ch. Big Boy of White Gate, came Princess Latona and Ch. Princess Latosca of Westphalia. Kurt v.d. Rheinperle had a record of twenty champions and nine producers, including among the latter his son Pericles of Westphalia. Pericles was a double grandson of Astor of Westphalia, his dam being Princess Latona. He sired six champions from one litter out of Ch. Jessy v.d. Sonnenhoehe, a Helios granddaughter, and a seventh champion out of a daughter of Ch. Napier of Rhinegold, a son of Kurt v.d. Rheinperle. Pericles' best son was Ch. Westphalia's Uranus, sire of eleven champions and seven producers, including three outstanding sons, Ch. Alcor v. Millsdod, Ch. Favoriet v. Franzhof and Ch. Kama of Westphalia. Besides Pericles, Kurt v.d. Rheinperle left five other sons who have carried on: Ch. Astor of Feuerstein out of Lady Hattie v. Tockstein, Ch. Black Ulan v.d. Rheinperle out of Ch. Mona v.d. Rheinperle (daughter of Ch. Troll v.d. Engelsburg and Kurt's

270

EDAH V. TRAIL
Sire: Bubi v. Verstaame   Dam: Lora v. Hays
Breeder-Owner: T. J. Holliday, Los Angeles, California

271

litter sister Kriemhilde v.d. Rheinperle) and the litter brothers Ch. Westphalia's Rajah, Ch. Westphalia's Rameses and Ch. Westphalia's Raswan out of Ch. Jessy v.d. Sonnenhoehe (a mating which also produced four champion bitches, three of them the dams or granddams of champions).

It is evident from the foregoing that the most important lines of descent from Prinz Carlo v.d. Köningstad was through his daughters Ilisa. Consequently, although the Köningstad blood is an important factor in most of the champions of today, there is not one of them in the past five years who traces to him in male line. It is astounding that such a dog as Prinz Favoriet v.d. Köningstad should not be represented by a single direct male descendant, yet such is the case. Two thirds of his champion get were daughters, and neither of his best sons, Ch. Hyde of Pontchartrain and Ch. Carlo of Rhinegold, proved an outstanding sire. Perhaps Troll v.d. Hoehen might have done so had he become a champion and had more opportunity at stud, but since all his actual champion get were daughters it might have made no difference.

Ch. Claus v.d. Spree, who finished his championship in 1924, the same year as Prinz Carlo and Prinzessin Elfrieda, was a striking dog with a peculiar head type, the skull domed above the eyes. Claus was a great grandson on his dam's side of Leuthold v. Hornegg, a dog whose head was almost totally lacking in stop. Leuthold transmitted this fault with great persistence, and when his inheritance was combined with three lines of descent from the half-greyhound bitch Stella (dam of Sybille v. Langen) it is not surprising that Claus' head type was severely criticized. Before leaving Germany Claus sired a litter out of Bona v. Sevira, a daughter of his maternal grandsire Artus v. Langerode, which contained the 1927 Sieger Gerd v. Sporthof and his sister Am. Ch. Gisela v. Sporthof. In America Claus sired twelve champions, a notable record for that time, and nineteen other sons and daughters who carried on his line more or less strongly. His mating to Prinzessin Elfrieda v.d. Köningstad produced five champions, Acto, Algard, Amerant, Asta and Big Boy of White Gate, but they failed to carry on with the exception of Big Boy. This dog, one of the best American-breds of his day, went Best in Show at the Rhode Island Kennel Club in 1928 and in 1930 was shown at the Nuremberg Sieger Show, where he was rated V (excellent) and placed 7th, having an off-day. It was generally considered that if he had shown his best he would have been one of the first three. Amerant, Big Boy's older full brother, had been one of the first trio of American-bred Dobermans exhibited in Europe in 1926, when he was 1st junior red and the only male of his color to receive a V.

Claus v.d. Spree has carried down to the present time over two different lines, and is the only son of Burschel v. Simmenau besides Lux v.d. Blankenburg who is represented in male line among the champions of the past five years. One of the lines from Claus comes through his Sieger son Gerd v. Sporthof, via Prinz Polivan v. Köningstad, Prinz Quitt v.d. Köningstad (whose dam was a sister to Prinz Polivan), to Ch. Carol v. Oevanes, Rolf v. Milde, and Ch. Carol v. Weiss, the sire of three champions. Ch. Carol v. Oevanes also sired Ch. Westphalia's Xerxes, who finished in 1947. Another male line from Claus ran through A. Rappo of Pontchartrain and Baron v. Simmineau to Ch. Dash of Bardo, the spectacular winner of Best of Breed under the German judge Herr Mueller at the Chicago Specialty Show in 1933. Dash left no known descendants, but his sister Sheila v. Blitzen was the dam of two champions by Ch. Figaro v. Sigalsburg.

Ch. Big Boy of White Gate was the best American-bred son of Claus v.d. Spree, although he sired only two champions. His daughter Ch. Sonia of Westphalia, had a successful show record unsurpassed by any American-bred bitch up to the middle 1930s but failed to carry on. Eight of Big Boy's eleven non-champion producers were sons, but only Yan of Pocahontas, sire of Ch. Rex of Northwood, has carried the male line down to the present time. However, it is through his daughters that Big Boy is chiefly represented today. Bajadere of High Larches has already been mentioned as the granddam of Pericles of Westphalia through her Astor of Westphalia daughter Princess Latona of Westphalia. Big

273

Boy was mated to his granddaughter Ch. Princess Latosca of Westphalia (litter sister to Princess Latona) and produced the bitch Adora v. Franzhof whose daughter by Ch. Ador v. Emschertal was Lady Arnette v. Maredegar. Lady Arnette was mated to Ch. Westphalia's Rajah and became the dam of Ch. Lady Valomar of Sugar Loaf. This bitch, who carried two lines to Big Boy, two to Astor of Westphalia and a third to Astor's sister Asta, was mated to Ch. Franz v. Franzhof, a grandson of her sire Ch. Rajah on one side and of Ch. Westphalia's Uranus (by Pericles, the double grandson of Astor and great grandson of Big Boy), on the other. Their daughter Valspar of Sugar Loaf was then mated to Ch. Damon of Jerry Run, a son of Ch. Westphalia's Rameses, litter brother to Ch. Rajah. This makes Ch. Chance Run's Town Talk trace ten times to Helios v. Siegestor and ten times to Claus v.d. Spree (through Ilisa of Westphalia and Big Boy of White Gate).

The strongest breeding to Big Boy among recent champions is found in Ch. Maja of Manor Park, dam of the 1948 Ch. Damasyn The Virginian. Maja is by Ch. Rex of Northwood, a Big Boy grandson, out of Linda del Rosario, a bitch who carries Big Boy five times in four generations including a sire and daughter mating. It is interesting to note that Linda del Rosario, not herself a champion, has no champions in her pedigree for three generations except for Big Boy, who appears once in the third.

The year 1924, which saw Claus v.d. Spree and Prinz Carlo v.d. Köningstad win their American championships, likewise saw Carlo's son Apollo v. Schuetzeneck win the red Sieger title in Germany. Apollo was a striking dog of excellent type and color, and with good temperament. However, on his dam's side he was a grandson of Salto v. Rottal and despite his individual quality he failed as a sire.

An interesting event of this year was the fact that the blue bitch Burga v. Kumpmuehl, by Artus v. Siegstor out of Flora Koch, won her championship. She seems to have been the first blue to complete the title, and for many years she was unrivaled. Indeed, there does not seem to have been

274

CH. STORM'S DONNER

Donner, a son of Ch. Rancho Dobe's Storm, is seen winning Best in Show at Westchester in 1959 under judge John W. Cross. Owned by Peter Mehlich of New York City, and handled by A. Peter Knoop.

another blue champion for twenty-five years, until Ch. Lucky Silver of Jerry Run in 1949.

Ch. Argos v. Vortrupp, an imported son of Dolf v. Wiesengrund out of the Lord v.d. Horstburg daughter Blüte Hoch-Warte, also finished in 1924. He was used fairly extensively at stud without producing anything notable.

Imported dogs continued to score during the next few years. 1925 saw three American-breds, Nero v. Telless, Red Roof Rowdy and Knight of Tidewater win their championships as against some ten imported dogs and bitches. Knight, by Peppo v. Marychel out of Gretel v. Römercastle, was the last champion entirely of the old, pre-war stock, but he left no winning descendants. Eidow v. Stresow (a litter brother to Ch. Freya v. Stresow the dam of Ch. Hyde of Pontchartrain and five other champions), was one of the first sons of Lux v.d. Blankenburg in this country and distinguished himself as one of the earliest Dobermans to win Best in Show. As a sire, however, he accomplished little.

In 1926 came the first American attempt to carry off the German Sieger titles. The late Howard K. Mohr of White Gate Kennels took a quartette to Berlin consisting of the German-bred Bajadere v. Zinsgut and two daughters and a son of Claus v.d. Spree and Prinzessin Elfrieda v.d. Köningstad. Bajadere received V and the red Siegerin title. She carried on through her daughter, Bajadere of High Larches by Big Boy. The dog, Amerant of White Gate, was the only red male receiving V but was too young to receive the Sieger title, which was not awarded that year. His two sisters received S. G. (very good) with Asta placing second in the junior black and tan class while Algarda was 1st junior red.

Under the German authority Franz Schulze in 1925 the winners dog at Westminster was Prinz Favoriet v.d. Koningstad, with Prinzessin Illisa v.d. Koningstad best of breed and first in the working Group. Ten days later at Boston the placings were reversed, and Prinz Favoriet won the Group. The November 1925 issue of the American Kennel Gazette carried a full page colored reproduction of

276

a painting of Prinz Favoriet by Henry Whitroy. The breed had definitely arrived.

The year 1926 saw the American-bred Ch. Trok v. Ulmeholz twice winner of Best in Show, while Mrs. Ellie Buckley tried her luck with three American-breeds at the Dortmund Sieger Show. Here Prinz Carlo of Westphalia placed 6th and V in Open blacks, with Elsa of Westphalia 7th and S.G. in Open black bitches. Princess Ilisa of Westphalia won the junior red bitch class, and three years later, in Hannover, annexed the red Siegerin title.

The number and quality of American-bred champions was on the increase, although imported champions still finished in a proportion of two to one.

In 1926 the Westminster entry under the third German judge to officiate, Otto Settegast, had risen to eighty-three. This was almost double the entry of two years before. The breed was spreading geographically, too, and there were active centers in Pittsburgh, Cincinnati, Chicago and Detroit, while the Pasadena show drew a four point entry headed by the Lux son Ch. Astor v. Thumshoehe. Ch. Druska v. Riga, who finished in this year, was bred in Russia by H. D. Anderson, who was later active in California. Druska was a litter sister to the dam of Ch. Altara v. Riga, also Russian-bred, who did not finish until 1931 but proved one of the outstanding brood bitches of the late 20's and early 30's, becoming the dam of seven champions bred by Mr. and Mrs. George Schroth of San Mateo, California.

Ch. Gisela v. Sporthof, daughter of Claus v.d. Spree and litter sister to the 1927 Sieger Gerd v. Sporthof, was perhaps the most outstanding show bitch of 1926, while from a breeding point of view the imported Ch. Elmar v.d. Rheinperle and the American-bred Ch. Hella of Pontchartrain were the two among the year's champions destined to carry on most strongly. Elmar left only one champion, the son Lindy v. Forsberg, but two of his daughters were important, and he sired ten producers in all. Elmar was a litter brother to Elfe v.d. Rheinperle, the paternal granddam of Siegerin Anita zur Immermannhoehe. He was sired by

Rolf Weiss, a direct male descendant of Edelblut v. Jaeger-hof, with two lines to the double Lord v. Ried granddaughter Wanda Knoll and one to Senta v. Hornegg, full sister to the dam of Burschel v. Simmenau. Elmar's dam was the blue Hertha II v. Golzheim by Jack v. Steubbenhaus, son of Graf Waldo v.d. Strengbach. Waldo was whelped in 1911 and like most dogs of his period had his breeding opportunities greatly restricted because of the war which occurred when he was in his prime. As a son of Prinz Modern v. Ilm Athen out of a double granddaughter of Prinz v. Ilm Athen he carried three lines to Prinz and was himself a grandson and great grandson of Sturmfried. Waldo transmitted his good build and head. His daughter Hertha II was also the dam of Achill v.d. Rheinperle who sired Egil zum Ziel, one of the leading sires of Switzerland, and his litter brother Eike zum Ziel who came to the United States. Egil's imported grand-daughter Toni v. Bärenburg was the granddam of Ch. Favoriet v. Franzhof, who will be considered in detail later on.

Elmar v.d. Rheinperle sired Burga v. Torrez and Patricia v. Milde both of whom have carried down successfully to the present time. Patricia's dam was a granddaughter of Arno v. Holstein who was strongly bred to Wanda Knoll (as was Elmar's grandsire Rolf Weiss), and likewise carried a line to Graf Waldo v. Strengbach. Burga v. Torrez was out of the imported Burga v. Scharflueck, a granddaughter of Burschel v. Simmenau and hence related to Elmar through the sisters Gudrun and Senta v. Hornegg. (A third sister, Dinoh v. Hornegg, was the granddam of Ch. Anneliessel Niessen, whose daughter bred to a son of Elfe v.d. Rhein-perle produced Siegerin Anita zur Immermannhoehe, the dam of Ch. Kurt v.d. Rheinperle.) Burga v. Scharflueck's sire was out of Asta v. Oststern, a litter sister to Adela v. Oststern, the dam of Claus v.d. Spree. Burga v. Torrez, the daughter of Burga and Elmar, was the dam of two champions, Alyse v. Sigalsburg and Alto v. Torrez and of two producers, Andree and Artiste v. Torrez, all in a single litter. Andree was the dam of Ch. Reinhardt of Randhof who descends in male line to Ch. Elblac's Blitz and other

278

INT. CH. RANCHO DOBE'S PRESTO
Owners: Bert and Bob Zacho, North Hollywood, California

winners of the present time. Artiste's daughter, Lady of Schroth Valley, was the dam of three champions and had many good descendants. Ch. Alto v. Torrez (by Ch. Claus v. Sigalsburg) was a Chicago-bred dog and the most successful American-bred sire up to this time. He sired six champions, was the grandsire of five more, and carried on through six non-champion sons and daughters. Alto's son Hanzar v. Hahn, bred to Hanzar's own daughter Roque's Nina, produced Puquette's Nina who has been the dam of three champions (Hans, Horst and Karla v. Koch) during the past five years. Ch. Glenna of Lawnwood was Alto's greatest show winner. She was a strikingly lovely brown bitch who went winners at the Chicago Specialty in 1933 and Best of Breed at Westminster the following year. Bred to Ch. Kanzler v. Sigalsburg and Ch. Kurt v.d. Rheinperle she produced a champion in each litter and has carried down to the present time through her son Ch. Milo of Garry Glen, the grandsire of Chs. Apache and Assemble of Eoghanviola and through Ch. Anne of Paulraine and her son Ch. Satan of Paulraine. Glenna's daughter Kiva of Lawnwood is the great granddam of Ch. Micah's Susie of Glen Ellyn, and Don of Lawnwood II carried down to Ch. Cella and Ch. Budi of Damhof.

Ch. Hella of Pontchartrain, who made her championship in the same year as Elmar v.d. Rheinperle, before she was two years old, was the first of her famous litter to finish. At three and a half she was bred to Lux v.d. Blankenburg, then ten years old, and produced Ch. Adonis of Pontchartrain who was Lux's most successful American-bred son. Adonis sired eleven champions and soon eclipsed his contemporary Alto v. Torrez. However, in spite of Adonis' success as a sire, none of his five champion sons has carried on in male line, though the brothers Ch. Cy and Ch. Cantor of Dobe Haven are by an Adonis grandson and great grandson. The Adonis daughter Baroness v. Kesterhoff produced two champions, one of them Black Duke v. Ernharkenburg, whose daughter Illkie v. Ernharkenburg is the dam and granddam of several champions.

Ch. Claus v. Sigalsburg, the 1926 German and Austrian Sieger, a son of Lux v.d. Blankenburg out of Siegerin Asta

280

v. Stolzenberg, was an outstanding show dog. This is said to have been the first instance of a Sieger and Siegerin producing a Sieger. Claus made a great show record in this country, going Best in Show all breeds five times in 1927 and eight times in 1928, while in 1929 he was Best Doberman at the Chicago Specialty. Unlike his grandsire, Troll v.d. Blankenburg and his sire Lux, Claus was imported young and left little or nothing behind him in Germany. He sired six champions, of whom the best producer was Ch. Alto v. Torrez. The latter's daughter, Ch. Glenna of Lawnwood, was a double granddaughter of Claus. His son Red Roof Exorcist out of his dam's full sister, Ch. Bella v. Stolzberg, sired three champions and was the grandsire of five more, while nineteen non-champion sons and daughters had at least one champion descendant apiece. Troll v. Blankenburg was whelped in 1917, and was already an old dog when he was imported. He went to California about 1926, and died in 1929 at the age of some twelve years. It is therefore hardly surprising that beginning at the age of nine he should not have produced many outstanding American-bred progeny. However, his Troll-Son v.d. Blankenburg, whelped when the sire was nearly ten out of his imported daughter 1920 Siegerin Asta v. Stolzenberg, did carry on through three sons, although the male line seems to have ended with Samson v. Strossen's son Max v. Haugaard's son Ch. Hans of Bavaria (who won his title in 1938) and Ch. Apollo of Silvergate's son Ch. Arno of Maunaloa, who finished in 1937. Both Max and Apollo are represented today through the dam of the 1949 champion Ventura Gypsy, who carried two additional lines to Troll v. Blankenburg through Ch. Marko v. Siegerpark and a fifth through another line from Asta v. Stolzenberg.

Perhaps Ch. Apollo of Silvergate would have carried on the Troll v. Blankenburg male line if he had remained in this country instead of going to Hawaii, where he was Best in Show in 1933. But if Troll had left no other get at all he would still be of prime importance through his daughter Dora v. Wiesengrund, dam of the most prepotent bitch in Doberman history up to her time. Dora was whelped in

1920, a litter sister to Ch. Dyno v. Wiesengrund, but she remained in Germany. Her dam, Lea v. Weissenfels, was out of the Sieger Lord v. Ried daughter Liesel v. Dambachtal, a beautiful blue bitch with very lovable character. Lea's sire was also a blue, Teja Herzynia, by Sturmfried. Although she came from a mating of two blue parents, Lea herself was black.

This is inconsistent with the known laws governing the inheritance of blue and there is some doubt as to the accuracy of this pedigree. Dora v. Wiesengrund was mated to Alex v.d. Finohoehe and produced in one litter Stolz v. Roeneckenstein and Lotte v. Roeneckenstein. Lotte bred to Sieger Lux v.d. Blankenburg produced Sieger Alto v. Sigalsburg, from whom 125 champions out of 245 in the last five years descend in male line alone (not counting other lines). Stolz was the sire of Ch. Helios v. Siegestor and Ch. Dewald v. Ludwigsburg, through whom 104 more of the remaining 120 descend in male line. (The other 16 are from Lux v.d. Blankenburg but not through Alto v. Sigalsburg, or from Lux' sire Burschel v. Simmenau. Most if not all of these last probably trace to Troll in some way or other.) And finally, before leaving Troll we should mention his litter out of Hela v. Goetterfelsen, a bitch of the Parthengrund strain, which included Astor, Alli and Anita v. Goldgrund. Astor was the sire (out of Blanka v. Halberstadt, a daughter of Hela and so his half-sister) of Ch. Fedor v. Buetersberg and his two sisters Flora and Freia v. Buetersberg (both dams of American champions). Anita was the dam of Ch. Anzac of Pontchartrain and several producers, while Ch. Alli v. Goldgrund was the dam of five champions by Prinz Favoriet v.d. Koningstad. This Favoriet-Alli litter was remarkable also for the fact that two of its members, Ch. Alli of Rhinegold and Ch. Carlo of Rhinegold, were winners dog and bitch at Westminster in 1928, the first such win by a litter brother and sister. Their achievement was repeated in 1936, when Ch. Nabob and Ch. Nana of Rhinegold, grandchildren of Ch. Alli of Rhinegold, were winners at Morris and Essex. Writing in 1930 in the American Kennel Gazette, Paul T.

Foley, then secretary of the Doberman Club of America, recalled Carlo as the best shower he remembered. Through his granddaughter, Toby v. Pohlindorf, Carlo appears three times in the pedigree of two recent champions, Komet and Kana of Pontchartrain.

The sensational bitch Mia v. Stresow, who won the Siegerin title in 1925 and 1926, was Best of Breed at Westminster in 1927 but left no important progeny. Ch. Fedor v. Buetersberg, although he sired the 1929 German Sieger Dankwart v. Erzgebirge, produced nothing of importance in this country. When Dankwart was later imported, although he sired three champion daughters he failed to carry on any better than his sire. Two American-bred champions who finished in 1927 were Max v. Strossen and Carlo v. Belger, both descendants of the early pre-war stock combined with later importations. More important from a breeding point of view, however, was Ch. Dietrich v.d. Barbarossahoehle, a son of Alto v. Sigalsburg (by Lux v.d. Blankenburg) out of Dilly v. Stolzenberg, another sister to Asta and Bella v. Stolzenberg. Dilly was an excellent producer and her son Edel v.d. Barbarossahoehle, a full brother to Dietrich, was an important sire in Switzerland. After winning his championship in 1927 at the age of three years, Dietrich apparently dropped out of sight. In 1932, when he was seven years old, he was acquired by the Dawn Kennels and thereafter sired eight champions and nine other producers, while a tenth non-champion producer came from the one earlier litter he is known to have sired in 1928. It was indeed a pity that a dog with such ability to transmit his good qualities was not available for use when in his prime. His son Ch. Dietrich of Dawn, whelped when his sire was within a few weeks of his ninth birthday, sired four champions, two of them out of his full sisters. Ch. Lady Lyle of Avernus (by Dietrich v.d. Barbarossahoehle) was the dam of three champions; his son Ch. Sona Dietrich v. Gragg sired two; and his daughter, Ch. Navigator's Girl, through her daughters, Lone Gold and Ch. Countess of Navigator, has many champion descendants.

Before leaving the year 1927 we ought to mention Rappo v.d. Blankenburg who finished his championship in that year at the age of nine! Rappo was by Graf Belling v. Berlin who was whelped in 1911 and thus goes far back to the early days of the breed. Rappo's dam was Asta Voss, a daughter of Edelblut v. Jaegerhof and one of the great producing bitches of Germany whose notable get included Lux v.d. Blankenburg, Leddy v.d. Blankenburg, Troll v.d. Blankenburg and Anita v.d. Blankenburg. He was mated at least twice in Germany, producing Asta v.d. Finohoehe out of his half-sister Leddy v. Blankenburg and Cora v.d. Eckhardtsburg out of Senta v. Gross Berlin. Asta became the paternal granddam of Comtess v. Steyerberg the dam of 1928 Sieger Ch. Hamlet v. Herthasee. Hamlet was an important sire whose get included a Sieger, two Siegerins and the dam of Ch. Blank v.d. Domstadt, one of the most influential American sires of the past two decades and a brother to Sieger Blitz v.d. Domstadt who remained in Germany. Cora v.d. Eckhardtsburg, the other Rappo daughter, was the dam of Asta v.d. Panke, a brown bitch owned by H. D. Anderson in Russia who later came to California. She was the dam of Ch. Druska v. Riga, Valuta v. Riga and Valuta v.d. Blankenburg and through Valuta v. Riga was the granddam of Ch. Altara v. Riga. Ch. Altara, sired by Alto v. Sigalsburg, was the dam of seven champions and five other producers, the granddam of at least nine champions, and one of the outstanding bitches of the early 1930s.

By 1928 the heavy importation of outstanding German winners had told. From 1923 to 1927 six leading German judges had officiated at American shows, and American breeders were acquiring the knowledge and experience to utilize the available material. Their homebreds were going to the top in the show ring and the proportion of imported champions dropped steadily. On four occasions from 1926 to 1930 American-breds were exhibited with success at German shows. Although a trickle of importations continued until 1939 they became relatively scarce.

Among the important kennels of this period may be men-

INT. CH. DIXIE VON MANNERHEIM
Sire: Ch. Cognac von Glenhugel   Dam: Aris of Pontchartrain
Breeder-Owner: Dr. Wilfrid E. Shute, London, Canada

tioned White Gate, Westphalia (still in existence in 1951), Pontchartrain (whose owner Glen Staines died July 7, 1951), Rhinegold, and Dawn. Later came Glenwood, Milde, Oxbo, Schroth, Rogerschmidt, Plantation Grove, Randhof, Silvergate and still later Glenhugel, Coldod, Millsdod, Damasyn, Elblac and Jerry Run.

Ch. Burschel v. Falkensee, who finished in 1927, was a son of Alto v. Sigalsburg out of a Troll v.d. Blankenburg daughter. Both sire and dam were grandchildren of Burschel v. Simmenau. Ch. Burschel v. Falkensee sired four champions and had a total of fifteen champion grandchildren. His son Ch. Graf v. Blankenburg, the California-bred son of Siegerin Bona v. Deckersburg, was himself the sire of six champions. Graf's line carried down to the present time through Krag v.d. Schroth, Byng v. Reichter and Erlheim's Rameses. A Graf daughter, Ch. Frieda v. Blankenburg (out of Ch. Altara v. Riga) was the dam of Ch. Midi of Silvergate who was mated to her great grand-sire Ch. Burschel v. Falkensee and produced Ch. Baron of Silvergate, the sire of three champions. Ch. Frieda was also the dam of Ch. Apollo of Silvergate, whose sire was Troll-Son v.d. Blankenburg. These dogs were owned on the West Coast. Ch. Baron of Silvergate sired Kurt v. Homburg whose son Ch. Koenig v. Heimdall sired four champions including the prepotent bitch Ch. Hannchen v. Gruenewald. Hannchen's dam, Cita v. Reyno, was by Hamlet v. Herthasee out of Lotte v. Berghofen, an imported daughter of Sieger Gerd v. Sporthof out of a Lux daughter. Although she never became a champion herself and had no champion get, Lotte was the dam of four producers, all by different sires, and had six champion grandchildren, and four other producing grandchildren of whom Ella v. Falkenstein was the most important. Ch. Hannchen v. Gruenewald was the dam of Ch. Votan v. Gruenewald II and of Isolde v. Gruenewald whose get includes one champion and the dams of two others, all bred by Damasyn Kennels.

1930 saw more than 150 Dobermans entered at the specialty Show in spite of the depression, while registrations for the year were 581. This was a tremendous in-

286

crease from ten years before when the year's total was only 56, though it looks small in comparison to the 3,704 registrations of 1950!

In 1930 the breed lost a good one in Ch. Anzac of Pontchartrain, a son of Lux and Anita v. Goldgrund (litter sister to the excellent producer Ch. Alli v. Goldgrund) who died shortly after completing his championship at the age of two. Anzac's litter brother Mikosch of Pontchartrain never finished, but he proved a fairly successful sire, carrying on through ten sons and daughters although only Elma of Middletown and Princess Pan of Pontchartrain became champions.

In 1931 old Lux v.d. Blankenburg himself died at the age of nearly thirteen years. Although he did not become a Sieger until 1923 when he was almost five years old, Lux was a sire of such tremendous dominance that in four years he sired the winners of six Sieger and Siegerin titles (Mia v. Stresow won twice), while 19 of his get became American champions and 20 more had champion descendants. Indeed, it is unlikely that there is a winning Doberman today without at least one line to Lux. Lux is described as somewhat loose in shoulder and too light in muzzle, as well as lacking sufficient depth of brisket. His progeny varied widely in quality, for he was used heavily at stud to all sorts and types of bitches. A slow maturer, he did not achieve fame until he was more than four years old. In America he was owned by Glen Staines of the Pontchartrain Kennels in Detroit. Out of the 245 Dobermans who finished their American championships from 1946 through 1950 more than half (134) trace in male line to Lux and many trace to him several times over. Of his tail male descendants, all but nine out of 134 trace through Alto v. Sigalsburg, whose dam, Lotte v. Roeneckenstein, seems to have surpassed even Asta Voss and Asta v. Starkenburg in prepotency. Her progeny included Sieger Alto v. Sigalsburg and his litter brother Ari. Lux II v. Simmenau and Lotte II v. Simmenau, the latter, though not a Siegerin, considered by some the best of the four, were also by Lux v.d. Blankenburg. Sieger Modern v. Simmenau and his litter brother Ch. Mars v. Simmenau were out of Lotte v. Roeneckenstein by the Lux son Lux v. Treidelschloss.

Sieger Hamlet v. Herthasee, who finished his American championship in 1931, was a son of Sieger Alto v. Sigalsburg. He sired the 1930 and 1932 red Sieger, Ikos v. Siegestor and 1930 red Siegerin Alraune v. Abendrot, as well as the 1931 black and tan Siegerin Bessie v. Brandenburg. His American-bred get included Ch. Reinhardt of Randhof, the sire of four champions, but his best producers were the imported Ch. Hans v. Tannenhaus and Cora v. Ruppertsburg, responsible for six and seven champions respectively, while Cora in addition left a Sieger son, Blitz v.d. Domstadt, behind her in Germany. Hans sired the 1933 red Siegerin Ella v. Graf Zeppelin and her litter sister Ch. Erna v. Graf Zeppelin, the latter being the dam of three champions. However, Hans seems to be carrying most strongly through his daughter Ch. Asta v. Oxbo, dam of Ch. King Adam v. Wagner, and through his imported daughter Asta v. Ulmer Spatz, dam of Ch. Gretl v. Kienlesberg whose three champion daughters, Dow's Cassie v. Kienlesberg, Dow's Cora v. Kienlesberg, and Assy v. Illerblick have three champions apiece to their credit. Ch. Gretl was by Cherloc v. Rauhfelsen, a son of Helios v. Siegestor and Prinzess v. Simmenau. This latter bitch was a daughter of Lotte v. Roeneckenstein by Kunz v. Roedeltal, a Lux v.d. Blankenburg son whose dam, Fee v. Roedeltal also produced Ch. Luz v. Roedeltal the sire of Sieger Muck Brunia and his sister Siegerin Mona v. Brunia. Cherloc was sold to Italy before his full value was realized, for besides Gretl v. Kienlesberg, whose early death was a sad loss to the breed, he was the sire of Ch. Jessy v.d. Sonnenhoehe. The greatest producing bitch in America to date, Jessy was best of breed at the Sieger shown for two successive years and was outstanding in every way. Before leaving Germany she was bred to Ch. Troll v.d. Engelsburg and produced in one litter the 1938 Sieger and Siegerin Ferry and Freya v. Rauhfelsen. In America she had six champions by Pericles of Westphalia and six more by Pericles' sire Ch. Kurt v.d. Rheinperle, making a record total of fourteen, while she has no less than forty-five champion grandchildren! Jessy's son Ch. Westphalia's Uranus (by Pericles) sired eleven champions, and Sieger Ferry v. Rauhfelsen and Ch. Westphalia's Rameses sired eight each, while her leading daughter, Ch. Westphalia's Rhemba, produced five. All this within sixteen years, for Jessy was not whelped until 1934.

With the advent of Obedience Training it was natural that the Doberman, with his long tradition of police work, should be a prominent contender. In 1929 these classes were a popular feature of the annual specialty show, where they were won by Aristo v. Ernst. The Doberman Pinscher Club of America has actively promoted Obedience Training and a considerable number of bench show winners are also the holders of training titles in this country, while in Germany a training degree is required of all Siegers. Obedience trained champions of the past few years include Ch. Danny v. Neckerheim C.D.X.; Ch. Gessner's Happy Jack C.D.; Ch. Schuffman's Seego C.D.; Ch. Elblac's Blitz C.D. whose sire Blitz v. Lauderbach U.D.T. and dam Spar of Elblac C.D. were both obedience trained; Ch. Elblac's Electra C.D. (daughter of Ulania of Elblac C.D.X.); Ch. Westphalia's Rameses C.D.X.; Ch. Linda of Lindengrus C.D.X.; Ch. Remus zur Bremengenhoff C.D.X.; Ch. Sieg v. Glenhugel. U.D.; Ch. Koline of Rancho Dobe C.D.; Ch. Bengel v. Grosshugel C.D.X.; Ch. Su-Deb's Daphne C.D.; and Ch. Wave v. Mulna U.D.—all proof that type and brains may be found in the same individual.

One of the outstanding American-bred bitches of this period was Ch. Tolla of Pontchartrain who won the Gisela v. Sporthof Trophy in 1930 for the bitch winning most points during the year, but died young in 1932. Tolla was a daughter of Ch. Figaro v. Sigalsburg, a son of Sieger Alto v. Sigalsburg and Siegerin Asta v. Stolzenberg. Figaro resembled his maternal grandsire, the robust and substantial Troll v.d. Blankenburg, and was the sire of fourteen champions. Figaro's get included Ch. Princess Flora of Pontchartrain (out of Ch. Tilly v. Melrap, a triple great grand-

289

daughter of Asta Voss), who was the dam of five champions, Ch. Figaro of Pontchartrain the sire of three, and imported Ch. Boby v. Hohenzollernpark the sire of seven. Boby's dam was Corina v. Sigalsburg, litter sister to Ch. Claus v. Sigalsburg, who was out of Figaro's dam by Lux v.d. Blankenburg, Figaro's paternal grandsire. Boby's best son, Ch. Carlo v. Bassewitz, carried on the inbreeding, for he was out of a daughter of Alto v. Sigalsburg, Fiffi v. Heimfeld, whose own dam was a granddaughter of Troll v.d. Blankenburg. Carlo v. Bassewitz sired thirteen champions, but seems to have carried on in male line only through Ch. Carlo of Bolcefield, whose son Ch. Carlo of Bolcefield II sired Chs. Cy and Cantor of Dobe Haven. Carlo v. Bassewitz' daughters include Kitty v. Theuer whose son Blitz v. Lauderbach is the paternal grandsire of Ch. Elblac's Blitz; Ch. Elsa v. Coldod, dam of Ch. Fritz v. Waltberg; and most important of all, Ch. Maida v. Coldod, dam of three champions including the outstanding Ch. Alcor v. Millsdod.

Ch. Kanzler v. Sigalsburg, who was by Figaro's sire Alto out of Fee v.d. Barbarossahoehle (by the Alto son Jockel v. Lobenstein out of Dilly v. Stolzenberg, full sister to Figaro's dam) sired five champions but with one exception, does not seem to be carrying on successfully. His son Bubi v. Verstaame (out of Lady Marta of Pontchartrain) sired the notable Ch. Edah v. Trail, dam of seven champions, five of them sons.

A dog who seems to have escaped the attention he deserved is Ch. Dewald v. Ludwigsburg. Whelped late in 1928, he finished his American championship in 1933, and was probably imported early the previous year, since his registration was published in June 1932. Dewald was owned by the Mildes of Chicago and his use seems to have been confined to that area and largely to his own kennel. He was both a Canadian and an American champion, and his picture shows a cleanly built, attractive dog with what looks like unusually good shoulder angulation. His American get included seven champions, six of them bitches, while he left behind him in Germany the dam of a double Siegerin. Nevertheless, although this would seem to suggest that Dewald

290

CHAMPION QUO SHMERK V. MARIENLAND
Sire: Emperor of Marienland   Dam: Fair to Middlin' of Marienland
Breeder: Marienland Kennel
Owner: W. H. Roach, Oklahoma City, Oklahoma

excelled as a sire of daughters the fact remains that two of his sons have carried on in male line and that among the sires of champions finished during the past five years are three grandsons and a great grandson. His grandchildren included fifteen champions. It is only necessary to state that Dewald's German-bred producing daughter was Alice (called Bella) v.d. Sonnenhoehe, the dam of the phenomenal producing bitch Siegerin Jessy v.d. Sonnenhoehe to understand both the high quality of Dewald's heredity and the opportunities which were lost by not utilizing his services more fully. In explanation, however, it should be pointed out that Jessy did not make her first Siegerin title until Dewald was already seven years old, and her tremendous breeding value did not become clearly apparent until later still, for none of her winning get were whelped until 1937. By the time Jessy's value became obvious it was too late to take advantage of her sire's prepotency.

Dewald was a son of Stolz v. Roeneckenstein and Cilly v. Rheinadler, the latter an Alto v. Sigalsburg daughter. His most successful mating was with the imported Kitty v.d. Residenz, which gave Ch. Maedchen v. Milde (the dam of five champions in one litter by Ch. Curt v.d. Schwarzwaldperle) and then to his granddaughter Ch. Hesta v. Gerdts (from the Curt-Maedchen litter) which produced his most prepotent son, Ch. Graf v. Gerdts. Graf (inbred to Dewald and carrying an additional line to Stolz v. Roeneckenstein through his dam's sire, the Helios v. Siegestor son Curt v.d. Schwarzwaldperle, as well as further Alto v. Sigalsburg and Troll v.d. Blankenburg through Curt's dam Adda v. Bad Heidelberg), sired seven champions. Four of them were out of two different Curt v.d. Schwarzwaldperle daughters, three out of Ch. Troll v.d. Engelsburg daughters, while the non-champion Hallwyre Hi-Chick, who sired three champions, was out of a Troll granddaughter. The dams of five of Graf's champions plus the granddam of Hi-Chick were also out of Ch. Countess of Navigator, a Canadian-bred daughter of Ch. Dietrich v.d. Barbarossahoehle.

Dewald's daughter Ch. Altara v. Milde and a non-champion son Itel v. Milde were out of the bitch Patricia v. Milde, a

292

daughter of Ch. Elmar v.d. Rheinperle, who has already been mentioned as the dam of Rolf v. Milde by Ch. Carol v. Oevanes. Itel sired Carla v. Falkenstein, the dam of one champion, and Gustl v. Falkenstein, the sire of three champions and two producers, and the Dewald male line was continued through Gustl's son Alex v. Falkenstein, whose dam was Ella v. Falkenstein, by Ch. Gustl v. Bad Heidelberg (whose sire was a brother to Adda v. Bad Heidelberg's sire and whose dam was a daughter of Helios v. Siegestor.)

It is clearly apparent that Dewald has carried on most successfully in combination with Helios v. Siegestor and Troll v.d. Blankenburg blood. It seems probable that a combination of Dewald with strong Helios through Gretl v. Kienlesberg or still better Jessy v.d. Sonnenhoehe should prove advantageous.

In addition to Astor of Westphalia who has already been discussed, two grandsons of Stolz v. Roeneckenstein, both by Helios v. Siegestor, have had tail male descendants siring champions of the past five years. They are Ch. Curt v.d. Schwarzwaldperle and Ch. Jockel v. Burgund. Both had excellent show records in Germany, although Jockel was set down at the Sieger Show for being over size. Jockel had a dazzling American career, winning the Group every time but one in twenty times shown (the exception being Westminster, where he was Best of Breed), and going on to Best in Show thirteen times. His dam was Jessy v. Lobenstein, a bitch who was also the granddam of Ch. Ossi v. Stahlhelm, the prepotent dam of seven Glenhugel champions, including Dictator. Jessy v. Lobenstein's dam was Hedda v. Margetenhof, a double granddaughter of Isolde v. Coeln (who was by the nearly perfect brown Marko v. Leutzellinden, otherwise known as Marko v. Hoernsheim and Marko v. Jaegerhof, the maternal grand sire of Edelblut v. Jaegerhof). Jockel v. Burgund sired four champions in America and his imported son Ch. Klaus v. Bayernstolz carried down the male line through Ch. Dietrich v. Koenigsheim (sire of three champions) and his son Ch. Alex v. Trail (sire of one). Curt v.d. Schwarzwaldperle, out of the double Alto v. Sigalsburg granddaughter Adda v. Bad Heidelberg (who

293

was also the dam of Ch. Olga v. Milde and the granddam of Ch. Kleta v.d. Schwarzwaldperle) had a more impressive record as a sire, with a total of thirteen champions, the last sired in 1941 when he was more than eight years old, but thus far none of his sons has carried on his record.

During the 1920s and 1930s a majority of Siegers and Siegerins found their way to this country. Sieger Modern v. Simmenau and his litter brother Mars were only moderately successful at stud, although Modern, through his mating to Ch. Alli of Rhinegold carries down via their daughter Chika of Silvergate to Heidi v. Heimdall, dam of Ch. Koenig v. Heimdall and others. Heidi's sire was Ch. Prinz Carlo of Plantation Grove, by Ch. Prinz Noah of Pontchartrain (the best American-bred son of Lux v.d. Blankenburg) out of Jouca of Middletown, a daughter of Ch. Rival v. Kranichstein who produced two champions and seven producers. Ch. Boby v. Hohenzollernpark and Ch. Kanzler v. Sigalsburg, Sieger in 1930 and 1931, have already been mentioned. They were followed by Sieger Muck v. Brunia, Sieger in 1932, Troll v.d. Engelsburg, winner of Best of Breed in 1934 and 1935, Moritz v. Roedeltal and Ferry v. Rauhfelsen. The Siegerins Bessie v. Brandenburg, Inita zur Immermannhoehe, Ella v. Graf Zepellin, Asta v.d. Domstadt, Jessy v.d. Sonnenhoehe, Ossi v. Stahlhelm were likewise imported during the 1930s. To these importations should be added a few others who proved important—the Dutch Ch. Carol v. Oevanes, Ch. Mona v.d. Rheinperle, Ch. Klaus v. Bayernstolz (a son of Ch. Jockel v. Burgund), Ch. Blank v.d. Domstadt, Ch. Carlo v. Fasanenheim, Ch. Roland v. Stahlhelm, Ch. Kleta v.d. Schwarzwaldperle, Ch. Ora v. Sandberg, and Ch. Assy v. Illerblick. Assy, who finished in 1941, was the last imported champion until 1950.

Troll v.d. Engelsburg was the outstanding sire of Germany from 1935 until he left for America in 1937. He was bred to all the best bitches, and his get dominated the Sieger Show of 1938, including the winning dog and bitch, Ferry and Freya v. Rauhfelsen, out of Jessy v. Lobenstein. Troll also sired the 1937 red Siegerin Ossi v. Stahlhelm, whose dam was Kleopatra v. Burgund, by Helios v. Siegestor out of Siegerin Freya v. Burgund. His show record in Germany was phenomenal, including two German Sieger titles and World Sieger, while over here he became a Canadian as well as an American champion, was 45 times Best of Breed, 34 times first in the Group, and 20 times Best in Show. His German get included the only World Siegerin, Alfa v. Hollingen and the American champions Kleta v.d. Schwarzwaldperle, Mona v.d. Rheinperle, Roland v. Stahlhelm and Kitty v. Hagenstolz. Altogether Troll sired thirteen American champions, five of which were American-bred, and ten others, eight of them American-bred, which appear in the pedigrees of champions of the last dozen years. Troll's dam was Adda v. Heek by Sieger Artus v. Thümshoehe, a Lux v.d. Blankenburg son who was a double grandson of Asta Voss. His sire was Sieger Muck v. Brunia who traces in male line to Lux v.d. Blankenburg through Ch. Luz v. Roedeltal and Alto v. Sigalsburg. Troll's most successful son has been Ferry v. Rauhfelsen, whose eight American champions and six producers exceed Troll's American-bred record. Ferry's three sons, Ch. Otto of Navigator, Ch. Baron of Lakewood and his grandson Ch. Danny v. Neckerheim (by Ch. Terry v. Neckerheim) account between them for eleven champions of the past five years. Another Troll son, Micah Birchwood v.d. Troll, sired a champion daughter, but though Troll has many champion descendants only Ferry seems to be carrying on in male line. Probably unique among American champions in its intense inbreeding is the pedigree of Ch. Thunderbolt v.d. Troll, who completed his championship in 1946. In 1938 Troll was bred to his half-sister, the Muck daughter Siegerin Asta v.d. Domstadt. Their daughter, Cissie v.d. Troll, was bred back to her sire and produced Missy Asta v.d. Troll in 1941. Finally, when Troll was nine and half years old he was mated to Missy Asta in 1943 and produced the son Ch. Thunderbolt.

Ch. Luz v. Roedeltal, who made his American championship in 1934 at the age of eight years, was a son of Alto v. Sigalsburg and Fee v. Roedeltal (a daughter of Faust v.d. Pleissenburg by Zeus v. Parthengrund) who was also the dam of the 1927 Siegerin Kitty v. Roedeltal. A Luz daughter, Bubina Deutschen Eck, was the dam of Sieger Moritz v. Roedeltal. This was decidedly a long-lived strain. Luz sired three American champions at eight and nine years of age, his son Udo v. Guestfalia sired two champions in his eighth year, another son, Sieger Muck Brunia, sired two champions in his eleventh year and one in his twelfth, and Muck's son Ch. Blank v.d. Domstadt sired his best son, Ch. Dictator v. Glenhugel at eight and half. Dictator, still vigorous at ten years old, already has a son, Ch. Ivan v. Trail, whelped when he was eight.

Sieger Muck v. Brunia came to America at the age of three, but managed to leave behind him two Sieger sons, Troll v.d. Egelsburg and Blitz v.d. Domstadt. His dam, Hella v.d. Winterburg, was a granddaughter of Sieger Benno v. Roemerhof who in everything but name belonged to the Dutch Köningstad strain. Her sire, Axel v. Haardtgebirge, was out of an Edelblut v. Jaegerhof daughter and was descended in male line from Lord v. Ried. Muck sired ten American-bred champions, five of them from a single litter out of Cora v.d. Ruppertsburg. The best of them was Ch. Falko v. Lindenhof, but he has not reproduced. Chs. Falk, Flaemmchen and Indra v. Lindenhof, and the non-champion Inka v. Lindenhof had a champion apiece. Indra's daughter, Ch. Maedl v. Randhof, by a son of Ferry v. Rauhfelsen, has three champion daughters bred by Rancho Dobe Kennels. Inka v. Lindenhof was the dam of Ch. Maida v. Coldod, whose two litters by Ch. Westphalia's Uranus included Ch. Merak v. Millsdod, Ch. Anieka v. Millsdod and Ch. Alcor v. Millsdod.

Muck's son Sieger Blitz v.d. Domstadt was the only outstanding male of the middle 1930s who remained in Germany. His brother Blank v.d. Domstadt was inferior to Blitz as a show dog but surpassed him as a sire. He made his championship in 1936 and is credited with thirteen American-bred champions and two imported sons, Sieger Moritz v. Roedeltal and Ch. Carlo v. Fasanenheim. Moritz, although he was criticized in Germany for tooth faults, is credited with seven champions and seven other producers, the best being the noted winner Ch. Ora v. Sandberg Lindenhof, Best Doberman twenty-five times and group winner nineteen times,

296

CH. SINGENWALDS PRINCE KUHIO
Best in Show winner, and one of the Top Ten Working Dogs in America
for 1962 and 1963. Sire of 27 champions. Owned by Mrs. Beatrice
Rickert of Angola, Ind., and handled by George Rood.

with three Best in Show awards during her first year in this country. Ora's dam was World Siegerin Alfa v. Hollingen (by Troll v.d. Engelsburg out of a Troll granddaughter), therefore, Ora carries three lines to Muck v. Brunia. Moritz' other imported daughter is Ch. Assy v. Illerblick, out of Ch. Gretl v. Kienlesberg. His son Ch. Punjab v. Lindengrus was sired when he was nine years old.

Blank's unique claim to fame, however, is his matings to Siegerin Ossi v. Stahlhelm, a daughter of Troll v.d. Engelsburg out of the Helios daughter, Kleoptra v. Burgund, whose granddam Jessy v. Lobenstein was the dam of Ch. Jockel v. Burgund. Ossi was mated to Blank at various times from 1936 to 1941. In six litters she produced a total of eleven champions and five others from whom champions are descended. The best litter contained five champions, Berta, Beth, Bengel and Binchen of Glenhugel, and Domossi of Marienland. This is sufficiently remarkable, but Blank's achievement does not stop there. No other sire has produced eleven champions from a single bitch, but still more striking is the degree to which they have bred on. Blank has no less than 94 champion grandchildren. No less than ten of his fifteen champion sons and daughters and seven non-champions have one or more champions each, while one additional champion has a champion granddaughter.

Blank is preeminently a sire of producing sons. Only five of his daughters are champions, compared to ten of his sons, and none of the daughters has produced more than two champions. On the other hand, eight sons have sired three or more champions each. Ch. Bengel v. Grosshugel sired three; Ch. Sieg v. Glenhugel four, Ch. Clipper v. Glenhugel five, Ch. Count Leo v.d Domstadt seven, Ch. Domossi of Marienland *twenty*, and Ch. Dictator v. Glenhugel the astounding number of *thirty-seven*—the record for the breed. Count Leo was out of the first Blank-Ossi litter, whelped in 1936, Domossi was in 1939, and Dictator in 1941, when Blank had already passed his eighth birthday.

World War II played a decisive part in the development

298

of the modern Doberman. In 1939, importations, which had dwindled to a trickle, ceased entirely. During the next ten years breeders were thrown entirely upon their own resources, but these were ample. Given the cream of the German dogs of the previous twenty years—a period in which Alto v. Sigalsburg and Alex v.d. Finohoehe were almost the only top ranking sires who never reached these shores—the highest accomplishment was possible and was dependent only on the skill of the breeders in selecting and combining their material. When the latest German winners no longer claimed the spotlight and the older importations had most of them had their day, American-bred sires of the finest bloodlines were available to take over. With unrivalled opportunity to demonstrate what they could produce, these dogs amply fulfilled the demands made upon them.

A considerable period of time is necessary before it is possible to adequately assess the long term value of any sire. Ten or twelve years is a minimum requirement and even then subsequent events may modify previous conclusions. It is not a sire's popularity in his own lifetime but the ability of his descendants to carry on down the generations which determines his final rank. Witness, for instance, Alex v.d. Finohoehe, who was largely overlooked in his own day in Germany and was sold to Czechoslovakia for a song, yet as the sire of Lotte and Stolz v. Roeneckenstein became one of the dominant influences upon future generations. Through his son Stolz, Alex heads the male lines of almost half today's champions, while the far more famous Prinz Carlo v.d. Koningstad, though his blood is widely diffused, is entirely lacking in tail male descendants. For this reason no final assessment of the dogs of ten or twelve years ago can yet be made, although the general pattern is too clear to make any drastic change seem likely.

The two dominant male lines of the 1940's trace to Blank v.d. Domstadt and Kurt v.d. Rheinperle. Blank goes in male line to Alto v. Sigalsburg and Lux v.d. Blankenburg; Kurt to Stolz v. Roeneckenstein and Alex v.d. Finohoehe. ALL the champions since 1945 trace in male line to Stolz or Burschel v. Simmenau (the sire of Lux v.d. Blankenburg). Muck v. Brunia was whelped in the same year as Astor of Westphalia (the half American-bred Helios v. Siegestor son out of the American born Siegerin Ilisa of Westphalia), who has done most to carry on the Stolz v. Roeneckenstein line. Stolz himself, like his sire Alex, seems to have had his value recognized too late, after the success of his son Helios and the phenomenal record of Alto v. Sigalsburg who was out of Stolz' sister. Helios was out of Ella v. Siegestor, who carried good blood through her dam Thessa v. Ostersee, an Edelblut daughter out of the prepotent Freya v. Ostersee (who combined the Ilm Athen blood of Waldo v. Strengbach with the double Lord v. Ried granddaughter Wanda Knoll). Ella v. Siegestor's sire was Bluto v. Isarstrand, a son of the severely criticized Roland v.d. Haide, who is generally considered to have done the breed no good. However, despite her sire's somewhat dubious heredity Ella was able to produce Sieger Ikos v. Siegestor when mated to Hamlet v. Herthasee, and Ikos in turn produced the dam of the 1938 red Siegerin Kleta v.d. Schwarzwaldperle. The fact that Ada v.d. Adelshoehe, the dam of Cora v. Ruppertsburg, was a granddaughter of Thessa v. Ostersee and that the latter's litter sister, Thela v. Ostersee, was the granddam of Sieger Apollo v. Schuetzeneck attests the hereditary value of this line. Unfortunately these excellently bred Ostersee bitches were usually combined with strong breeding to Roland v.d. Haide and his son Salto v. Rottal, so that their usefulness was greatly impaired. That they carried on as they have in spite of this handicap speaks volumes for their worth.

Helios v. Siegestor was the subject of controversy as a young dog because while beautifully correct in type he had several cream-colored toes on one of his hind feet. Despite this tendency to a color defect (or in some cases a missing toe) on the right hind foot of Dora v. Wiesengrund's descendants, the sum total of their quality is so tremendously great that the fault, though it has to be

MARC ZORN OF SOLBO
Sire of Ch. Marc's Diana of Solbo
"Solbo" means "Sunny Home" in Swedish
Owner: Margit Anderson, Chicago, Illinois

reckoned with, especially when inbreeding, is outweighed by the preponderating values of the line. Helios, although he sired the record breaking bench winner Jockel v. Burgund and the apparently more prepotent Ch. Curt v.d. Schwarzwaldperle, holds his place today as one of the two dominating tail male lines through his non-champion son Astor of Westphalia and this entirely through Astor's son Ch. Kurt v.d. Rheinperle, a dog who despite his title was described twenty years ago as "not prepossessing in appearance and indifferently successful in the show ring; nevertheless, due to his heredity has had a large measure of success at stud." This is certainly faint praise for the sire of twenty champions (the first individual of the breed to attain that figure and great grandsire of one of the two later dogs who have surpassed it), but it is proof were any needed that the prepotency which enables a dog to transmit outstanding quality is not necessarily linked to top performance in the ring. Nevertheless, though a great sire need not be in the top flight of show performers he needs to be good, and to carry close behind him the high quality which he is expected to hand on. It must not be forgotten that Kurt's dam was the Siegerin Anita zur Immermannhoehe, whose own pedigree was an imposing one. Anita was by Bodo v. Siegerpark whose sire was by Troll v.d. Blankenburg while his dam was Elfe v.d. Rheinperle, a sister to Ch. Elmar v.d. Rheinperle. Anita's dam, Asta v. Burghofplatz, was by Sieger Benno v. Roemerhof (whose blood of the Dutch Koningstad strain was identical with that carried by Kurt's great granddam Ch. Prinzessin Ilisa v.d. Koningstad) out of Anneliesel v.d. Düsselquelle (also called Anneliesel Niessen, under which name she came to America and made her championship in 1926), who carried the rare but highly esteemed Rheinerft blood.

Kurt v.d. Rheinperle undoubtedly owed a great measure of his extraordinary success to two factors. One was the knowledge and breeding skill gained by more than fifteen years experience at Westphalia Kennels. The other was Jessy v.d. Sonnenhoehe. Jessy had already produced a sieger and siegerin from her mating to Troll v.d. Engelsburg. Troll and his sire Muck were both at stud in this country. Nevertheless, Jessy was mated in 1939 to the far less prominent Kurt, producing a litter of seven champions in 1938, while fourteen months later she was mated to Pericles of Westphalia, an unknown two year old son of Kurt who never made his championship. Pericles was a double grandson of Kurt's sire Astor of Westphalia, and carried in addition on his dam's side, through Ch. Big Boy of White Gate, the same combination of Claus v.d. Spree and Koningstad blood which Astor received from his dam Siegerin Ilisa of Westphalia, plus two further lines to Edelblut. Six out of the seven champions which Pericles sired were out of this mating to Jessy, as were all his producers except the non-champion Sandra Helveron, whose dam was by the Kurt v.d. Rheinperle son Ch. Napier of Rhinegold.

Jessy's forty-five champion grandchildren were all but eight (sired by Ferry v. Rauhfelsen) from individuals whelped in these two matings, and the balance between them is still fairly even. If the Kurt litter has the larger total—twenty-three champions from six individuals (three sons and three daughters)—the Pericles litter scores in that it contained Ch. Westphalia's Uranus, whose eleven champions (out of fifteen for this whole litter) is the highest number for a single individual. If the average number of champion get for the R litter (by Kurt) was four each for six individuals as against four and two thirds for three individuals in the Pericles litter on the one hand, on the other hand, out of seven champions in the R litter six have carried on, while out of six champions in the U litter only three produced champion get, though a fourth had one champion grandson. Nevertheless, Uranus' achievement was so outstanding that it probably outweighs the combined record of the R litter, for among his eleven champion get were three outstanding stud dogs— Ch. Kama of Westphalia the sire of seven champions; Ch. Favoriet v. Franzhof, the sire of thirteen and topping them all, Ch. Alcor v. Millsdod, the sire of twenty-six. And it should be noted in passing that Uranus was the only champion male in his litter, while the R litter contained three. Westphalia's Rameses was the sire of nine champions; Raswan and Rajah the sires of four each, and a sister, Ch. Westphalia's Rembha produced five champions while establishing a noteworthy show record as well.

Alcor v. Millsdod's dam, Ch. Maida v. Coldod, was sired by Ch. Carlo v. Bassewitz, who was by the Figaro v. Sigalsburg son, Sieger Boby v. Hohenzollernpark out of an Alto v. Sigalsburg daughter. Her dam, Inka v. Lindenhof, was a younger full sister to Ch. Blank v.d. Domstadt. Maida's rank as a producer is high and would perhaps rival other great bitches of the breed if she had had more ample opportunity. Her first litter contained Alcor and his brother Ch. Merak v. Millsdod, the remainder being sold as pets and neither shown nor bred from. When nearly nine she was bred back to Uranus and whelped a single bitch puppy, Ch. Anieka v. Millsdod, whose first litter is still unshown. The fact that Alcor and Merak were both retained by their breeder also had the effect of restricting Merak's opportunities, since breeders in the locality preferred to use his more famous brother. His only reported litter contained two bitches who were the dams of three champions.

Alcor v. Millsdod got a slow start at stud. His first litter was not whelped until he was nearly three years old, so that he was already five when his first two champions appeared. Three more champions were whelped in 1945, four in 1946, and by 1947, the year in which he went Best of Breed at Westminster, his reputation was fully established. In that year he sired fourteen individuals which were to complete their championships, and three more followed in 1948. Ch. Duke v.d. Ravensburg III, who has a record of numerous group wins and three Best in Shows, was out of the third Alcor litter whelped in 1948, when Alcor was seven and a half. A number of his get are still young enough so that his list of winners may still receive further additions. The last litter which he sired, a few months before his death at just short of ten years old, was whelped in 1950 out of his full sister Ch. Anieka v. Millsdod.

Alcor was the first Doberman who was twice Best of Breed at Westminster. He won permanent possession of the Doberman Pinscher Club of America trophy on which the first win was made by his granddam Ch. Jessy v.d. Sonnenhoehe, and his son Ch. Jet v.d. Ravensburg retired the subsequent trophy offered in Alcor's name. Eight Alcor sons and one daughter have gone Best in Show a total of seventeen times. The largest number of wins was scored by Ch. Ardexter v. Valtheim (4), Ch. Duke v.d. Ravensburg III comes second with three, while Ch. Kilburn Conqueror, Ch. Jet v.d. Ravensburg, and Ch. Ranco Dobe's Presto have two wins each. Alcor was shown 53 times, under 47 different judges, and was 44 times Best of Breed, with 15 firsts in the Group and six Bests in Show. He was the first dog to twice win the Doberman Pinscher Club of America Specialty Show, in 1946 and 1948. His litter brother Merak was the only dog to defeat him twice. Alcor sired 61 litters and was evidently a dominant black and tan, for all of his puppies were black and tan, though his brother Merak, with far more limited opportunities, sired some reds. Alcor's most outstanding single litter contained five champions, four of them sons, out of Ch. Dow's Dame of Kilburn, a daughter of Dictator and Ch. Dow's Dodie v. Kienlesberg. Dodie was a daughter of Dictator's older brother, Ch. Domossi of Marienland and Ch. Dow's Cassie v. Kienlesberg, by Kurt v.d. Rheinperle out of Ch. Gretl v. Kienlesberg who was a half-sister to Jessy v.d. Sonnenhoehe. This Alcor-Dame litter contained Chs. Brown's Armand, Archer, Admiral, Achilles, and Adventuress. The bitch, Ch. Brown's Adventuress, was bred at two years old and produced the 1950 champion Berger's Blue-Beard. Another litter by Alcor, out of Ch. Lucinda v. Valtheim (daughter of the Blank v.d. Domstadt son Ch. Carlo v. Fasanenheim) contained four champions, Alcindor, Amneris, Arturo and Ardexter v.d. Valtheim, while a fifth bitch, Alexandrina v.d. Valtheim, lacked only a couple of points needed to finish when she was severely injured while saving a child from the path of a souped-up car.

Two other matings to Alcor produced four champions each, but not in a single litter. Ch. Flora of Collenburg II was the dam of Chs. Jet and Carlo v.d. Ravensburg in one litter and of Chs. Beowulf and Duke v.d. Ravensburg III in a second. She was by Ch. Favoriet v. Franzhof, a Uranus son, out of Frieda v.d. Rheinperle-Musbro, the daughter of Ch. Moritz v. Roedeltal and Ch. Mona v.d. Rheinperle, who was out of Kriemhilde v.d. Rheinperle, a litter sister to Kurt. Three sons, Chs. Kilburn Cameron, Conqueror and Jingo, plus a daughter Ch. Kilburn Jest came from two litters by Alcor out of Ch. Kilburn Audacity. Audacity was by Ch. Emperor of Marienland, a son of Ch. Domossi of Marienland and Ch. Westphalia's Rembha, out of Ch. Dow's Illena of Marienland, who was by Ch. Westphalia's Rameses out of Ch. Dow's Cora v. Kienlesberg, a litter sister to Ch. Dow's Cassie v. Kienlesberg.

Alcor's first champions, Florizel and Francesca of Jerry Run, were out of Ch. Assy v. Illerblick, the imported daughter of Moritz v. Roedeltal and Gretl v. Kienlesberg. All of his champion get were closely related to Alcor on the dam's side, some through Kurt v.d. Rheinperle or Cherloc v. Rauhfelsen (the sire of Jessy v.d. Sonnenhoehe and Gretl v. Kienlesberg), some through Jessy's son Ferry v. Rauhfelsen, and the Westphalia R or U litters, and some through Maida v. Coldod's dam Inka v. Lindenhof, the sister of Blank v.d. Domstadt. In some of the brood bitches these lines have already been combined several times over. The one apparent exception is th litter by Alcor out of Ch. Astrid v. Stifthub which produced Ch. Ascor v. Brauseestadt. Astrid, who was whelped in 1946, made her championship in 1949 and was the first Doberman imported since World War II to do so. She is by Nestor v. Simmenau, a great grandson in tail male of Troll v.d. Engelsburg who carries at least two additional lines to Troll, one of them through Siegerin Freya v. Rauhfelsen, the litter sister to Ch. Ferry v. Rauhfelsen. Since Troll was himself a son of Muck v. Brunia, the sire of Inka v. Lindenhof, Astrid actually goes back to much the same stock as the other bitches mated to Alcor.

Ch. Kilburn Cameron, his oldest champion son, and Ch.

Rancho Dobe's Presto, whelped in June 1947, have each sired three champion daughters. Cameron's litter brother Ch. Kilburn Conqueror has also sired a champion daughter. Most of his other sons are too young to have many get of an age to appear in the ring, so that it is impossible to forecast which ones will carry on the line. Any selection would be no more than a guess.

The brown Ch. Favoriet v. Franzhof was whelped in 1941, the same year as his half-brother Alcor, his dam being Adele v. Meigel, a daughter of Ch. Westphalia's Rajah and the Swiss bitch Toni v.d. Baerenburg. This line through Toni gives Favoriet some excellent blood not generally available, and in his mating to Lona of Somerville, a Toni daughter, this is capitalized to produce Pinckney Farms Ranee, the dam of Ch. Pinckney Farms Archon, a brown like his grandsire Favoriet. Another son, Ch. Christie's Barrier, was the only black and tan in a litter of seven males. Their dam was Ch. Christie v. Klosterholz, a younger full sister to Ch. Kama of Westphalia's dam, Alma v. Molnar. The Swiss line recurs again in the mating of Favoriet to another daughter of Lona of Somerville, Liselotte of Westphalia, who like Favoriet himself was a grandchild of Toni v. Baerenburg but was sired by Ch. Westphalia's Rajah. From this mating came Ch. Gunther v. Westphalia, the sire of two champions, Brenda and Caesar of Vernon View, both out of Dow's Dorette of Kilburn. Caesar of Vernon View and Ch. Helmut v. Klosterholz by Ch. Christie's Barrier carry on the male line from Favoriet v. Franzhof, who sired thirteen champions in all and ranked next to Alcor v. Millsdod among the sons of Ch. Westphalia's Uranus.

Ch. Kama of Westphalia, the third outstanding son of Uranus, was two years younger than Alcor and Favoriet, having been whelped in 1943. His dam, Alma v. Molnar, was by Westphalia's Rajah, as has been mentioned, giving Kama two lines to Kurt v.d. Rheinperle and two to Jessy v.d. Sonnenhoehe. Through her dam, Tessa v. Hirschberg, Alma v. Molnar carried two lines to Claus v.d. Spree (one of them through Big Boy of White Gate) and four to Sieger Benno v. Roemerhof. With four additional lines to

307

CH. HIGHBRIAR WILLO OF ALLENWOOD
Best in Show winner and one of the Top Ten Working Dogs of 1965.
Owned by Betsy R. Thomas of Gambier, Ohio, and
handled by Eugene Haupt.

Prinz Carlo v.d. Köningstad, Tessa, like her sister Ch. Christie v. Klosterholz, is very strong in the Dutch Köningstad strain and entirely lacking in the Blankenburg blood except for a single appearance of Troll v.d. Blankenburg in the sixth generation. This is as complete an outcross as is obtainable anywhere today.

Ch. Westphalia's Rameses, whelped in 1938 by Kurt out of Jessy, sired nine champions, four of which were sons, and fourteen other sons and daughters who left champion descendants. Six of Rameses' sons have champion descendants, but only two of them have sons. Ch. Barney of Nanja heads the list, with two sons, Ch. An-Joe's Anthon and Ch. Amar of Wesley's. Ch. Damon of Jerry Run has a son, Ch. Chance Run's Town Talk, and a daughter, Ch. Chance Run's Roulette. Barney's dam, Nanja's Show Girl, is by Ch. Blixen of Barlynn, a son of Moritz v. Roedeltal. Blixen also sired Angie's Fair Lady, the dam of Ch. An-Joe's Anthon, while the Moritz daughter Gret'l v. Kohlson was the dam of Ch. Amar of Wesley's. Ch. Chance Run's Town Talk is out of Valspar of Sugar Loaf, a daughter of Favoriet v. Franzhof with an additional line through her dam to Westphalia's Rajah, and through her dam's dam two lines to Big Boy of White Gate and one to Asta of Westphalia.

The other line from Kurt v.d. Rheinperle which shows some likelihood of carrying on is that of his son, Ch. Black Ulan v.d. Rheinperle, out of Ch. Mona v.d. Rheinperle. Mona is by Troll v.d. Engelsburg out of Kurt's sister Kriemhilde v.d. Rheinperle, but has no line to Jessy v.d. Sonnenhoehe. Black Ulan sired three champions, two sons and a daughter, while another son and daughter have produced three champions between them. Ulan's daughter Ch. Wave v. Mulna (dam of Ch. Rajah v. Halfritz) and the non-champions Admiral v. Mulna and Ruby Wac v. Mulna were all three out of Mona (without a kennel name), a daughter of Ch. Westphalia's Rameses and Illkie v. Ernharkenburg, a granddaughter of Ch. Dewald v. Ludwigsburg. Admiral v. Mulna sired two champion daughters. The two Ulan champion sons are Charlie Boy v.d. Rheinperle, out of a granddaughter of Ulan's dam and Ch. Wittland's Black

Knight, whose sire is a grandson of Jockel v. Burgund and Ilse v. Lindenhof (litter sister to Ch. Maida v. Coldod's dam) on one side, with Muck v. Brunia, Figaro v. Sigalsburg, and two lines to Ch. Prince Claus of Pontchartrain on the other. The only male line from Helios v. Siegestor via Jockel v. Burgund which seems to be carrying on today goes through Jockel's son Ch. Klaus v. Bayernstolz to Ch. Dietrich v. Koenigsheim and the latter's son Ch. Alex v. Trail, the sire in his turn of the 1950 champion male Colla v. Pittman.

The outstanding group of dogs belonging to the other principal line, that of Blank v.d. Domstadt and his sons who trace in tail male to Lux v.d. Blankenburg, has already been mentioned. Ch. Dictator v. Glennhugel established a breed record of 52 champion progeny to well surpass his nearest competitor, Alcor v. Millsdod, while his older brother Domossi of Marienland, with twenty champions, is also close to the top. Being two and a half years older than Dictator, Domossi has had a certain advantage in that his sons have had more time in which to prove their powers. Of Domossi of Marienland's three producing sons the best is Ch. Emperor of Marienland out of Ch. Westphalia's Rembha (herself the dam of five champions). Emperor, with eighteen champions, has four producing sons, including Nicholas of Marienland, Ch. Kilburn Award (sire of three champions), Ch. Quo Shmerk of Marienland, adjudged the "dog of the year" in 1945 and sire of two champions, and Roxanna's Emperor v. Reemon (out of Ch. Westphalia's Roxanna), the sire of seven champions, six of them sons. Two additional producing sons of Domossi are Roxanna's Darius v. Reemon and Ch. Dow's Dash v. Kienlesberg.

It is interesting to note some of the bitches from whom have come the champions sired by the red Dictator. Five are out of Ch. Edah v. Trail, while one of the youngest, Ch. Ivan v. Trail, is out of a daughter of Edah and Alcor v. Millsdod. The Emperor of Marienland daughter, Kay of Reklaw (whose dam is Ch. Nana of Rhinegold by Kurt v.d. Rheinperle) is the dam of three champions by Dictator, while Ch. Dow's Dodie v. Kienlesberg is also the dam of three. Altogether there are ten champions out of six different daugh-

310

ters of Dictator's older brother Domossi. Two more are from a daughter of Dictator's sire, Blank v.d. Domstadt. One is out of Ch. Kleta v.d. Schwarzwaldperle, a daughter of Troll v.d. Engelsburg and granddaughter of Ikös v. Siegestor. Ch. Satan of Paulraine is already the sire of two champions, while Dow's Dickdie of Kilburn and Ch. Dolf v. Blau Türe have one each.

During six years at stud, Dictator sired 77 litters. He was withdrawn from public stud in 1950 at the age of nine years but at ten was still active and in use on bitches at the Damasyn Kennels. From Cleveland in 1944 through Westminster in 1945 Dictator was Best of Breed for fifteen consecutive times and was five times Best in Show. Renowned for his exceptional temperament, Dictator's influence upon the breed during the years since 1944 has been decisive and his descendants are certain to play important roles during the years to come.

The remaining sons of Blank v.d. Domstadt who deserve mention are Dictator's full brother, Ch. Clipper v. Glenhugel, six months older and the sire of five champions, and Ch. Sieg v. Glenhugel whelped in 1938 out of Roeslein Rot v.d. Heide, a daughter of Ch. Prinz Claus of Pontchartrain. Sieg sired four champions, including Gessner's Happy Jack and Gessner's Rolf v. Siegzell. Happy Jack has sired two champion sons, Hans and Horst v. Koch, while Rolf's son Major v. Huffmanheim is the sire of Ch. Adonis v. Huffmanheim. The non-champion Bayern v.d. Heide sired Ch. Patroon v. Rensselaer. The Gessner dogs carry lines to both Dewald v. Ludwigsburg and Ch. Kaspar v. Lobenstein.

The lines tracing down from Burschel v. Simmenau outnumber the lines from Stolz v. Roeneckenstein in a proportion of roughly six to five. Both lines lead back eventually to Hellegraf, and through daughters and granddaughters the two are inextricably interrelated. Starting from Hellegraf, one line goes to Sieger Lord v. Ried, Prinz Leuthold v. Hornegg, Achim v. Langerode and Alex v.d. Finchoehe to Stolz v. Roeneckenstein in the sixth generation. An interval of

311

CH. PINCKNEY FARM'S ARCHON AKC 14312
Breeder-Owner: Dr. Chas. P. Horton, Carmel, New York
Best of Breed: Morris and Essex   Best of Winners: Westminster

312

eighteen years separated the birth of Hellegraf in 1904 from that of Stolz in 1922. Nineteen more years and six further generations brings us to the birth of Alcor v. Millsdod in 1941. The male line goes from Stolz to Helios v. Siegestor, Astor of Westphalia, Pericles of Westphalia and Westphalia's Uranus to Alcor. It should be noted that both Uranus and Pericles were American bred, while on his dam's side Pericles goes back three more generations to Big Boy of White Gate before coming to the end of the American-breds.

The other principal male line from Hellegraf goes by way of Lux Edelblut v. Ilm Athen, Prinz Modern v. Ilm Athen, Bayard v. Silberberg, and Arno v.d. Gluecksburg to Burschel v. Simmenau. Although like Stolz he is the sixth generation from Hellegraf, Burschel was whelped late in 1915 and was more than six years older. At Burschel the line divides, one branch going by way of Ch. Claus v.d. Spree and then dividing again. By far the larger and stronger branch goes to Lux v.d. Blankenburg, whelped in 1918, and his son Alto v. Sigalsburg whelped in 1923. The lines from Lux through Prinz Noah and Prinz Claus of Pontchartrain are stronger than the branch from Claus v.d. Spree, but the main line continues through Alto, where it divides into four parts. Ch. Burschel v. Falkensee, Ch. Hamlet v. Herthasee, and Ch. Figaro v. Sigalsburg are fairly comparable in strength. Ch. Luz v. Roedeltal carries on only through Muck v. Brunia. Muck's line through Troll v.d. Engelsburg is still fairly vigorous over here, while indications are that it is still more prominent in Germany. However, it is the Blank v.d. Domstadt line which is strongly in the ascendancy. Blank's outstanding son, Ch. Dictator v. Glenhugel, is the sixth generation from Burschel and the twelfth from Hellegraf. Like Alcor, he was whelped in 1941.

Let us place these two lines side by side, with the bitch mated to each dog indicated, as follows:

CH. HEDGE'S DACQUIRI
Best in Show winner and one of the Top Ten Working Dogs of 1961.
Owned by Lovell Moore, Los Angeles, Calif.

1.
   to Schnuppe v.d. Saale
2. Lux Edelblut v. Ilm Athen
   to Lotte v. Ilm Athen
3. Prinz Modern v. Ilm Athen
   to Sybille v. Langen
4. Bayard v. Silberberg
   to Fee v.d. Boerde
5. Arno v.d. Gluecksburg
   to Gudrun v. Hornegg
6. Burschel v. Simmenau
   to Asta Voss
7. Lux v.d. Blankenburg
   to Lotte v. Roeneckenstein
8. Alto v. Sigalsburg
   to Fee v.d. Roedeltal

9. Luz v. Roedeltal
   Hella v.d. Winterburg

10. Muck v. Brunia
    to Cora v.d. Ruppertsburg
11. Blank v.d. Domstadt
    to Ossi v. Stahlhelm

   to Beda Frischauf
2. Lord v. Ried
   to Helga v.d. Pfalz
3. Prinz Leuthold v. Hornegg
   to Asta v. Starkenburg
4. Achim v. Langerode
   to Leddy v.d. Blankenburg
5. Alex v.d. Finohoehe
   to Dora v. Wiesengrund
6. Stolz v. Roeneckenstein
   to Ella v. Siegestor
7. Helios v. Siegestor
   to Ilisa of Westphalia
8. Astor of Westphalia
   to Anita zur Immermannhoehe
9. Kurt v.d. Rheinperle
   to Princess Latona of Westphalia
10. Pericles of Westphalia
    to Jessy v.d. Sonnenhoehe
11. Westphalia's Uranus
    to Madiz v. Millsdod

The relationship becomes much closer, however, when it is observed that Helga v.d. Pfalz was the dam of Gudrun v. Hornegg as well as of Prinz Leuthold; Leddy v.d. Blankenburg was a litter sister to Lux; and Lotte v. Roeneckenstein was a litter sister to Stolz. Lord v. Ried was also the sire of Sybille v. Langen as well as of Prinz Leuthold v. Hornegg. The principal sires have been mentioned. It remains now to stress a few of the more important dams. Helga v.d. Pfalz was a black daughter of Lord v. Ried and Luna (or Lina) II v.d. Pfalz. Her daughter Gudrun v. Hornegg, by Moritz v. Burgwall, was through Burschel v. Simmenau the granddam of Lux v.d. Blankenburg, and through his sister Leddy was the great granddam of Alex v.d. Finohoehe. Gudrun was also the dam of Lotte I v. Simmenau, dam of the Stolzenberg bitches. Prinz Leuthold v. Hornegg was by Helga's own sire, Lord v. Ried, and is important as the sire of Achim and Artus v. Langerode. Through Achim, her grandson, Helga is found a second time in Alex v.d. Fino-

315

hoehe. Another Helga daughter, Dinorah v. Hornegg by Prinz Modern v. Ilm Athen, is found occasionally in pedigrees tracing to the Rheinerft dogs, in particular as the granddam of Anneliesel v. Dusselquelle, the granddam of Siegerin Anita zur Immermannhoehe.

Asta v. Starkenburg, by Edelblut v. Jaegerhof out of Betty v. Jaegerhof, was the dam of all the Langerode dogs and also of several litters bred by the Hindendorff kennels, including Diethelm v. Hindendorff and Axel v. Hindendorff, the latter sire of the important Swiss Axel Kirchbühl. Through Achim v. Langerode she was the granddam of Alex v.d. Finohoehe and through Artus the granddam of Adele v. Oststern (dam of Claus v.d. Spree) and of Anita v.d. Blankenburg, dam of Asko, Artus and Astor v.d. Thumshoehe.

Asta Voss attains first rank as the dam of Lux and Leddy v.d. Blankenburg, Troll v.d. Blankenburg, and the less important Anita and Rappo. Through Leddy she was the granddam of Alex v.d. Finohoehe, and the great granddam of Stolz and Lotte v. Roeneckenstein.

Lotte v. Roeneckenstein was perhaps even more important as the dam of Alto v. Sigalsburg, Ari v. Sigalsburg, Lux II v. Simmenau and Lotte II v. Simmenau, Modern and Mars v. Simmenau, and Pia and Prinzess v. Simmenau.

Then there was the remarkable bitch Sybille v. Langen, by Lord v. Ried out of the part greyhound bitch Stella. Mated to Prinz Modern v. Ilm Athen she produced Hispa, Heidi and Bayard v. Silberberg. From the mating of Heidi and Bayard (the most inbreeding possible) came Sybille v. Silberberg, dam of Adela v. Oststern and granddam of Claus v.d. Spree. Bayard mated to Fee v.d. Boerde produced Arno v.d. Gluecksburg, the East German sire of Burschel v. Simmenau, who became the grandsire of Lux and Leddy v.d. Blankenburg and also sired Claus v.d. Spree. The other sister, Hispa v. Silberberg, was mated to the Moritz v. Burgwall son Bodo v. Elfenfeld, by whom she was the dam of Borste v. Falkenhain (dam of Alex v. Simmenau) and of Brunhilde v. Falkenhain (also called Brunhilde v. Silberberg, dam of Salto v. Rottal, the grandsire of Apollo v. Schuetze-neck).

The generations follow one after another. Fashion plays its part, and the much touted favorite of today may be forgotten by tomorrow—or the day after. It is the long view which counts; all too often when a dog's true worth is realized it is too late, for good or ill, to make direct use of the knowledge. Nevertheless, to study the bloodlines of the past helps a breeder to plan wisely for the future. With dogs as with men, "By their fruits shall ye know them." Knowingly or not we build the future upon the foundation of the past.

CH. PINCKNEY FARM'S ARCHON
This picture was taken when 10 months old
Breeder-Owners: Dr. and Mrs. Charles P.
Horton, Carmel, New York

317

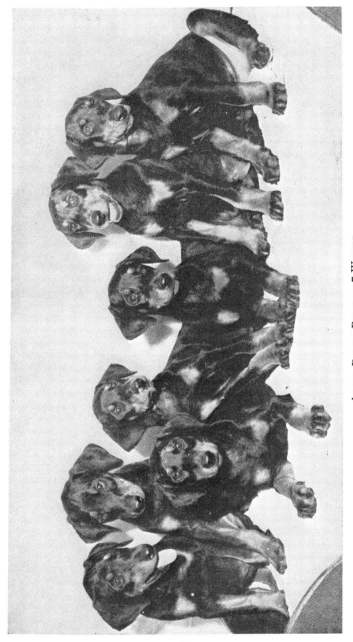

ALCOR-DIANA PUPS AT 7 WEEKS

ALCOR-DIANA PUPS AT 10 WEEKS

*The puppies shown at three stages of early develop-
ment on this and the preceding two pages are from
a litter sired by Ch. Alcor of Millsdod out of Ch.
Marc's Diana of Solbo. Owned by Margit Anderson,
Chicago, Ill.*